Continuing Your Professional
Development in Lifelong Learning

Also available from Continuum:

FE Lecturer's Survival Guide – Angela Steward
Getting the Buggers to Learn in FE – Angela Steward
How to Teach in FE with a Hangover – Angela Steward
FE Lecturer's Survival Guide – Angela Steward
A to Z of Teaching in FE – Angela Steward
Reflective Teaching in Further and Adult Education, 2nd Edition – Yvonne Hillier
Teaching in Post-Compulsory Education, 2nd Edition – Fred Fawbert

Continuing Your Professional Development in Lifelong Learning

Angela Steward

network
continuum

Continuum International Publishing Group

The Tower Building 80 Maiden Lane, Suite 704
11 York Road New York, NY 10038
London, SE1 7NX

www.continuumbooks.com

British Library Cataloguing-in-Publication Data
A catalogue record for this book is available from the British Library.

ISBN: 9780826425164 (hardcover)
9780826445872 (paperback)

Library of Congress Cataloging-in-Publication Data
Steward, Angela.
  Continuing your professional development in lifelong learning / Angela Steward.
     p. cm.
  ISBN 978-0-8264-2516-4 (hardcover : alk. paper) – ISBN 978-0-8264-4587-2 (pbk. : alk. paper)
1. Teachers–Education (Continuing education)–United States. 2. Teachers–In-service training–United States. 3. Teacher effectiveness–United States. I. Title.

LB1715.S7183 2009
370.71′5–dc22

2009007516

Typeset by YHT Ltd, London
Printed and bound in Great Britain by Bell & Bain Ltd, Glasgow

Mixed Sources
Product group from well-managed forests and other controlled sources
www.fsc.org Cert no. TT-COC-002769
© 1996 Forest Stewardship Council

To Dave

Contents

Acknowledgements   ix

List of Abbreviations and Acronyms   xi

Introduction – Personalisation and Constructive Practice   1

Part I – Past Policies

1   Workforce Reforms   11

Part II – The Role of the Teacher

2   Professional Standards and Code of Practice   35

3   The Role of the Teacher and the Teaching and Learning Environment   35

Part III – Constructive Practice

4   Approaches to Continuing Professional Development   85

5   Professional Development as Constructive Practice   114

6   Constructing a Professional Role   132

7   Constructing Professional Knowledge   157

8   Constructing Professional Relationships   190

9   Constructing a Repertoire of Intellectual Skills   209

Part IV – Future Practice

Conclusion – Continuing Your Professional Development   233

References   244

Index   253

Acknowledgements

Special thanks to my friends and colleagues in Education Studies at City College Norwich for their continued encouragement and support.

Many teachers, CPD professionals and students have generously shared their experiences, success stories and viewpoints with me. Some wish to remain anonymous, but I would like to offer my sincere thanks to the following for their contributions: Ercan Aslan, Karl Aubrey, Julia Cameron, Bunny Catchpole, John Chow, Coral Drane, Carol Fells, Eileen Gartside, Terry Gentry, Ruth Harrison, Vicki Hingley, Kim King, Wendy Knipe, Rachel Kirk, Danusia Latosinski, Steve Moseley, Celia Nicholson, Lesley Oliver, Hari Patel, Rachel Paul, Amanda Reeve, Mark Winston and Christina Yates.

I would like to thank the following for permission to reproduce copyright material:

Assessment Standards Knowledge exchange, Centre for Excellence in Teaching and Learning based in the Business School at Oxford Brookes University – 'Using generic feedback effectively'

Institute for Learning – Model of dual professionalism

Lifelong Learning UK – Professional standards for teachers, tutors and trainers in the lifelong learning sector.

My thanks to Christina Garbutt and Alice Eddowes at Continuum and Sue Cope and Tracey Smith for editing and proofreading.

The illustrations are by Nicola O'Reilly who achieved her MA at the University College of the Arts Norwich.

Grateful thanks to Professor Rob Fiddy, East of England Centre for Excellence in Teacher Training, for sponsoring my own CPD through research and study.

Finally, many thanks for caring to Sue, Sue, Sue, Cindy and Vera – a special group of friends.

Abbreviations and Acronyms

ABC	Antecedent, Behaviour, Consequences – understanding behaviour
ACL	Adult and Community Learning
ASKe	Assessment Standards Knowledge exchange
BRR	Behavioural, Reflective, Relationship – behaviour management
CEL	Centre for Excellence in Leadership
Cert. Ed.	Certificate in Education
CETT	Centre for Excellence in Teacher Training
CLASS	Challenging, Linked, Action, Structured, Supported – lesson plans
CPD	Continuing Professional Development
CTLLS	Certificate in Teaching in the Lifelong Learning Sector
CV	Curriculum Vitae
DBERR	Department for Business, Enterprise and Regulatory Reform
DCSF	Department for Children, Schools and Families
DDP	Diploma Development Partnership
DfEE	Department for Education and Employment
DfES	Department for Education and Skills
DIUS	Department for Innovation, Universities and Skills
DTLLS	Diploma in Teaching in the Lifelong Learning Sector
EAG	Expert Advisory Group for Diplomas
FD	Foundation Degree
FE	Further Education
FEFC	Further Education Funding Council
FENTO	Further Education National Training Organisation
FESDF	Further Education Staff Development Forum
GCSE	General Certificate in Secondary Education
GROW	Goals, Reality, Options, Way forward – model of coaching
HE in FE	Higher Education in Further Education
ICT	Information and Communications Technology
IfL	Institute for Learning
LEA	Local Education Authority
LLS	Lifelong Learning Sector
LLUK	Lifelong Learning UK
LSC	Learning and Skills Council
LSIS	Learning and Skills Improvement Service
NIACE	National Institute for Adult and Continuing Education

NVG   National Vocational Qualification
Ofqual   Office of the Qualifications and Examinations Regulator
Ofsted   Office for Standards in Education
PAR   Present, Apply, Review – components of effective lesson
PDJ   Professional Development Journal
PGCE   Postgraduate Certificate in Education
PTLLS   Preparing to Teach in the Lifelong Learning Sector
QCDA   Qualifications and Curriculum Development Agency
QCF   Qualifications and Credit Framework
QIA   Qualifications Improvement Agency
QTLS   Qualified Teacher Learning and Skills
SFA   Skills Funding Agency
SMART   Specific, Measurable, Achievable, Realistic, Timebound
SOLO   Structure of Observed Learning Outcomes – classification
SPERT   Success, Purpose, Enjoyment, Reinforcement, Target setting – planning
SWOT   Strengths, Weaknesses, Opportunities, Threats – analysis
T2G   Train to Gain
YPLA   Young People's Learning Agency

Introduction – Personalisation and Constructive Practice

> In the introduction you will find:
> - personalisation of continuing professional development (CPD);
> - constructive practice as a way of achieving CPD;
> - use of the generic terms 'teacher' and 'classroom';
> - ideas for strategies for your own CPD.

Personalisation of continuing professional development (CPD)

In case study research into professionalising the workforce in the Lifelong Learning Sector in England, Peeke identifies that personalisation has yet to be accepted as an approach to CPD for staff:

> Personalisation for learners within organisations is well recognised, but has yet to be widely applied as a concept to approaches to continuing professional development for staff. (Peeke, 2008: 10)

A key theme, which he draws attention to, is the need for education and training organisations in the sector to explore and support more informal methods of continuing personal and professional development for their staff. In this book, I shall argue that more informal approaches to continuing personal and professional development not only acknowledge the diversity of professional practice in the Lifelong Learning Sector but also that the personalisation of the professional development agenda recognises an individual's professional needs and engages them in activities that are important and relevant to them. Personalisation of continuing personal and professional development arises from the individual's professional needs and is a way of enabling staff to engage in lifelong learning themselves – whether it is through formal or informal learning – and of enabling the result of their efforts to have an immediate impact on their day-to-day professional practice, thus improving their learners' experience and contributing to the raising of their learners' achievement.

If you were able to spend time on deciding on the structure and development of the subject matter for a new learning programme or training course or improving the design of materials for presentations or workplace assessments then you would see that:

- *your organisation* would benefit from offering up-to-date programmes and courses;
- *your learners* would benefit from improved resources;
- the whole experience would have contributed to *your own professional learning* as you updated your knowledge and tested out your own organisational and management skills.

That's what personalisation of continuing personal and professional development would mean for you. You would be able to demonstrate a commitment to improving the quality of your practice whilst working on something that was relevant and important to you.

However, it must be remembered that individuals within organisations and across the sector are likely to make *similar choices* about what is relevant and important to them to focus on for their professional development. Despite the diversity of the sector and the range of different roles that individuals play, it is asserted that 'professional development processes share a common goal: improved practice' (Osterman and Kottkamp, 1993: 29). Meeting the needs of the individual does not mean that there has to be customised professional development activities to create a product which is 'fit for purpose' for every individual's needs. There are no 'general recipes' (James and Biesta, 2007: 37) for improved practice and it is not something that can be generally applied across the sector to all organisations and classrooms. It is acknowledged that there may be many different strategies or routes taken towards the common goal of improved practice, but what meeting the needs of the individual does mean is that particular conditions need to be in place for individual members of staff to engage in professional development activities.

Personalised learning, according to Pollard and James (2004: 1) is 'a question of developing social practices that enable people to become all that they are capable of being'. Therefore, to accomplish the common goal of improved practice across the Lifelong Learning Sector, the aim must be to develop *social practices* that achieve professional and personal development, which requires a shift in mindset from primarily focusing on the needs of the organisation to acknowledging that professional development comes about through both organisational and individual development. There must be a shared and public commitment to CPD within the organisation.

Improvement in quality requires the ability to align organisational priorities and the learning needs of the individual – and that is the real challenge.

Before social practices create a learning culture which enables individuals to become all that they are capable of being, individuals need to be committed to and see the relevance of personalised learning, not just to organisational needs but also to their own professional needs:

> By the term 'learning cultures', the researchers [James and Biesta, 2007] mean the social practices through which tutors and students learn and not the contexts or environments in which they learn, although people's working conditions are obviously important too. Individuals are part of learning cultures and so exert their influence on them; and vice-versa, so learning cultures are part of individuals and influence them in turn. Learning cultures permit, promote, inhibit or rule out certain kinds of learning. (Coffield, 2008: 16)

The question this provokes for James and Biesta is how social practices enable or disable different learning possibilities and Coffield questions which practices tutors should be holding on to and which ones should be abandoned. These are pertinent questions to address because if organisations are holding on to outdated practices then they are not always open to improvement. Whilst accepting that there is no one best way of achieving the common goal of improved practice, if continuing personal and professional development is designed to address local and personal needs and it affords individual members of staff the opportunity to identify their own developmental requirements and activities then, as Peeke reports, it is an empowering experience for staff and an effective way for organisations to demonstrate their support as staff respond to the changes and developments across the Lifelong Learning Sector. The personalisation of professional development helps address Coffield's question as organisations and staff jointly consider which practices should be improved and developed and which ones should be abandoned.

Constructive practice as a way of achieving CPD

But what if you do not have a special project to work on or new initiatives that you can identify? Perhaps you are working on learning programmes or training courses that someone else has developed or using materials in your presentations or assessments that others have prepared previously. What would happen then? In these circumstances, how would you show your commitment to improving the quality of your practice? How would you fulfil the compulsory requirement for CPD now introduced in the Lifelong Learning Sector?

There is an increasing emphasis placed on continuing personal and professional development in the Lifelong Learning Sector and this book is a response to that. Its purpose is to introduce and develop the idea that there is an opportunity for every one of you in the sector to engage in your own professional development through your everyday workload – regardless of whether you are on a training placement, a volunteer or in paid employment. The ideas in the book will demonstrate that your current workload is a ready-made vehicle for your continuing personal and professional development. Throughout this book, ways to achieve this are identified through what I call 'constructive practice' which is a term I coined after exploring and studying the practice of experienced and successful professionals in the Lifelong Learning Sector.

Constructive practice is identified in individuals who have an intention to continue to learn and who also control their workload so that they can apply that learning to achieve personal and professional development.

In a nutshell, the concept of construction has three broad elements:

- building;
- creation;
- interpretation.

The way successful individuals in the Lifelong Learning Sector approach professional learning fits these three elements: they build, create and interpret not only their role but also their knowledge, skills and workplace relationships. Successful individuals approach their continuing personal and professional development in a constructive way through positive activity which is beneficial to themselves and others in that it is productive and practical. Successful individuals also recognise that their personal and professional development is worth investing in and the ways in which they do this are offered throughout the book as guidelines for you to try out or adapt for yourself in your own setting.

- If you are a pre-service or in-service trainee studying for Preparing to Teach in the Lifelong Learning Sector (PTLLS), Certificate in Teaching in the Lifelong Learning Sector (CTLLS) or Diploma in Teaching in the Lifelong Learning Sector (DTLLS), you will find plenty of ideas to help you fulfil Domain A of the qualifications – standards relating to professional values and practice.
- If you are working in an FE College, Sixth-form College or as a private training provider and are wondering what to focus on for your annual obligation to undertake continuing personal and professional development, then reading the case studies about the ways in which successful teachers in the sector engage in their own personal and professional development through

constructive practice are worth considering and should provide plenty of ideas for you to think about.

> **Check It Out   0.1**
>
> ### Planning your professional development
> As you begin reading this book, start to think about aspects of your current workload – or activities in your work placement – which would provide excellent learning opportunities that you could focus on for your own continuing personal and professional development.
>
> Your first task is to set up your CPD records for your annual professional development cycle.
>
> **Links To CPD**
> - Create a folder for your annual CPD records.
> - Design a Professional Development Log to record dates, activities completed and the time spent on them.
> - Open a file for your Professional Development Journal, which will incorporate your descriptions of activities and reflections on the process over the year.
> - Start to collate any learner evaluations or observer evaluations.
> - Enter your initial ideas and thoughts about learning opportunities. To start with these may be brief notes about problems and difficulties or dilemmas you face that need resolving. You may consider updating your subject specialism or incorporating new policies into your teaching and learning.
> - Identifying these is an important first step in order to gain insights into your own workload which can help you grow and develop in your workplace. You may have some action points, but at this stage may not necessarily be able to identify goals or activities.
> - If you are undertaking your initial teacher training, collate your mentor evaluations, observer evaluations and assessment results from your course and develop an Action Plan for the next stage of your placement through discussion with your mentor and course tutors.

Use of the generic terms 'teacher' and 'classroom'

Lifelong Learning United Kingdom (LLUK), the organisation which developed qualifications underpinned by new professional standards introduced in the Further Education Workforce Reforms (LLUK, 2007a), uses the term 'teacher' generically. The term teacher is used by LLUK to represent not just teachers but also:

- tutors;
- trainers;

- lecturers;
- practitioners;
- facilitators;
- instructors.

Do you recognise your own job role in the list? Maybe you are in a teacher-related role such as human resource manager, workplace trainer and assessor or have set up your own training agency or consultancy? The term 'teacher' includes anyone whose role involves aspects of teaching even if the role is combined with other non-teaching work, but it does not include anyone whose role is exclusively non-teaching, e.g. as a verifier, assessor or learning support practitioner. Whether you work in a college, a public service organisation, an offenders' learning and skills unit or the armed services, are employed in work-based learning, are a community-based provider or are a volunteer, the common role among the different job titles is that of supporting learning.

You can now see why 'teacher' has, therefore, been chosen as the generic term by LLUK as, even if you are not described as a teacher in your job description, your role inevitably involves aspects of teaching and a commitment to deliver high standards and the skills or qualifications which people and business need in these increasingly competitive times (LLUK, 2007b). Throughout this book I shall follow the LLUK's lead and use the term 'teacher' to cover the many roles described above.

Just as it is evident that the generic use of the term 'teacher' covers many roles for individuals working in the Lifelong Learning Sector, so it follow that the use of the term 'classroom' covers many different learning environments. Throughout the book the term 'classroom' is used for simplicity and this could be where you undertake your professional practice, but it could also mean a simulated work environment or a:

- workshop;
- studio;
- office;
- salon;
- resource centre;
- community centre;
- nursery;
- library;
- museum;
- training centre.

The learning environment might not even be inside and may be a:

- farm premises;
- building site;
- garden;
- sports field.

Has your teaching and learning environment been identified in the list? Perhaps you use a different term in your organisation to the ones identified here. The range of possibilities illustrates the breadth of the Lifelong Learning Sector.

Ideas for strategies for your own CPD

Nearly 40 years after I qualified as a teacher, I still have a foothold in the classroom! I am the first to admit that experience alone does not make you an expert, but this book contains ideas I have developed over time through practice and research which I would like to share with you. It is a personal approach to CPD and contains elements of a 'how to' book, a 'self-help' manual and also a textbook. Whilst I do not attempt to cover comprehensively the theories of CPD or every aspect of teaching and learning, throughout the book I have introduced models and frameworks produced by experts in the field of professional development and teacher training that I have found useful, and which I have tried out in my own practice. I draw on them extensively and invite you to assess how relevant they are to your own context. You may find some familiar names among them and recognise some of your favourite authors.

I focus explicitly on one theory of teaching and learning, a constructivist approach, because I consider its principles are pertinent to young people, adults and work-based learners. I have also included numerous case studies about different approaches to continuing professional development from individuals currently working in the sector. These all provide you with first-hand accounts of what teachers have learned from practice and are an opportunity for:

- *outside-in* learning, i.e. you can learn from experts and colleagues in the sector who are outside your immediate working environment by sharing their theories and ideas and thinking about how you might put them into practice.

You are also encouraged to reflect on your personal theories and ideas and there is an opportunity for:

- *inside-out* learning, i.e. learning about how you act out your own theories and ideas in practice.

I take the view that CPD should be ongoing, and in each chapter there are ideas and activities to enable you to focus on aspects of your own personal and professional development by completing tasks, reading about examples from colleagues who practice in the sector and making links to practical teaching and learning situations as well as the LLUK standards. These might include:

- **Case Study Research** – Accounts of my primary research with teachers in the sector.
- **Check It Out** – The tasks provide an opportunity for you to assess how much you already know and check out how information relates to your own workplace.
- **Keep Up To Date** – Keeping up to date is important in a fast-changing sector and these activities provide an opportunity for you to make sure that the information presented in the book is still current.
- **Links To CPD** – Ideas for tasks to fulfil your annual continuing professional requirement for the Institute for Learning are suggested. If you are undertaking initial teacher training there is an opportunity to match your workplace and placement experiences against the LLUK standards.
- **Success Stories** – Case studies from a wide range of people from across the sector, e.g. learners, teachers, mentors and managers, describing their own personal and professional development experiences and decisions which provide advice, guidelines and inspiration for the reader.
- **Successful Strategies** – Summarises the chapters and provides ideas and approaches for planning your successful professional development.
- **Viewpoint** – Personal perspectives and opinions from experts in the field of initial teacher training and professional development.

Your responses to the activities in each chapter will depend on the kind of organisation in which you work and your own role within it.

Now you know what's in store in the book, it would be a good idea to make a start on Chapter 1 and to focus on the past events and policies that shed light on the present culture of organisations that come under the remit of the Department for Innovation, Universities and Skills (DIUS) in England and Wales. Looking back helps you understand and appreciate how your organisation works and why your colleagues think about teaching, learning and professional development in the way they do today. Developing your awareness in this way is an important aspect of your own personal and professional development.

Part I – Past Policies

1 Workforce Reforms

In this chapter you will find sections on:

- workforce practices and workplace culture;
- moving towards the professionalisation of the workforce;
- occupational standards and qualifications for FE teachers;
- the creation of the Learning and Skills Sector;
- reforming initial teacher training;
- teaching standards for the Lifelong Learning Sector;
- policies shaping new qualifications for teachers;
- restructuring of government departments;
- workforce strategy;
- preparing to meet the challenges ahead;
- an awareness of wider educational issues.

The chapter addresses issues relating to Domain A: AS4 Reflection and evaluation of their own practice and their CPD as teachers.

For those undertaking initial teacher training, the chapter provides opportunities to generate evidence for LLUK standards AS1, AK1.1, AP1.1, AS4, AP4.2 and elements of Domains B, C, D and E. (You will find full details of Domains A – E in Chapter 2.)

Workforce practices and workplace culture

Lincoln and Denzin point out that, although you cannot foresee what the future will hold, you can imagine it, because what happens in the future stems from what has happened in the past:

> We cannot predict the future, but we can speculate about it, because the future never represents a clean break with the past. (Lincoln and Denzin, 1998: 420)

Although you cannot say exactly what will happen in the future, you can take an educated guess because events from the past influence the way things turn out in the future. In this way, policies and strategies introduced in the past have a critical impact on workforce reforms in the Lifelong Learning Sector today and influence how they are received by individuals currently working in the sector and, subsequently, how they will be implemented in the future.

- When you joined your organisation did you wonder why teaching and training sessions were done the way they were and how they came to be like that?
- If you are undertaking an initial teacher training qualification, have you thought about why certain things came to be included in the learning programme and why they are considered so important?

Check It Out 1.1

Workforce practices

Think back to the particular ways of working you wondered about when you joined your organisation or started your teaching placement. Make a note of what you found different from what you expected, or what you found difficult to understand, and try to remember what it was that struck you about these differences and difficulties at the time. For example, it could have been:

- the way teaching and learning sessions were organised;
- how teachers related to their learners;
- how teachers engaged in developing programmes;
- the way managers organised the resources.

What surprised you about these workforce practices or others that you identified?

Have you any experiences of other organisations to compare them with?

What do these ways of working convey about the ethos of the organisation you are thinking about?

Links To CPD

- Identify workforce practices in your current organisation that may have contributed to the difficulties, problems or dilemmas that you identified (in Check It Out 0.1) as possibilities for CPD activities and possible inclusion in your Action Plan.
- Make additions and edit your Action Plan appropriately.
- Analysing these issues helps you evaluate workforce practices more effectively.

Workforce practices within organisations do not usually come about by chance and those within the Lifelong Learning Sector are no exception. New policies are often instigated to rectify past problems but their introduction often imposes further challenges for you as an individual as you are required to implement the changes and, more generally, it can affect the workplace culture of organisations in the sector. Undertaking continuing personal and professional development is a way of responding positively to the challenges which changes in policy bring, with benefits both to you and to your organisation. However, being well informed so that you can take an educated guess about future practices and focus on the important issues is the secret of success.

Towards the professionalisation of the workforce

To help you understand how the present qualifications for teachers in the Lifelong Learning Sector in England came into force and why emphasis is now being placed on continuing personal and professional development beyond initial teacher training, I look back on the recent past and provide a brief historical review of the events over the last few years that played a part in the professionalisation of the workforce. I address issues about how professionalisation of the workforce developed to its position today, how qualifications for teachers developed and how there is now a requirement for professional registration and a commitment by individuals to continuing personal and professional development in the future.

To an outsider, it may seem incredible that until the first year of the twenty-first century holding a teaching qualification was not a compulsory requirement for those teaching in colleges in the Further Education Sector (FE). Teaching appointments in the sector (and in adult training and education generally) were made on the strength of an individual's industrial experience, and their professional or craft expertise and teaching experience and teaching qualifications (or the lack of them) were not always taken into account. Teaching qualifications for the Further Education Sector had been in existence for many years, and indeed the majority of teachers in the sector held them. However, they were considered desirable for teachers in colleges and training organisations – but not a necessary requirement. Although new-style, criterion-based, occupational standards for teachers in the sector were first drafted in 1991, it took almost a decade of development, debate and disputes before they were introduced.

It was envisaged that the use of national standards – derived from analysing teachers' work content and defining performance criteria and assessment specifications based on objectives – would provide a basis for initial teacher training and accredited staff development with clear progression routes into qualifications for teaching. However, this functional approach based on typical National Vocational Qualification (NVQ) specifications was challenged by various stakeholders, e.g. employers' bodies, FE staff and their union representatives and teacher trainers. The period following the incorporation of the Further Education Sector in 1993, with a move away from the control of local education authorities (LEAs) as colleges became independent business corporations, saw the polarisation of these stakeholders about workforce issues into what Elliott and Crossley (1997) later called 'oppositional cultures'. The opposing perspectives from different stakeholders were based on divergent values and principles and so no mutually acceptable solutions were readily forthcoming. The way the FE teacher's role was defined, what their workload should be and how it was to be assessed was problematic from the outset and agreement on new occupational standards for teachers appeared insoluble for a considerable time, which meant their development and introduction took several years.

The move to incorporated status outside the control of the LEAs and the radical reforms in the Further Education Sector, which were implemented during the 1990s, were intended to put colleges on to a commercial footing. The reforms fundamentally impacted on the way FE Colleges were organised, funded and managed: there was a shift from traditional education structures to new systems derived from business and industry. A traditional ethos of public service was supplanted by one of competition, where market forces were introduced into colleges in a series of policies which gave rise to quality and accountability systems. All these measures changed the culture of colleges and the working conditions of teachers in the Further Education Sector.

Occupational standards and qualifications for FE teachers

Moving towards a qualified workforce became government strategy in 1998 (DfEE, 1998) but it was not until 1999 that the first occupational standards for the sector were launched by the Further Education National Training Organisation (FENTO, 1999) and they only became effective in 2001. The occupational standards were intended to inform the design of accredited qualifications for teachers in the Further Education Sector. Despite the protracted development period, they were generally accepted by providers and accreditors of FE teacher training qualifications by the time they were launched. However, this was achieved only after a consultation process with stakeholders in the sector after which revisions were made by the Further Education Staff Development Forum (FESDF), which was the body charged with strategic responsibility for taking the development of the occupational standards forward. Even so, after all this work and development there were still disputed elements within the FENTO standards.

Interestingly, at the same time as the first occupational standards for the Further Education Sector were launched, the National Institute for Adult and Continuing Education (NIACE, 1999) drew attention to the fact that not all qualifications need be based on national standards, e.g. National Vocational Qualifications (NVQs). NIACE considered NVQs were narrow and limiting, especially at a time when education was being increasingly aimed at the needs of the individual. The report published by NIACE also asserted that any reformed qualifications must be 'future-proof'. NIACE demonstrated foresight in:

- identifying that it would be increasingly important to focus training on skills which might be needed by the workforce in the future;
- recognising the trend in education to meet the needs of the individual.

These two factors highlighted the emerging personalisation agenda that is today at the forefront of teaching and learning strategies. The need for personalised learning and training for future employability was not widely recognised by stakeholders and policymakers at the time. However, looking back the germ of the idea was already beginning to take hold several years before the personalisation agenda was implemented and became widespread practice. It did not just suddenly appear: looking back enables you to see where its roots lie and why the concept evolved as a widespread practice.

The creation of the Learning and Skills Sector

A new policy on qualifications and professional development for teachers was announced to coincide with the government's plans for the new Learning and Skills Council which came into force in 2001 under the Learning and Skills Act (2000). The main elements of the Act concerned the funding of post-school education and training (excluding university education) and brought into being the Learning and Skills Sector.

The Learning and Skills Sector included not just FE Colleges, which had been the main sites of post-school learning and vocational training up to this point, but also:

- Sixth-form Colleges;
- work-based training and workforce development;

- adult and community learning;
- guidance services for adults;
- business links.

The expansion of the post-school sector was part of the government's strategy already articulated in *The Learning Age: A Renaissance for a New Britain* (DfEE, 1998). The priorities for this newly expanded sector were to implement the strategy by encouraging participation in learning, improving the basic skills of adults, making a contribution to the economy through updating skills, raising standards in post-school learning and ensuring excellence in teaching and training. The strategy enshrined a commitment by government to fund learning and skills provision in the sector – but this had to be in partnership with employers and individuals.

If the purpose and main consequence of the publication of *The Learning Age* signalled a markedly new approach to learning and skills through lifelong learning, then the publication of *Learning to Succeed: A New Framework for Post-16 Learning* (DfEE, 1999) signalled a decisive shift towards policies promoting social cohesion. The government was clearly intent on changing the nature of the learners staying on in the education system after the compulsory school-leaving age and widening participation in post-school education and training. They accelerated the pace of reform with a remit to the Learning and Skills Council to build a 'new culture of learning and aspiration' (DfEE, 1999: 13). The responsibility of the Learning and Skills Sector was to attract and involve people in education and training who in the past would have left school at 16 and who would have had no further connection with formal education or training after that. The raising of the school-leaving age from 16 years to 18 years becomes effective in 2015 but, as can be seen, the idea was raised and introduced in policies years earlier.

The priorities for the new sector were not only widening participation in education and training by recruiting so-called non-traditional learners and improving retention rates but also raising the achievement of learners in the whole sector. Teachers in the sector were under pressure to meet these often clashing targets as learners struggled to achieve qualifications and frequently required more support and guidance than the traditional learners who had customarily stayed in the education system beyond the age of 16. Incidentally, achieving retention targets with more diverse learners, who tended to be young people with little or no family experience of education and training beyond the age of 16 years and with few or no qualifications gained at school, began to change the approaches to teaching and training in the sector as traditional 'chalk and talk' methods were no longer effective in the new learning environment.

Dutton assessed the consequences of the government's drive towards the professionalisation of the teaching workforce at the time the Learning and Skills Council was created:

> The challenges that teachers and leaders alike will face in the new LSC [Learning and Skills Council] environment are not just about quality and standards. Equally important for them will be the stronger emphasis on the 'curriculum offer' and its position in the new 'supplier' market-place. Aligning strategies to LSC requirements will mean that college staff, all of whom contribute to teaching and learning, will require new skills, new understanding, new motivation and considerable re-alignment in the way things are done. (Dutton, 2000: 5)

Dutton noted the challenge for the Learning and Skills Sector of developing the curriculum offer and the link between supply and quality. She also identified the need for greater consistency and value for money in the sector alongside the need for quality throughout organisations in the new sector. The task for the sector was to initiate a demand-led system so that employer-demand could lead education and training organisations as suppliers and so ensure that teaching and learning were better aligned to the future requirements of employers and individual learners. So, not only would new teaching qualifications have to be delivered by teacher-educators in colleges and universities and achieved by those teaching in the new Learning and Skills Sector, but also all those involved would need to quickly get up to speed with the changing requirements of the Learning and Skills Council to take into account employers' and learners' needs if the qualifications were to be fit for purpose.

At this stage, the way teachers were currently being trained for employment in the sector was not seen as inconsistent with the emphasis on a demand-led curriculum offer. The need to realign the way teachers practised, which Dutton identified, was not connected at the time to the primary focus in teacher training programmes on *generic teaching skills* for everyone, whatever they planned to teach, rather than on *specialist teaching skills* for specific curriculum areas and specialised subjects – but it would not be too long before it was.

Reforming initial teacher training

Indeed, it was not long after the introduction of the FENTO standards that concerns were raised about greater choice for learners, raising standards and meeting the skills needs of employers. A discussion document *Success for All: Reforming Further Education and Training – Our Vision for the Future* (DfES, 2002) introduced four so-called 'pillars' on which the government's policy for the sector was based:

1. strategic planning;
2. a major programme of training and professional development;
3. improving teaching methods;
4. new targets setting minimum levels of performance.

These four pillars were the mainstay of the government's policy and implementation of the discussion document *Success for All* was a blueprint for the expanded sector, which influenced the day-to-day working lives of those in the sector as colleges and other Learning and Skills providers had to accede to a three-year funding regime with incentives for achieving targets – and possible intervention or penalties if they did not. In the discussion document, the government was critical of the Further Education Sector for lack of overall quality and for standards which it considered were not as high as learners deserved. To rectify this perceived lack of quality, a Post-16 Standards Unit was set up to improve standards in teaching. Additionally, a major programme of training and professional development in the sector was announced with the target that, by 2006, 90 per cent of all full-time teachers and 60 per cent of part-time teachers were to be qualified and by 2010 all teachers must be qualified.

> **Keep Up To Date   1.1**
> When you read this, check out on the government's website whether the government is meeting the targets it set – or have new ones been announced?

The *Success for All* strategy also emphasised the need for staff development across the whole workforce in the Learning and Skills Sector and a major programme of staff training formed the cornerstone of a framework for developing quality and achieving success by putting teaching, training and learning at the heart of what the sector did. At this juncture, staff training and development were declared a priority for raising the standards in the sector but CPD was not made a compulsory aspect of professional practice.

However, concerns about teaching and training in the Learning and Skills Sector did not abate and the following year the Department for Education and Skills (DfES) invited the Office for Standards in Education (Ofsted) to carry out a review of teacher education for the post-compulsory sector. Ofsted's review (2003) revealed that teacher training was concerned with *generic teaching skills* and not with the *specific teaching skills* required by vocational subject specialism. This was considered by government to be a real weakness that needed to be addressed and, although the FENTO standards had only been in use for about three years, at this point it was decided that the FENTO standards were to be replaced with new and clearer professional standards, which would include an emphasis on:

- competence in teaching in an area of specialism, i.e. the professional, vocational or subject area in which the individual planned to teach;
- continuing personal and professional development.

Check It Out   1.2

Self-assessment of teaching may be the most valuable form of assessment from a professional standpoint according to Moran (2001). He provides a list of nine factors of effective teaching, which it is suggested would be a good starting point for addressing ideas for continuing personal and professional development.

Begin the self-assessment process by identifying which factor(s) match any of your initial thoughts about activities for your Action Plan for CPD that you have already considered.

1. **Learning/Value** – The learners find the learning worthwhile.
2. **Instructor enthusiasm** – The teaching attracts and maintains attention. Teaching conveys high expectations.
3. **Organisation/Clarity** – Presentations are easily understood.
4. **Group interaction** – Learners interact and learn from each other.
5. **Individual rapport** – The teacher has good relationships with individual learners.
6. **Breadth of coverage** – The material is covered from more than one perspective. It is current and unbiased.
7. **Examinations/Grading** – Examinations are fair. They encourage critical thinking. Feedback is thorough, supportive and prompt.
8. **Assignments/Readings** – Assignments are challenging and encourage active learning and creativity.
9. **Workload/Difficulty** – The workload is reasonable and well paced. It accommodates diverse ways of learning. (Adapted from Moran, 2001: 46–7)

- How does your competence in teaching match up to the teaching behaviours identified?
- How do these teaching behaviours match ways of teaching in your specialist area?

Links To CPD

- Factors 1–9 above identify teaching performance and if you provide full responses to each you will produce an excellent self-assessment.
- If you are already employed as a teacher, select which factor(s) you wish to prioritise for your annual CPD activities relating to teaching and learning, e.g. will you prioritise improving Organisation/Clarity or does Breadth of Coverage need attention?
- Identify your priorities as targets in your Action Plan.
- If you are undertaking initial teaching training, your responses to factors 1–9 provide evidence for LLUK standards AS4, AP4.2 and elements of Domains B, C, D and E. (You will find full details of Domains A–E in Chapter 2.)

Teaching standards for the Lifelong Learning Sector

In 2004 proposals for the reform of initial teacher training in the Further Education Sector were announced. The impetus for reform arose from the acknowledgement that the FENTO standards were not appropriate for the expanded Learning and Skills Sector and that the generic approach to initial teacher training was not fitting for the range of training providers across the whole sector. The publication *Equipping Our Teachers for the Future: Reforming Initial Teacher Training for the Learning and Skills Sector* (DfES, 2004a) pointed out that the standards now needed to meet the requirements of training providers from:

- industry;
- public services;
- private providers.

The standards needed to be fit for purpose across the sector – not just fit for the requirements of FE Colleges.

To achieve the government's commitment to the training and development of a well-qualified and professional workforce, important reforms were initiated and new professional standards for teachers in the sector began to be developed by LLUK, which is one of the 25 Sector Skills Councils set up by employers to raise skills levels among the workforce as a whole through better training and development. LLUK is responsible for the professional development of those working in the Lifelong Learning Sector.

The Lifelong Learning Sector covers:

- further education;
- higher education;
- work-based learning;
- community-based learning and development;
- youth work;
- libraries, archives and other information services.

The reformed standards were introduced in the White Paper *Further Education: Raising Skills, Improving Life Chances* (DfES, 2006) and, just like the FENTO standards before them, went through a process of consultation and change before implementation.

Policies shaping new standards for teachers' qualifications

Whilst the development of the new standards was being undertaken and during the period of consultation before implementation, important policies and strategies were published which were key in changing not only the priorities of the Lifelong Learning Sector but also in influencing the shape of the new teacher qualifications for the sector.

In 2005, the government published a White Paper *14–19 Education and Skills* (DfES, 2005) after challenges in the changes to the Tomlinson Report, *14–19 Curriculum and Qualifications Reform* (DfES, 2004b). The government had commissioned a review of the curriculum for 14–19 year-olds and Tomlinson advocated that A levels, GCSEs and vocational examinations should be phased out and be replaced by a Diploma offering four different levels of attainment for candidates. The proposals for the Diplomas included the recommendation that there should be less coursework and fewer examinations and at advanced Diploma level there should be extra and more demanding questions that would stretch the most able candidates. The proposal for the reduction in the number of public examinations was generally welcomed, especially if the new Diplomas allowed greater differentiation between candidates and prepared them for their future – whether it was to be in the workplace, further education or higher education. However, implementing the reforms would require massive curriculum development and different organisational structures to cater for delivering the new Diplomas to 14–19 year-olds. The reformed assessment system would require different ways of working for teachers in the sector.

Following that, Foster carried out a review of the future role of FE Colleges and called for the FE sector to put its house in order (Foster, 2005). A crucial recommendation in his report *Realising the Potential* was that the focus of colleges should be on the provision of skills and ensuring employability for learners and it identified a key role for the Further Education Sector in implementing the 14–19 reforms and rationalising the diversity of the qualifications offered in the sector. Additionally, Foster recommended a more streamlined Learning and Skills Council with a change in its role and funding and criticised the bureaucracy created by a plethora of organisations in the sector charged with inspection, improvement and regulatory functions.

Yet another influential report was published at the end of 2006. The Leitch Review of Skills was also a government commission; this time the review was to identify the optimal skills mix for 2020 to maximise the UK's economic growth, productivity and social justice. The final report *Prosperity for All in the Global*

Economy – World Class Skills (HM Treasury, 2006) recommends that the UK should aim to be a world leader in skills by 2020 and identified the strategies to achieve this. Basically, to become a world leader in skills, the report indicated that the UK needs to spend much more money on increasing skills for everybody at every level. A recommendation was that all public funding for adult vocational skills (apart from community learning and some provision for individuals with learning disabilities) should be through the new Train to Gain (T2G) programme and through Skills Accounts.

- The T2G programme subsidises training in an individual's place of work and compensates their employer for the time it takes.
- Skills Accounts offer learners choice in training. The Skills Accounts are a vehicle to address a problem arising from a previous policy: they are a modified version of the previous Individual Learning Accounts which were so problematic and open to fraud that the government had to withdraw them.

The notion of shared responsibility between employers and individuals, as well as government, was stressed and it was emphasised that increased investment needed to come from employers and individuals because skills training gives them 'private' benefits, whereas the government should invest in promoting skills training for everyone, i.e. for 'public' benefits.

Another of Leitch's recommendations was the creation of a Commission for Employment and Skills. The main task of the Commission would be re-licensing the Sector Skills Councils and strengthening their powers to give employers a voice in the workforce needs of their industries as well as advising government on skills and employment strategies. The overall message of Leitch's report is that skills are the key to unlocking the individual's potential and his warning is that without increased skills the UK will face a decline in competitiveness and a bleak future for its workforce.

It was also recommended that apprenticeships for young people should double and efforts should be made to improve completion rates. Although Leitch accepted that government could not *compel* employers to run apprenticeships he felt that they should increase their investment in skills and be convinced of the benefit of skills training. Public Service Agreements are planned to be used to improve the attainment of 16–19 year-olds and raise adult skills levels. However, Leitch did propose that if by 2010 adequate progress was not being made voluntarily then the government should introduce an entitlement for anyone in the workforce without a Level 2 qualification to get the training needed to achieve it. This is where the notion of needing a license to practise, i.e. the possession by an individual of an approved qualification in order to perform, was introduced and this is now incorporated in the professional standards for teachers in the Lifelong Learning Sector. These recommendations were later included in the Children, Skills and Learning Bill (2008) which legislates to give all suitably qualified young people the right to an apprenticeship by 2013, to create the National Apprenticeship Service and a statutory framework for an apprenticeship and also to ensure that all young people get adequate advice and guidance at school about apprenticeships (DIUS and DCSF, 2008a).

One recommendation that received much attention at the time was to raise the compulsory age for participation in education or workplace training from 16 years to 18 years by 2015 after the new Diplomas recommended by Tomlinson (DfES, 2004b) are implemented. Whether the young people targeted by this change in policy will see this as an entitlement to education and an opportunity to gain skills and qualifications, which would enhance their future prospects and contribute to the nation's prosperity, or regard it as an imposition is another thing!

Restructuring of government departments

In 2007 there was a change of leadership in government and a restructuring of government departments. Ministerial responsibilities were reorganised and three new departments emerged:

- Department for Children, Schools and Families (DCSF) responsible for education, children and youth issues up to the age of 19.
- Department for Innovation, Universities and Skills (DIUS) responsible for adult learning, further and higher education, skills, science and innovation.
- Department for Business, Enterprise and Regulatory Reform (DBERRR) responsible for promoting productivity, enterprise, competition and trade.

The result of the restructuring is that two government departments now share responsibility for learners in the Lifelong Learning Sector: the DCSF and the DIUS. The establishment of the Department for Innovation, Universities and Skills under a secretary of state is in line with a recommendation made many years previously that universities and science should be brought together in government. This new partnership of science and innovation with further and higher education does mean, however, the separation of school and further and higher education, as the responsibility for schools now lies within another government department.

According to the government, the rationale behind the changes was to sharpen the focus of central government on the different and difficult challenges now facing the UK. The DIUS is to take a lead on expanding graduate skills and raising the skills of the wider adult workforce. Within the DIUS there is a minister with responsibility for Lifelong Learning, Further and Higher Education and one of the director-generals appointed in the Department has specific responsibility for Further Education and Skills. The latter's responsibilities include developing the government's Skills Agenda and ensuring employers are involved in the design and delivery of adult training.

Keep Up To Date   1.2

When you read about the staffing and structure of the DIUS, check on the government's website whether there has been any reorganisation since 2007 and find out the names of those in government who are currently responsible for education and training in your sector.

Remember the famous phrase 'a week is a long time in politics'. You need to keep yourself up to date!

Key aspects of the reforms to increase participation and achievement in the FE system, including the standards for initial teacher training, were included in the Further Education and Training Act (2007). The Act will make it easier for new delivery models, e.g. trusts and mergers, to be set up and gives powers to FE institutions in England to award their own Foundation Degrees. To enable the Further Education system to play a full part in accomplishing the government's Skills Agenda and the challenges posed by *Implementing the Leitch Review: World Class Skills* (DIUS, 2007) there was a restructuring of the Learning and Skills Council and provision for new strategy-making bodies. These legislative changes are intended to make the sector more responsive to the changing needs of employers and learners.

Workforce strategy

The government introduced the Further Education (FE) Workforce Reforms in England in 2007, which include:

- the introduction of new qualifications for principals;
- a new professional status and associated qualifications for teachers, tutors and trainers across colleges and other LSC-funded providers;
- a requirement for CPD for teachers, tutors and trainers;
- a prerequisite to register with the Institute for Learning (IfL).

On the government's behalf, the Sector Skills Council LLUK developed the Workforce Strategy for the Further Education Sector in England 2007–12. The key priority of this strategy is stated as 'professionalising the workforce from initial training to continuing professional development' (Hunter, 2008: 2). The way the strategy is implemented will be reviewed and updated annually to ensure its currency and relevance.

The FE White Paper *Further Education: Raising Skills, Improving Life Chances* (DfES, 2006) had identified the need for the sector to have a workforce with up-to-date skills and recommended broader recruitment policies and CPD. The Workforce Strategy sets out four priorities for action:

1. understanding the nature of the workforce;
2. attracting and recruiting the best people;
3. retaining and developing the modern professionalised workforce;
4. ensuring equality and diversity is at the heart of strategy, policy-making, planning and training. (LLUK, 2007: 19)

The strategy also identifies the vision for 2007–12: a focus on quality, participation, partnership, promotion and flexible delivery and design.

In Chapter 2 you will find details of the six Domains A–F of the LLUK professional standards for teachers, tutors and trainers in the Lifelong Learning Sector, which are considered a linchpin of the Workforce Strategy and central to professionalising the role of teachers.

Preparing to meet the challenges ahead

A consequence of the reviews and reforms over recent years is two interesting developments. First, the intervention of government appears to be changing. Within policies there is a new emphasis on empowering learners and employers as 'customers', e.g. enabling access to training for individuals across a range of providers with a wider choice of subjects available, thus enabling a demand-led system to materialise. All this requires different organisational structures. A more competitive element to provision and funding of customers is now evident. The document *FE Colleges: Models for Success* (DIUS, 2008) set out the government's requirements to ensure that the Further Education system can respond to the challenges ahead. These include the development of new business models which reflect and respond to the new training environment and are capable of making the most of the new opportunities open to schools, colleges and other training providers. This requires more collaboration and innovation as new partnerships between employers and training providers are encouraged and new ways of working are forged.

Second, two separate systems are becoming apparent: one concerning the education and training of 14–19 year-olds from the academic year 2010–2011 and one which concerns adults. The intention to raise the school-leaving age from 16 years to 18 years by 2015 is influencing government policy. The government announced plans to give local education authorities more say in the education of 14–19 year-olds and to rationalise the skills system for adults. A joint publication by the DIUS and the DCSF, *Raising Expectations: Enabling the System to Deliver* (2008), provided information about proposed new arrangements for funding. These changes mean different funding bodies, new ways of working and, particularly, an emphasis on demand-led education and training. Two new agencies have been set up:

1. **Young People's Learning Agency (YPLA)** – This agency will work with local authorities in funding schools and colleges more equitably through a National Funding Formula. The YPLA is also responsible for overseeing 14–19 provision and planning and commissioning education and training for 16–19 year-olds. In the academic year 2010–11, local authorities will become the single point of accountability for all 0–19 children's services.

2. **Skills Funding Agency (SFA)** – This agency will work with colleges and training organisations and will oversee the performance of the whole FE service. The SFA will fund, but not plan, adult education.

The rationale behind the establishment of two agencies is to provide a system that meets the demands of both learners and employers. The joint consultation between the DIUS and the DCSF marks:

> The creation of two complementary systems for young people and adults which will provide colleges with more opportunities and challenges in delivering excellent provision across a changing landscape. (2008b: 6)

The intention behind the proposals is to make sure that the money gets where it is needed. It is considered that local authorities – because they are local and already administer educational provision to sixth-form level – are able to respond to the needs of young people in their locality and ensure that they can access the right programmes and qualifications to fulfil their potential. The reality is that most colleges recruit learners from more than one local authority so sub-regional groups of authorities will need to be created to cope with this.

One outcome of the reforms to make the most of the talents of young people and enable them to participate in the education and training they need to get a good job is that public funding is being directed towards Level 2 skills. This decision means that adult education is to be increasingly market-led and adults wanting to enhance their skills at Level 3 or above have to pay more. This particular reform has provoked discussion about whether there will be a downturn in adult learning and whether achieving world-class skills for young people will be at the expense of lifelong learning for adults. These changes mean that the responsibilities of the Learning and Skills Council will be taken over by new organisations. However the Learning and Skills Council is effective until 2010 when it is to be abolished and the Skills Funding Agency will take over responsibility.

The government has proposed an ambitious plan to introduce 14 new Diplomas for 14–19 year-olds between 2008 and 2011. The first five Diplomas were offered in September 2008:

- Construction and the Built Environment;
- Creative and Media;
- Engineering;
- Information Technology and Society;
- Health and Development.

These first Diplomas were offered to nearly 40,000 young people in nearly 900 schools and colleges around the country. The remaining nine Diplomas will be introduced in stages and all will be on offer by 2011:

- Administration and Finance;
- Business;
- Hair and Beauty;
- Hospitality;
- Environmental and Land Based Studies;
- Manufacturing and Produce Design;
- Public Services;
- Sport and Leisure;
- Travel and Tourism.

The government asserts that the Diplomas will provide opportunities for combining academic and practical options and allow young people to make the most of their talents, whether they are progressing to further study, work or an apprenticeship. The Secretary of State stated:

> We are confident that these new subject-based Diplomas will secure the benefits of Diplomas for all young people. They will provide a wider curriculum offer for those young people who want to secure both the theory and practical skills they need to

excel in study, work and life. We need the business and academic worlds to continue to back these qualifications and help make them a success. With their support, I believe that Diplomas could emerge as the jewel of our education system. (DCSF, 2007: 1)

Three additional Diplomas were announced in 2008 which will be implemented for the first time in 2011:

- Humanities;
- Languages;
- Science.

These additional Diplomas are designed to provide a core of functional skills in English, Maths and ICT as well as in-depth subject knowledge and practical skills. They are substantially different to the previous 14 Diplomas as they are not sector specific. Instead they combine learning related to a particular discipline, e.g. science, with generic learning including personal learning and thinking skills. When they are introduced they will also include an extended project and additional or specialist learning. This will allow learners to deepen their subject knowledge or broaden their studies. The Department for Children, Schools and Families states that the Diplomas will incorporate the best aspects of existing GCSE and A level qualifications alongside specially designed content and will require the same academic rigour as GCSEs and A levels, and standards will be ensured by an independent regulator. The Children, Skills and Learning Bill (2008) legislated to establish an independent regulator of examinations and tests (Ofqual) and a development agency for curriculum, assessment and qualifications (QCDA).

- An Expert Advisory Group will specify the design structure and principles for the new Diplomas and advise on the implications for the strategic direction of 14–19 qualifications offer.
- A Diploma Development Partnership (DDP) will specify the content for each of the new Diplomas.

The government's intention is that the new Diplomas will provide a balance of academic rigour, practical knowledge and generic skills and produce the supply of talented young people that businesses need in the future to compete globally. Perhaps this is a move away from the vocational–academic divide so prevalent in this country's education system and the Diplomas will allow young people to develop all their talents and prepare them for entry to higher education and/or their chosen future in the world of work.

When introducing the new Diplomas, it was also announced that the 2008 Review of A Levels was postponed and the first review of 14–19 qualifications will be held in 2013 instead so that the success of the Diplomas and the changes already made to

A levels and GCSEs can be assessed. It was also announced in 2008 that the Qualifications and Credit Framework (QCF) was approved for implementation and this will enable people to gain qualifications in the Further Education Sector at their own pace in a more flexible and accessible way. The QCF will record them on an Individual Learner Record, which has the potential to remove the need for paper records in the future.

In June 2008 a new body dedicated to the development of Further Education and the Skills Sector was officially named and its purpose highlighted. This new body was formed by the amalgamation of the Quality Improvement Agency (QIA) and the Centre for Excellence in Leadership (CEL) and is called the Learning and Skills Improvement Service (LSIS), which is dedicated to development.

The structural changes have been put in place by government and the published strategy for the whole sector is now firmly committed to *development* and this book focuses on personal and professional development for teachers in the sector.

An awareness of wider educational issues

At the beginning of this chapter, I drew your attention to the notion that the future is never a clean break with the past. Nevertheless, when you are evaluating your progress during your initial teacher training or reflecting on your performance in teaching in the Lifelong Learning Sector, you are usually concerned just with the present. All your energies probably go into coping with your daily tasks in your organisation – or preparing, planning and delivering your allocated sessions when in a placement organisation.

Strangely enough, if you want to improve your teaching and support learners more effectively and don't want to end up exhausted after putting all your energies into coping with the 'daily grind', you need to widen your focus beyond your present day-to-day duties. You must try not to shut the classroom door and forget about everything else and work in isolation. To improve and be successful, what you really need is to be more open to issues outside your immediate classroom, office, workroom or training centre.

An approach to professional development that is promoted in this chapter is one that is not limited to acquisition of the technical skills or methods teachers need in order to perform effectively in the future. Rather, it is an approach which Cranton (1996: 165) advocates should place an emphasis on the need for individuals to understand both the 'big picture' of the field of education and training and how each one of you can make a unique contribution to the 'big picture' in your day-to-day work in your college, school or training organisation. Cranton turns on its head the idea that you cannot contribute to the 'big picture' and illustrates that, if you focus on what is important to you and make positive changes, then these influence what goes on in your organisation, and in turn your organisation influences what is going on in your local community for the better; positive change has an influence far beyond the classroom or training workshop. I am not saying that you can change the whole world for the better single-handedly, but perhaps you can make your little bit of it a better place to be. That's why when you focus on professional development that's important and personal to you, you need to be aware of organisational priorities and government policies for society and you also need to be aware of how they connect with your day-to-day work in the classroom. You need to have a knowledge of wider educational issues to understand your professional practice.

Keep Up To Date   1.3

You may have been surprised by the number of changes that have been described in this chapter and, indeed, there may be many more by the time you read this! Lots of people resist change, but being aware of why the changes are introduced helps you understand the sector you are working in or training for, so identify policy changes that have taken place in the sector since the publication of this book.

Keeping up to date with what is going on in the wider world of education and training increases your confidence to contribute to current discussions with colleagues about how new initiatives are to be introduced and delivered in the future.

Successful Strategies

- The knowledge you acquire by reading about past policies provides a framework for thinking about education and training and raises your awareness that educational initiatives are driven by a political agenda.
- To put your textbook knowledge and practical experience of teaching and learning into context look beyond what's happening from day to day in your organisation to gain an understanding of past events and how they directly influence your workplace practice today and be aware of wider issues of education and of the rationale behind the curriculum.
- An understanding of policies enables you to evaluate your organisation's new initiatives more realistically and ensures you are better informed about the reasons behind changes in teaching and learning introduced into your specialist area.
- Identifying the links between policies and your practice in the classroom or training workshop helps you make better choices about which aspects of your work to focus on for your professional development and helps you make sound decisions about how to develop your practice in the future.
- Informed professional development means you are able to contribute in a positive way to individual, organisational and, potentially, social change.

In Chapter 2 you will have an opportunity to examine in more detail the LLUK standards for teachers, trainers and tutors and learn about the role of the Institute for Learning.

Part II The Role of the Teacher

2 Professional Standards and Code of Practice

In this chapter you will find sections on:

- an introduction to the Lifelong Learning UK (LLUK) standards;
- the Institute for Learning – Code of Professional Practice;
- LLUK standards – Domains A–F.

The chapter addresses issues relating to Domain A: AS6 Teachers in the Lifelong Learning Sector are committed to the application of agreed codes of practice and the maintenance of a safe environment.

An introduction to the Lifelong Learning UK (LLUK) standards

The government recognises that there are already many excellent staff in the sector but considers that learners and employers deserve the best, which is excellence from everybody:

> There are already many excellent teachers, tutors and trainers working in further education. We want all to aspire to excellence – learners and employers deserve the best. That is why Government, LLUK and the further education system, with its diverse range of providers from colleges and work based learning to prisons and the voluntary and community sector, support the professionalization of the workforce.
> (Rammell, 2006: I)

A major part of the FE Workforce Reforms is the introduction of a new professional status and associated qualifications for teachers. The LLUK standards for teachers in the Lifelong Learning Sector incorporate the skills, knowledge and attributes required by individuals who perform a wide range of teaching and training roles in the sector. The professional standards incorporate three components and cover six teaching domains which encompass three major categories.

Levels	Threshold (Award in preparing to teach in the LLS) Associate Teacher (Certificate in teaching in the LLS) Full Teacher Role (Diploma in teaching in the LLS or PGCE)
*Domains	A Professional values and practice B Learning and teaching C Specialist learning and teaching D Planning for learning E Assessment for learning F Access and progression
Categories	Scope – range of responsibilities Knowledge – depth and breadth of understanding of processes and practices used to encourage learning Practice – learning situations capable of being assessed

*The full details of Domains A–F can be found at the end of this chapter.

Viewpoint

Planning is to enable learning

Although I don't think the LLUK standards are as complicated as the former FENTO standards, I don't think they are any less excessive. Overall, the six identified domains are a helpful framework which have streamlined the standards and make them more accessible to our trainees, which is an improvement.

The standards do highlight that planning is to enable learning and provide pointers for the indicative characteristics of effective teaching and learning. Trainees with the most potential not only refer to the standards and criteria to plan and prepare to a very high standard but, what is important, they deliver to the same very high standard and engage their learners. What the best trainees do is to take on board ideas that are discussed during the course sessions, they listen to suggestions from tutors and mentors and try them out. They are receptive to new ideas and use their imagination to create excellent activities and resources themselves which engage the learners' interest. Even though they're aware of the criteria for achieving a distinction level for an observation, other students don't seem to take on board new ideas and so don't progress in the same way.

Engaging learners

I think what the best trainees have is self-awareness and an understanding of their role and can recognise in themselves what's required to engage learners, and have the confidence to try things out. But, at the same time, they're critical of what they do –

and you can see this in their evaluations – and reflective. So, in this way, they keep on learning through thinking about what they've done and developing it.

If you asked me ...

If I was observing a trainee, I would be hoping to see them:

- able to engage with learners – relate to them and value them for what they are;
- use a range of resources – but be realistic and aware of practical resource constraints;
- create interesting tasks for learners – which address different learning styles;
- give positive feedback throughout to learners;
- encourage learners to share experiences and information;
- highly regarded by learners for their teaching skills and specialist subject knowledge.

In my view, some factors for success for those already working in the Learning and Skills Sector would be to:

- develop a team approach – share resources, plan together;
- learn from your peers – review and evaluate sessions, modify resources;
- support each other – listen to each other, encourage each other;
- value your learners – put them first, love what you're doing;
- develop yourself – do qualifications or further study related to work; find a role that suits your temperament.

(Course Leader for Part-time Diploma in Teaching in the Lifelong Learning Sector)

This viewpoint provides an individual perspective and overview of an initial teacher training course and it highlights the importance of creating links between theoretical ideas introduced on the course and through discussion with mentors about professional knowledge and their practical application in the classroom. It is clear from this viewpoint that the standards can be used both for teacher training and for the purpose of CPD. There are excellent pointers here for trainees to be aware of when being observed and useful ideas for staff already employed who want to develop their practice.

The LLUK standards have been developed specifically in response to Ofsted's appraisal of the Further Education National Training Organisation (FENTO) standards which identified a need for clearer standards, which are relevant across the whole of the sector and emphasise teaching in a particular area of specialism.

One significant change in the new standards was the identification of two distinct teacher roles. The first is a full teaching role encompassing the full range of responsibilities. Teachers in this category are expected to attain the status of Qualified Teacher, Learning and Skills (QTLS). The second role identified is that of an associate teacher which carries fewer teaching responsibilities, although the quality of the teaching is expected to be of an equally high standard. An example of this associate teacher role might be someone who teaches from work-packs or resources which have been designed and developed by others. Another significant change was the inclusion of criteria designed to strengthen the teaching in an area of specialism, which was a need previously highlighted by Ofsted. The standards are not only designed to provide support and guidance for new teachers to the Lifelong Learning Sector but also for CPD purposes.

A new requirement for CPD of 30 hours at the very least for full-time teachers has been introduced alongside the professional standards together with revised standards for leadership and management within the sector. Centres for Excellence in Teacher Training (CETTS) were set up in each region in the sector in 2007 to support these new ventures.

The overarching standards, therefore, provide benchmarks for performance in a variety of roles that teachers, trainers, tutors and lecturers in the sector undertake. A new qualification framework for teachers in the Lifelong Learning Sector provides units of assessment setting out the learning outcomes and assessment criteria, which when grouped together will form qualifications for specified teacher roles – some of which will be mandatory and some optional.

Viewpoint

Teacher training should encourage lifelong learning

In my view, the FENTO standards were prescriptive and seemed to be exclusive; they did not provide an opportunity for teacher-trainees to apply them to their own working contexts. In this way, I felt that they disadvantaged teacher-trainees. What they seemed to encourage everyone to do was to break down everything they did and try to tick off as many criteria as they could and not look at the teacher's role in a holistic way.

To some extent the LLUK standards appear to exclude some student-teachers, but they are probably not so bad in this respect. However, I still feel that the multi-faceted nature of the standards even now does not encourage lifelong learning as it should – although the inclusion of the 'Professional Values' module is a good idea and was obviously introduced for this purpose as part of the package of workforce reforms for the sector.

Vocational training or academic education

What the LLUK standards do seem to have done is perpetuate the debate about vocational competence versus academic excellence, which is not in line with the modern-day environment that teacher-trainees will go on to work in. The Lifelong Learning Sector is promoting inclusion and widening participation amongst non-traditional learners and it is a pity that the strategy for the professionalisation of teachers perpetuates the long-standing lack of parity between vocational training and academic education.

A need for greater embedding of the theoretical concepts of pedagogy

From my point of view, there needs to be a greater embedding of the theoretical concepts of pedagogy so teacher-trainees can explore not only the 'how?', which is very important, but also the 'why?' of learning and teaching. This would, perhaps, give the trainees a greater holistic understanding of how their students learn and how they themselves learn and develop in their profession as teachers. Reflective practice has always had a place in teacher training; however, I suggest its value and centrality in improving practice has not been uniformly stressed. This I feel could be developed by greater emphasis on encouraging the role of the 'researcher/reflective practitioner' through small action research projects, for example during teacher training. This would personalise study and empower teacher-trainees in improving their particular pedagogical practice and sharing this with others. An induction of practitioner research within the supportive confines of the teacher training environment – which gives focus to the individuals and their own subject area and student body – should then be taken forward and encouraged in the time allotted CPD element post qualification. Hopefully, this will eventually evolve into creating a practitioner research community within FE, which would, I suggest, go some way to establishing parity with other sectors of education.

(Teacher-trainer and University Lecturer)

The viewpoint expressed above captures the notion of the teacher as a researcher and reflective practitioner, and encouraging this within the supportive confines of their initial teacher training course is an excellent idea, which may go some way to addressing the importance of lifelong learning for professionals. The ongoing debate about the vocational–academic divide raises justifiable issues about how well the criteria will meet the requirements of the diverse and widening sector. Exploring why teaching and learning is done in the way it is is essential to provide a holistic understanding of practice and, as the Viewpoint reveals, helps teacher-trainees develop in their profession as teachers themselves from the outset of their career.

The Institute for Learning – Code of Professional Practice

The role of the LLUK standards for teachers in the sector is to inform the development of qualifications and set expectations for CPD and the construction of individual development plans. Working in any profession entails meeting strict criteria, including holding entry qualifications before being able to practise. After gaining a teaching qualification, the IfL conducts a process of professional formation and awards QTLS status.

Another part of the reform agenda emanating originally from the government publication *Success for All* (DfES, 2002) was the establishment of a professional body for teachers in the Lifelong Learning Sector. Teachers in the sector have to register with the IfL and remain in good standing through CPD. For the first time, there is a Code of Professional Practice to adhere to for teachers in the sector.

Institute for Learning: Code of Professional Practice

The Code is based on six core principles or behaviours: integrity, respect, care, practice, disclosure, responsibility.

Behaviour 1: PROFESSIONAL INTEGRITY

The members shall:

1. meet their professional responsibilities consistent with the Institute's Professional Values;
2. use reasonable professional judgement when discharging differing responsibilities and obligations to learners, colleagues, institution and the wider profession;
3. uphold the reputation of the profession by never unjustly or knowingly damaging the professional reputation of another or furthering their own position unfairly at the expense of another;
4. comply with all reasonable assessment and quality procedures and obligations;
5. uphold the standing and reputation of the Institute and not knowingly undermine or misrepresent its views nor their Institute membership, any qualification or professional status.

Behaviour 2: RESPECT

The members shall at all times:

1. respect the rights of learners and colleagues in accordance with relevant legislation and organisation requirements;
2. act in a manner which recognises diversity as an asset and does not discriminate in respect of race, gender, disability and/or learning difficulty, age, sexual orientation or religion and belief.

Behaviour 3: REASONABLE CARE

The members shall take reasonable care to ensure the safety and welfare of learners and comply with relevant statutory provisions to support their well-being and development.

Behaviour 4: PROFESSIONAL PRACTICE

The members shall provide evidence to the Institute that they have complied with the current Institute CPD policy and guidelines.

Behaviour 5: CRIMINAL OFFENCE DISCLOSURE

Any member shall notify the Institute as soon as practicable after cautioning or conviction for a criminal offence. The Institute reserves the right to act on such information through its disciplinary process.

Behaviour 6: RESPONSIBILITY DURING INSTITUTE INVESTIGATIONS

A member shall use their best endeavours to assist in any investigation and shall not seek to dissuade, penalise or discourage a person from bringing a complaint against any member, interfere with or otherwise compromise due process.

As well as the professional code, the IfL has developed an online tool – REFLECT – to help teachers keep a log of progress over one year, help plan development activities in a structured way and provide an up-to-date record of CPD hours logged.

What is not prescribed in the new standards is what professional development entails, although guidelines are suggested by the IfL. This presents an opportunity for teachers to negotiate their own professional development activities. Continuing personal and professional development is not about notional standards but what an individual in a particular organisation needs. Also, it is not just a matter of logging continuing professional activities to comply with requirements – but learning from them and making improvements to practice:

> The time spent can be meaningless unless it makes a difference to you and your learners. You might spend half a day at a workshop, listening, taking notes and discussing ideas that go nowhere once you are back at work, or you may return full of ideas that you can put into practice and that has a real impact on learning, which makes the exercise worthwhile, and has CPD value. Measuring the 'so what' factor by analysing what you have changed and learners' feedback is an important part of the process too. (Kelly, 2008: 7)

Improvement of quality in teaching and learning in the sector is not achieved exclusively through short-term external professional development and training activities but requires ongoing workplace learning which is long term in focus, practice-oriented and work-based to improve future practice and needs to be embedded in critical reflection and evaluation of workloads. It is suggested that CPD can be thought of positively as continually updating a curriculum vitae.

Success Story

Making a difference through a team approach to coaching teaching and learning

In 2008 the senior management agreed to the appointment of five Teaching and Learning Coaches and there was competition for the posts which had an enhanced payment and three hours a week for carrying out the duties. We are planning to train one of the Teaching and Learning Coaches as an Advanced Coach, to enable further coaches to be trained in-house. One of the benefits of the appointments is that we now have the beginnings of a team of mentors for those staff in the college who undergo teacher training and another is that we can now make better use of Coaches throughout the college. The appointment of Teaching and Learning Coaches has enabled the team to instigate and develop several initiatives which encourage a whole-college approach to supporting academic staff and a 'joined-up' approach to their CPD.

Frank Coffield said that where individuals choose from a long list of options for CPD – what he describes as a 'smorgasbord' approach* – it is unlikely to have much effect on the work of the teaching teams. Individuals and teams need time after CPD sessions to take on board new ideas that have been presented so that they can work out how they can assimilate them into their teaching in order to improve the quality of students' learning, e.g. time for professional conversations. That's why we encourage CPD opportunities such as active learning and activities that have relevance to practice, e.g. embedding Skills for Life is a priority for us as the college is surrounded by some of the most deprived wards and boroughs in the country.

We have experienced staff in the college who are good teachers and don't necessarily see the need to change and who don't always want to alter their approach to teaching and learning. But they may have done their teacher training several years ago and things have moved on so their experience isn't necessarily in tune with the current criteria for external inspection and internal observation or, nowadays, considered good practice. So we want to bring teachers up to date but, more importantly, we want them *to feel excited about teaching again* – just as new teachers are – and get back some of that energy they had when they started out. We feel it's there – just buried – and we want to guide them to opportunities to feel enthusiastic about teaching and learning again.

Teachers talking

The team have identified certain themes which arise, first, from feedback from Ofsted inspection reports, second, from the evaluation of internal lesson observations and, third, from appraisals. Looking at the issues about teaching and learning that arise from these, and following discussion about them, we have been able to put on a series of professional development workshops called 'Teachers Talking' for staff, which are really relevant. For example, one of the themes identified by Ofsted was that targets were not challenging enough and another was the need for embedding equality and diversity in the classroom. We developed two active learning training sessions with the aim of leading by example.

In a session called 'Challenging Targets' we demonstrated ways that teachers were actually doing this and encouraged colleagues to relate the session to their own practice. It was an opportunity for us to say to colleagues look at what you're doing and a chance for them to pick up ideas from us and from each other and see how they could adapt them. The workshop enabled staff to have thinking time and share issues and good practice. The group was very mixed with staff at different levels of experience and expertise and we provided something for everybody. The core idea was that they had time in the workshop to start developing resources and materials that they could actually take away and immediately use in their sessions. This was a particularly successful element and their execution enabled the teachers to start talking and raise questions and ideas just snowballed. The feedback showed that staff felt the workshop was really relevant to their day-to-day teaching, they learned from talking to each other and they did use the materials, so the session was successfully run again with different groups.

Teaching and Learning Coaches

We have a subject specific coach in each team each of whom acts as a coach to their colleagues and a mentor to new staff. A new initiative is that before a team is internally observed, the Teaching and Learning Coaches go in *en masse* and provide intensive support for individuals to whom they are matched. They provide coaching about anything that an individual asks about, but it is usually about how to prepare for the observation session itself and how to get their paperwork in order. But it could be anything – whatever they want. It's coaching in its true sense and it is already starting to make an impact on the quality of teaching and learning observed.

Using e-skills in the classroom

Lots of staff have been in the college a long time and are not comfortable with IT. The sessions were multi-levelled and for those who didn't tend to use e-skills in the classroom the sessions started off so that staff could access material and delete and/or superimpose information so that they could personalise it and produce resources that they could use in the classroom straight away. Again, staff had time to do something practical in the session that was relevant to them, however small, and they could ask each other or the team for support without feeling they were imposing on another's time. They became engrossed in the activities and so excited when they achieved a good result. It was really nice to witness them going back to their staffrooms and waving what they had done around and saying 'Look what I've done'. On a more serious note, monitoring during internal observations did show that there was definitely more use of e-skills in the classroom and staff appeared more confident.

Every Learner Matters

We invited someone from every team in the college to come to a session. We asked them to bring along a scheme of learning and then got them to identify areas that were relevant and where they could actually start to embed strategies. They were thinking about documentation that they actually use and taking away ideas for improvement.

After this, what we did was to email the materials, which had been produced by individuals on the day from all the different sessions we held, to everyone. There were several reasons behind this. We wanted to remind people what they actually did and jog them to continue what they'd started. Also, we wanted them to see what others did across all the sessions, and so be exposed to ideas that their colleagues had instigated – rather than us telling them what others did or what to do themselves. This follow-up by email moved embedding Every Learner Matters on another notch.

Institute for Learning and REFLECT

We have always held CPD records centrally for each member of staff and they are used when staff apply for a job or there's a course revalidation. Now we are encouraging each team to explore the use of the IfL's REFLECT database. We are focusing on CPD in the teams and, interestingly enough, staff are actually asking about how they can use REFLECT and pushing us for workshops so that they can get competent with. Obviously, although we are advocating that individuals and teams identify relevant professional development activities, we are still directing some aspects, such as Child Protection and Race, Equality and Disability legislation which are cross-college requirements. Staff are now discussing their CPD activities, which is brilliant and it does indicate that there is a changing culture taking place in the college toward CPD.

If you asked us ...

The team thought about what they would say about how to be successful when teachers start out on their career and how to approach CPD, and came up with the following guidance:

- To make things work better you have to be open and take risks and accept that sometimes things which might look great on paper don't work out as planned. It happens to us all. Sometimes you need someone else to say 'Have a go!' or 'Don't worry!' before you try out new things, so share your concerns with other teachers.
- Start looking around you and see what's good. Observe a teacher you admire and aspire to be like. Have professional conversations with them and learn from them and reflect on what they say. You don't have to look far to find examples of good practice. Be like a sponge and take in what's around you.
- Start small. Make little changes and you will soon build up a repertoire of resources and skills. Always think how you can improve things or make something right.

(Team Leader and Team Member for Teaching and Learning – FE College)
[*Coffield, 2008: 23]

The case study supports the contention that improvement of quality requires ongoing workplace learning and is long term and practice-oriented. Understanding how to be successful at continuing personal and professional development throughout your career needs support from your organisation and the team approach illustrated here is an excellent example of a whole-college commitment to their staff's professional learning. It illustrates Mullin's concept of strategic training whereby an organisation recognises and practises training as an integral part of the management of human resources and plans training in the light of both individual and organisational needs:

> Training should be viewed as an investment in people. It must be real, operational and rewarding. Training requires the co-operation of line managers, adequate finance and resources, time, skilled staff and a supporting appraisal system. There has to be a genuine commitment – from top management and throughout all levels of the organisation. (Mullins, 2007: 490)

Mullins argues that 'one size will not fit all' and a complementary range of learning opportunities that will make sure new skills and learning are properly embedded is what is required, and the case study illustrates this with the range of activities described and the provision of time for embedding new ideas into practice.

Unilateral solutions to problems tend to be self-defeating so improvement strategies need to be collaborative and cooperative; it is no good individual members of staff all trying to solve problems on their own. What makes this case study such a success story is that the incentive behind all the team's hard work in establishing a 'joined-up' approach to coaching teaching and learning through active learning and relevant tasks is to get every member of staff *to feel excited about teaching again* – just as new teachers are! Now if every organisation had a whole staff who worked with the enthusiasm of newcomers, the workforce reforms and professionalisation policies would certainly be validated.

LLUK standards – Domains A–F

The standards are listed below so that you can familiarise yourself with them and use them to identify activities for your own CPD.

Table 2.1 Domain A: Professional values and practice

Scope: Teachers in the Lifelong Learning Sector value:	Knowledge: Teachers in the Lifelong Learning Sector know and understand:	Practice: Teachers in the Lifelong Learning Sector understand that aspects of professional practice:
AS1 learners, their progress and development, their learning goals and aspirations and the experience they bring to their learning.	AK1.1 what motivates learners to learn and the importance of learners' experience and aspirations.	AP1.1 encourage the development and progression of all learners through recognising, valuing and responding to individual motivation, experience and aspirations.
AS2 learning, its potential to benefit people emotionally, intellectually, socially and economically, and its contribution to community sustainability.	AK2.1 ways in which learning has the potential to change lives. AK2.2 ways in which learning promotes the emotional, intellectual, social and economic well-being of individuals and the population as a whole.	AP2.1 use opportunities to highlight the potential for learning to positively transform lives and contribute to effective citizenship. AP2.2 encourage learners to recognise and reflect on ways in which learning can empower them as individuals and make a difference in their communities.
AS3 equality, diversity and inclusion in relation to learners, the workforce and the community.	AK3.1 issues of equality, diversity and inclusion.	AP3.1 apply principles to evaluate and develop own practice in promoting equality and inclusive learning and engaging with diversity.

Scope: Teachers in the Lifelong Learning Sector value:	Knowledge: Teachers in the Lifelong Learning Sector know and understand:	Practice: Teachers in the Lifelong Learning Sector understand that aspects of professional practice:
AS4 reflection and evaluation of their own practice and their CPD as teachers.	AK4.1 principles, frameworks and theories which underpin good practice in learning and teaching. AK4.2 the impact of own practice on individuals and their learning. AK4.3 ways to reflect, evaluate and use research to develop own practice and to share good practice with others.	AP4.1 use relevant theories of learning to support the development of practice in learning. AP4.2 reflect on and demonstrate commitment to improvement of own personal and teaching skills through regular evaluation and use of feedback. AP4.3 share good practice with others and engage in CPD through reflection, evaluation and the appropriate use of research.
AS5 collaboration with other individuals, groups and/or organisations with a legitimate interest in the progress and development of the learners.	AK5.1 ways to communicate and collaborate with colleagues and/or others to enhance learners' experience. AK5.2 the need for confidentiality, respect and trust in communicating with others about learners.	AP5.1 communicate and collaborate with colleagues and/or others, within and outside the organisation, to enhance learners' experience. AP5.2 communicate information and feedback about learners to others with a legitimate interest, appropriately and in a manner which encourages trust between those communicating and respects confidentially where necessary.
AS6 teachers in the Lifelong Learning Sector are committed to the application of agreed codes of practice and the maintenance of a safe environment.	AK6.1 relevant statutory requirements and codes of practice. AK6.2 ways to apply relevant statutory requirements and the underpinning principles.	AP6.1 conform to statutory requirements and apply codes of practice. AP6.2 demonstrate good practice through maintaining a learning environment which conforms to statutory requirements and promotes equality, including appropriate consideration of the needs of children, young people and vulnerable adults.

Scope: Teachers in the Lifelong Learning Sector value:	Knowledge: Teachers in the Lifelong Learning Sector know and understand:	Practice: Teachers in the Lifelong Learning Sector understand that aspects of professional practice:
AS7 teachers in the Lifelong Learning Sector are committed to improving the quality of their practice.	AK7.1 organisational systems and processes for recording learner information. AK7.2 their own role in the quality cycle. AK7.3 ways to implement improvements based on feedback received.	AP7.1 keep accurate records which contribute to organisational procedure. AP7.2 evaluate own contribution to the organisation's quality cycle. AP7.3 use feedback to develop own practice within the organisation's systems.

Table 2.2 Domain B: Standards relating to learning and teaching

Scope: Teachers in the Lifelong Learning Sector know and understand (Scope targets from Domain A plus BS commitments added below) and are committed to:	Knowledge: Teachers in the Lifelong Learning Sector know and understand:	Practice: Teachers in the Lifelong Learning Sector understand that aspects of professional practice:
BS1 maintaining an inclusive, equitable and motivating learning environment.	BK1.1 ways to maintain a learning environment in which learners feel safe and supported. BK1.2 ways to develop and manage behaviours which promote respect for and between others and create an equitable and inclusive learning environment. BK1.3 ways of creating a motivating learning environment.	BP1.1 establish a purposeful environment where learners feel safe, secure, confident and valued. BP1.2 establish and maintain procedures with learners which promote and maintain appropriate behaviour, communication and respect for others, while challenging discriminatory behaviour and attitudes. BP1.3 create a motivating environment which encourages learners to reflect on, evaluate and make decisions about their learning.
BS2 applying and developing own professional skills to enable learners to achieve their goals.	BK2.1 principles of learning and ways to provide learning activities to meet curriculum requirements and the needs of all learners. BK2.2 ways to engage, motivate and encourage active participation of	BP2.1 provide learning activities which meet curriculum requirements and the needs of the learners. BP2.2 use a range of effective and appropriate teaching and learning techniques to engage and motivate learners and encourage independence.

Scope: Teachers in the Lifelong Learning Sector know and understand (Scope targets from Domain A plus BS commitments added below) and are committed to:	Knowledge: Teachers in the Lifelong Learning Sector know and understand:	Practice: Teachers in the Lifelong Learning Sector understand that aspects of professional practice:
	learners and learner independence. BK2.3 the relevance of learning approaches, preferences and skills to learner progress. BK2.4 flexible delivery of learning, including open and distance learning and online learning. BK2.5 ways of using learners' own experiences as a foundation for learning. BK2.6 ways to evaluate own practice in terms of efficiency and effectiveness. BK2.7 ways in which mentoring and/or coaching can support the development of professional skills and knowledge.	BP2.3 implement learning activities which develop the skills and approaches of all learners and promote learner autonomy. BP2.4 apply flexible and varied delivery methods as appropriate to teaching and learning practice. BP2.5 encourage learners to use their own life experience as a foundation for their development. BP2.6 evaluate the efficiency and effectiveness of own teaching including consideration of learner feedback and learning theories. BP2.7 use mentoring and/or coaching to support own and others' professional development as appropriate.
BS3 communicating effectively and appropriately with learners to achieve their goals.	BK3.1 effective and appropriate use of different forms of communication informed by relevant theories and principles. BK3.2 a range of listening and questioning techniques to support learning. BK3.3 ways to structure and present information and ideas clearly and effectively to learners. BK3.4 barriers and aids to effective communication. BK3.5 systems for communication within own organisation.	BP3.1 communicate effectively and appropriately using different forms of language and media, including written, oral and non-verbal communication, and new and emerging technologies to enhance learning. BP3.2 use listening and questioning techniques appropriately and effectively in a range of learning contexts. BP3.3 structure and present information clearly and effectively.

Scope: Teachers in the Lifelong Learning Sector know and understand (Scope targets from Domain A plus BS commitments added below) and are committed to:	Knowledge: Teachers in the Lifelong Learning Sector know and understand:	Practice: Teachers in the Lifelong Learning Sector understand that aspects of professional practice:
		BP3.4 evaluate and improve own communication skills to maximise effective communications and overcome identifiable barriers to communication. BP3.5 identify and use appropriate organisational systems for communicating with learners and colleagues.
BS4 collaboration with colleagues to support the needs of learners.	BK4.1 good practice in meeting the needs of learners in collaboration with colleagues.	BP4.1 collaborate with colleagues to encourage learner progress.
BS5 using a range of learning resources to support learners.	BK5.1 the impact of resources on effective learning. BK5.2 ways to ensure that resources used are inclusive, promote equality and support diversity.	BP5.1 select and develop a range of effective resources, including appropriate use of new and emerging technologies. BP5.2 select, develop and evaluate resources to ensure they are inclusive, promote equality and engage with diversity.

Table 2.3 Domain C: Standards relating to specialist learning and teaching

Scope: Teachers in the Lifelong Learning Sector know and understand (Scope targets for Domain A) plus CS commitments added below and are committed to:	Knowledge: Teachers in the Lifelong Learning Sector know and understand:	Practice: Teachers in the Lifelong Learning Sector understand that aspects of professional practice:
CS1 understanding and keeping up to date with current knowledge in respect of own specialist area.	CK1.1 own specialist area including current developments. CK1.2 ways in which own specialism relates to the wider social, economic and environmental context.	CP1.1 ensure that knowledge of own specialist area is current and appropriate to the teaching context. CP1.2 provide opportunities for learners to understand how the specialist area relates to the wider social, economic and environmental context.

Scope: Teachers in the Lifelong Learning Sector know and understand (Scope targets for Domain A) plus CS commitments added below and are committed to:	Knowledge: Teachers in the Lifelong Learning Sector know and understand:	Practice: Teachers in the Lifelong Learning Sector understand that aspects of professional practice:
CS2 enthusing and motivating learners in own specialist area.	CK2.1 ways to convey enthusiasm for own specialist area to learners.	CP2.1 implement appropriate and innovative ways to enthuse and motivate learners about own specialist area.
CS3 fulfilling the statutory responsibility associated with own specialist area of teaching.	CK3.1 teaching and learning theories and strategies relevant to own specialist area.	CP3.1 apply appropriate strategies and theories of teaching and learning to own specialist area.
	CK3.2 ways to identify individual learning in own specialist area.	CP3.2 work with learners to address particular individual learning needs and overcome identified barriers to learning in own specialist area.
	CK3.3 the different ways in which language, literacy and numeracy skills are integral to learners' achievement in own specialist area.	CP3.3 work with colleagues with relevant learner expertise to identify and address literacy, language and numeracy in own specialist area.
	CK3.4 the language, literacy and numeracy skills required to support own specialist teaching.	CP3.4 ensure own personal skills in literacy, language and numeracy are appropriate for the effective support of learners.
	CK3.5 ways to support learners in the use of new and emerging technologies in own specialist area.	CP3.5 make appropriate use of, and promote the benefits of, new and emerging technologies.
CS4 developing good practice in teaching own specialist area.	CK4.1 ways to keep up to date with developments in teaching in own specialist area.	CP4.1 access sources for professional development in specialist area.
	CK4.2 potential transferable skills and employment opportunities relating to own specialist area.	CP4.2 work with learners to identify the transferable skills they are developing, and how these might relate to employment opportunities.

Table 2.4 Domain D: Standards relating to planning for learning

Scope: Teachers in the Lifelong Learning Sector know and understand (Scope targets from Domain A plus DS commitments added below) and are committed to:	Knowledge: Teachers in the Lifelong Learning Sector know and understand:	Practice: Teachers in the Lifelong Learning Sector understand that aspects of professional practice:
DS1 planning to promote equality, support diversity and to meet the aims and learning needs of learners.	DK1.1 how to plan appropriate, effective, coherent and inclusive learning programmes that promote equality and engage with diversity. DK1.2 how to plan teaching session. DK1.3 strategies for flexibility in planning and delivery.	DP1.1 plan coherent and inclusive learning programmes that meet learners' needs and curriculum requirements, promote equality and engage with diversity effectively. DP1.2 plan teaching sessions which meet the aims and needs of individual learners and groups, using a variety of resources, including new and emerging technologies. DP1.3 prepare flexible learning session plans to adjust to the individual needs of learners.
DS2 learner participation in the planning of learning.	DK2.1 the importance of including learners in the planning process. DK2.2 ways to negotiate appropriate individual goals with learners.	DP2.1 plan for opportunities for learner feedback to inform planning and practice. DP2.2 negotiate and record appropriate learning goals and strategies with learners.
DS3 evaluation of own effectiveness in planning learning.	DK3.1 ways to evaluate own role and performance in planning learning. DK3.2 ways to evaluate own role and performance as a member of a team in planning learning.	DP3.1 evaluate the success of planned learning activities. DP3.2 evaluate the effectiveness of own contributions to planning as a member of a team.

Table 2.5 Domain E: Standards relating to assessment for learning

Scope: Teachers in the Lifelong Learning Sector know and understand (Scope targets from Domain A plus ES commitments added below) and are committed to:	Knowledge: Teachers in the Lifelong Learning Sector know and understand:	Practice: Teachers in the Lifelong Learning Sector understand that aspects of professional practice:
ES1 designing and using assessment as a tool for learning and progression.	EK1.1 theories and principles of assessment and the application of different forms of assessment, including initial, formative and summative assessment in teaching and learning. EK1.2 ways to devise, select, use and appraise assessment tools, including, where appropriate, those which exploit new and emerging technologies. EK1.3 ways to develop, establish and promote peer and self-assessment.	EP1.1 use appropriate forms of assessment and evaluate their effectiveness in producing information useful to the teacher and the learner. EP1.2 devise, select, use and appraise assessment tools, including, where appropriate, those which exploit new and emerging technologies. EP1.3 develop, establish and promote peer and self-assessment as a tool for learning and progression.
ES2 assessing the work of learners in a fair and equitable manner.	EK2.1 issues of equality and diversity in assessment. EK2.2 concepts of validity, reliability and sufficiency in assessment. EK2.3 the principles of assessment design in relation to own specialist area. EK2.4 how to work as part of a team to establish equitable assessment processes.	EP2.1 apply appropriate methods of assessment fairly and effectively. EP2.2 apply appropriate assessment methods to produce valid, reliable and sufficient evidence. EP2.3 design appropriate assessment activities for own specialist area. EP2.4 collaborate with others, as appropriate, to promote equity and consistency in assessment processes.
ES3 learner involvement and shared responsibility in the assessment process.	EK3.1 ways to establish learner involvement in and personal responsibility for assessment of their learning. EK3.2 ways to ensure access to assessment within a learning programme.	EP3.1 ensure that learners understand, are involved and share in responsibility for assessment of their learning. EP3.2 ensure that access to assessment is appropriate to learner need.

Scope: *Teachers in the Lifelong Learning Sector know and understand (Scope targets from Domain A plus ES commitments added below) and are committed to:*	Knowledge: *Teachers in the Lifelong Learning Sector know and understand:*	Practice: *Teachers in the Lifelong Learning Sector understand that aspects of professional practice:*
ES4 using feedback as a tool for learning and progression.	EK4.1 the role of feedback and questioning in assessment for learning. EK4.2 the role of feedback in effective evaluation and improvement of own assessment skills.	EP4.1 use assessment information to promote learning through questioning and constructive feedback, and involve learners in feedback activities. EP4.2 use feedback to evaluate and improve own skills in assessment.
ES5 working within the systems and quality requirements of the organisation in relation to assessment and monitoring of learner progress.	EK5.1 the role of assessment and associated organisational procedures in relation to the quality cycle. EK5.2 the assessment requirements of individual learning programmes and procedures for conducting and recording internal and/or external assessments. EK5.3 the necessary/ appropriate assessment information to communicate to others who have a legitimate interest in learner achievement.	EP5.1 contribute to the organisation's quality cycle by producing accurate and standardised assessment information, and keeping appropriate records of assessment decisions and learners' progress. EP5.2 conduct and record assessment information to those with a legitimate interest in learner achievement, as necessary/ appropriate.

Table 2.6 Domain F: Standards relating to access and progression

Scope: *Teachers in the Lifelong Learning Sector know and understand (Scope targets from Domain A plus FS commitments added below) and are committed to:*	Knowledge: Teachers in the Lifelong Learning Sector know and understand:	Practice: *Teachers in the Lifelong Learning Sector understand that aspects of professional practice:*
FS1 encouraging learners to seek initial and further learning opportunities, and to use services within the organisation.	FK1.1 sources of information, advice, guidance and support to which learners might be referred. FK1.2 internal services which learners might access.	FP1.1 refer learners to information on potential current and future learning opportunities and appropriate specialist support services. FP1.2 provide learners with appropriate information about the organisation and its facilities,

Scope: Teachers in the Lifelong Learning Sector know and understand (Scope targets from Domain A plus FS commitments added below) and are committed to:	Knowledge: Teachers in the Lifelong Learning Sector know and understand:	Practice: Teachers in the Lifelong Learning Sector understand that aspects of professional practice:
		and encourage learners to use the organisation's services, as appropriate.
FS2 providing support for learners within the boundaries of the teacher role.	FK2.1 boundaries of own role in supporting learners.	FP 2.1 provide effective learning support, within the boundaries of the teaching role.
FS3 maintaining own professional knowledge to provide information on opportunities for progression in own specialist area.	FK3.1 progression and career opportunities within own specialist area.	FP3.1 provide general and current information about potential education, training and/or career opportunities in relation to own specialist area.
FS4 a multi-agency approach to support development and progression opportunities for learners.	FK4.1 professional specialist services available to learners and how to access them. FK4.2 processes for liaison with colleagues and other professionals to provide effective guidance and support for learners.	FP4.1 provide general and current information about a range of relevant external services. FP4.2 work with colleagues to provide guidance and support for learners.

Successful Strategies
- Understanding how to be successful at continuing personal and professional development throughout your career needs to start during initial teacher training.
- Professionalisation policies in the sector need to be implemented with creativity.
- Individual teachers who have organisational support are more likely to benefit from professional development opportunities.
- CPD should provide something for everyone in the organisation through active learning opportunities and relevant tasks.

Chapter 3 explores the role of the teacher and the teaching and learning environment and provides an opportunity for you to see how the LLUK standards apply in practice.

3

The Role of the Teacher and the Teaching and Learning Environment

In this chapter you will find sections on:

- the changing nature of teachers' professional practice;
- teachers' work as educational practice;
- the diversity of the teacher's role;
- professional compromise and the teacher's role;
- managers' perspectives on the role of the teacher and the teaching and learning environment;
- teachers' professional identity;
- a reframed perspective of the role of the teacher.

The chapter addresses issues relating to Domain A: AS7 Teachers in the Lifelong Learning Sector are committed to improving the quality of their practice.

For those undertaking initial teacher training, the chapter provides opportunities to generate evidence for LLUK standards AS4, AK4.1, AK4.2, AP4.1, AP4.2, AS5, AK5.1, AP5.1, AP5.2, AS6, AK6.1, AP6.1, AS7, AK7.1, AK7.2, AP7.1, AP7.2 and elements of Domains B, C and D.

The changing nature of teachers' professional practice

Petty jokes that, if in years to come you look back on the way that you teach today, you will either laugh or groan!

> I am convinced that by the end of this century people will look back at our present ... practice and laugh – or groan – just as we do when we hear of 19th-century

teaching. And they may even envy us that we were born in a time when old methods were abandoned for exciting new and powerful ones, and when teachers had the challenge and fun of working out the teaching of the future. And seeing the results.

The future is in sight, but the path is not yet clear, and it is the present generation of teachers who will forge these new ways. That's you. Our students have a lot to gain, and so will the economy and social inclusion. We teachers have a lot to gain too, as the new methods often make teaching less tiring, and much more interesting. (Petty, 2006: 2)

The radical change in the teacher's role in the Lifelong Learning Sector over recent years is widely recognised. The move away from the traditional role of the teacher as someone who imparts knowledge to a view of the main role of the teacher as being one of supporting learning has gained pace in the twenty-first century, and has been experienced by those already working in the sector. A reappraisal of the teacher's role affects the relationship between teacher and learner and means the whole body of professional practices is potentially subject to change. Abandoning old methods and developing new ones does not have to be daunting. Petty suggests that forging new ways of working may be challenging but can also be fun, and if the new methods make teaching less tiring and more interesting, as he promises, then it's more than worth the effort of investing in CPD that delivers these promises and enjoying the results for yourself!

Remember, in this book the term 'teacher' is used in a generic sense and represents not just teachers but also tutors, trainers, lecturers and instructors. You may be engaged in teaching in a wide range of organisations, e.g. private training organisations, commercial companies, colleges, Sixth-form Colleges, prisons, armed services or other organisations which come under the remit of the Lifelong Learning Sector and your classroom could be one of a number of different environments. In Chapters 1 and 2, the changing practices in the Lifelong Learning Sector were set in the context of a framework of national policies to raise standards in the sector. These have emerged at a time when there is a shift in values within government policies towards those promoting future economic prosperity and social cohesion through lifelong learning. Petty asserts that, on the one hand, the economy and social inclusion initiatives will gain from new ways of teaching and, on the other hand, our learners have a lot to gain from both the government's policies promoting inclusion and new ways of teaching.

As well as providing education and training for a more skilled and flexible workforce, employees in the Lifelong Learning Sector are also part of the government's strategy to raise the nation's vocational skills. Those of you who have been working in the sector for some time will be aware that the notion of what is considered to be good professional practice has changed in the last few years. The sector now values meeting the needs of both learners and employers and what is now considered as important is a learner-centred curriculum which is vocationally relevant. There is a focus on the key skills of communication, numeracy, problem-solving, information technology and team work. The efforts to modernise teaching and learning and encourage the value-added nature of any education or training for employers and learners (and thereby the competitiveness of the economy) do not place importance on traditional teaching methods, such as lectures or formal presentations and cramming for tests and examinations, all of which were previously regarded as central to teachers' professional practice. At the end of the twentieth-century, Avis (1999) described the labour process in the Further Education Sector as being transformed and with this change new identities are generated of what it is to be a teacher in the sector. Many of you will have experienced this shifting identity first-hand as you encountered the numerous changes required of you in your role as teacher during the first decade of the twenty-first century.

Check It Out   3.1

Changes to professional practice

- If you have been working in the sector for any length of time, identify and list the changes that you have experienced in your role as a teacher and the impact they have had on your day-to-day working and the progress and development of your learners.
- If you are undertaking initial teacher training, ask your mentor to talk about the changes that they have experienced, the ways in which they keep up to date with current knowledge and how they respond to changing practices to enhance their learners' experience.
- Identify any initial improvements you have made to your teaching as a result of developing your Action Plan.
- Identify any 'old' methods of teaching that you could bring up to date and would improve the quality of your practice.
- Evaluate your learner's feedback and identify ways to respond to it and develop your own practice.
- Identify changes and amend your teaching and learning records, e.g. schemes of learning or session plans.
- Record your activities and reflections on your personal log and/or IfL REFLECT account.
- If you are undertaking initial teacher training, your responses provide evidence for AS5, AK5.1, AP5.1, AS7, AK7.2 and AP7.3 and elements of Domains B and C.

Although the introduction of policies for lifelong learning include a strategy for further developing a more professional and highly regarded workforce, the unintended consequence of this same framework of policies is that they have created conditions (perhaps more so within colleges than other organisations in the Lifelong

Learning Sector) that, in some cases, seem to militate against an essential requirement for personal and professional development: the energy and time teachers need to embark on projects for improvement and undertake their own CPD. On the one hand, the pressure on teachers to respond to new policies, take on new occupational responsibilities and implement change *stimulates* the need for CPD to cope with the change. On the other hand, the pace of change itself and the intensification of workloads *creates barriers* to improvement as opportunities for reflection are limited and time for discussion with colleagues diminished in the workplace 'as it is often too easy to become bogged down with all the day-to-day activities' (Hillier, 2005: 215).

There is no doubt that the issue of how to improve the quality of teaching and learning in the Lifelong Learning Sector has had high political, professional and managerial priority for some years, yet the goals imposed on the sector through government policies are not always consistent with the aims of individuals working in the sector. There seems to be a contradiction between the sector's desire to view the introduction of the LLUK standards for teachers in the sector as a positive move to contributing to raising the standards of teaching and learning in the sector and the reality of everyday practice for teachers in the sector. Teachers experience successive changes to conditions of work, significant changes brought about by new funding methodologies and more often than not an increase in workloads. For many teachers, all of these factors seem to jeopardise standards of teaching and learning. The low morale of those working in the Further Education Sector has been well documented over the years and the Workforce Strategy for the Further Education Sector in England 2007–2012 is a welcome development to make the Lifelong Learning Sector a more attractive place in which to work and promote Further Education as a career of choice (LLUK, 2007a).

The performance of the sector has been linked to the achievement of government objectives and is overseen by the Young People's Learning Agency and the Skills Funding Agency, but it is not just *structural or organisational changes* in the last decade that have consequences for the teacher's role in the sector today, it is also *educational changes*. The tensions between the twin demands of managers outside the classroom or training workshop and of learners inside them have contributed to changing the nature of teachers' workloads and their occupational role and thus, it is suggested, the skills and attributes needed by teachers to practise successfully in the future.

If the nature of the individual teacher's role is changing, then it is important to be able to identify how it is changing and the characteristics of the skills and attributes that are required now and in the future, so that you can benefit from this knowledge when considering your own professional and personal development. What you need to know is how successful teachers continue to develop their role as they undertake new tasks and work in different situations and how they develop their professional practice through opportunities embedded in their everyday workloads. This knowledge will help you to make choices about engaging in activities that will contribute to your own success in the future. After all, as Petty says, it is up to you to work out the teaching of the future!

Teachers' work as educational practice

In spite of the need to identify what teachers need to know and do to be successful, defining teachers' professional practice and what makes it successful is problematic. It could be argued that professional practice is all that is not theory – as theory deals with abstract ideas and success involves practical tasks, activities, capacities and skills connected to teaching and learning. It is suggested by Carr (1993: 162) that this view of practice is unsatisfactory as the 'general weakness of this "oppositional" view is that it generates criteria for "practice" which, when applied to the notion of *educational* practice, excludes too much' (Carr, 1993: 162).

Carr's perspective is that this approach always underestimates the extent to which individuals like yourself, who are engaged professionally in educational practices, have to reflect upon, and hence theorise about, what you are trying to do. What you do as a teacher and what you think about and reflect on to help you make decisions about how to improve what you subsequently do cannot be separated – these elements are an integral part of your role as a teacher, i.e. your work is educational practice. If you accept the view taken by Carr, professional practice is not opposed to theory but is governed by an implicit theoretical framework, which has been developed through reflection and which structures and guides the activities of individuals engaged in educational practice. The activities are, in essence, made up of practical tasks which individual teachers reflect on but it is important to remember that they are about education – not just to keep learners busy.

Consequently, concepts such as educational practice are subject to change as political, economic and social changes occur. I have previously advocated that one way of understanding the concept of educational practice is to identify the changes that are occurring in the *wider environment*, and this was addressed through the discussion of policies in Chapter 1 and the LLUK standards in Chapter 2. Another way of understanding the concept is by noting changes in the *organisational environment* that influence how you as a teacher approach your role – which is the main focus of this chapter.

What often happens, however, is that organisational goals and your individual goals may not always align, and what has been known for some time is that an organisation cannot operate efficiently unless there is *synergy* between the goals of the organisation and the individual. According to Hannagan (2008: 12) departments and teams are more productive when they work together rather than as separate units. In the Lifelong Learning Sector this is not always necessarily the case because:

- job descriptions have limitations in revealing what teachers in the sector actually do from day to day and many routine, and regular tasks which are carried out remain unwritten in the formal document;
- the psychological contract (consisting of a teacher's perceived expectations of their role and what the organisation expects to receive) is largely assumed on both sides and unspoken;
- individual teachers (just like many employees in other organisations) tend to organise their workload to satisfy their own needs and work on tasks that they feel comfortable with and avoid tasks they don't like;
- nationally agreed conditions of service have been replaced by locally agreed contracts which may vary from organisation to organisation and working hours and rates of pay may vary from public sector to private sector organisations.

If you take all these factors into account, it is evident that approaches to the role of teacher may differ widely from organisation to organisation and person to person. Therefore, your criteria for success and what counts as suitable for CPD will probably differ from someone else's criteria for success and their choice for CPD.

Check It Out   3.2

The following questions might help you discover whether there is synergy between organisational goals and your individual goals.

- Do you do precisely what is written down on your job description and nothing else?
- Have you ever been unaware that certain duties or tasks were expected of you – and only became aware of them when it was pointed out by a manager or colleague that you hadn't done them?
- Have you noticed a tendency in yourself to concentrate on tasks that you are familiar with and put off undertaking new responsibilities or making changes that your managers or colleagues request and would like to see you carry out?
- Do you actually know what your organisation's goals are and, if so, do your own personal goals for the current year align with the organisation's goals?

Links To CPD

- Formulate your own goals from the ideas you have been developing on your Action Plan and where possible link them specifically to your organisation's goals. Also consider your commitment to the application of relevant statutory requirements and how you conform to agreed codes of practice, e.g. in assessment. Edit your Action Plan to include your own personal goals for the current year.
- If you are undertaking initial teacher training, your responses to the above activity provide evidence for LLUK standards AS6, AK6.1, AP6.1 and elements of Domain E.

Although you might think that what comprises teachers' own professional practice could simply be defined as *the amount of work that is performed*, there are many complex issues surrounding the work performed and the tasks teachers carry out, for example:

- the division of labour within the workforce;
- the emotional labour involved;
- the nature of the tasks carried out.

These issues have to be considered as well as the way tasks are allocated, selected and prioritised by the individual and the organisation. The content of teachers' practice is influenced by a range of factors within the organisation, such as:

- the resources available;
- teaching methods adopted;
- the make-up of learner groups;
- assessment systems;
- management styles.

Such factors are themselves influenced to a significant degree by the policies and frameworks for governance within which organisations in the Lifelong Learning Sector operate, and it is obvious that the nature of teachers' practice is continually subject to change to take account of these demands. These demands in turn are also influenced by an individual's disposition, for example:

- the professional commitment of individual teachers to their job;
- how much time and effort they invest in their job;
- the values that they bring to their job which underpin their day-to-day professional practice.

No doubt you have probably come across teachers who are devoted to their job, who are hard-working and go 'the extra mile' for their learners. You have probably also met other teachers who appear disinterested and disillusioned about the expectations of their role and wish they were working anywhere but with learners in the Lifelong Learning Sector.

To sum up these ideas, educational practice can be said to be everything you do as a teacher as part of your working life including the way you reflect and theorise about your job. Hence, to develop your knowledge of professional practice it is necessary to examine what you *currently do*. Cooper and McIntyre (1996) stress that any serious attempts to improve the quality and effectiveness of teaching and learning must start with deepening your understanding of what you do in the classroom at present but they advise that, to be successful, your initial and CPD also needs to be informed by an understanding of how *experienced* teachers do their work, preferably in your subject specialism.

Check It Out   3.3

Develop your understandings of educational practice

- Examine your learning plans or training documents for one week and evaluate each one in depth.
- Identify the particular tasks that contribute to the effectiveness of your teaching.
- Organise an observation of a teaching/training session by an experienced teacher in your subject specialism and record what they do (this will be part of your programme if you are undertaking initial teacher training).
- Analyse the experienced teacher's session, then discuss the content, methods, etc. with them and invite them to share with you what makes their session effective.
- Compare your ideas with those of the experienced teacher and identify which of their effective elements you could incorporate into your own sessions in the future to improve your practice.

Links To CPD

- Critical reflection is an important tool for professional learning. How do the above activities contribute to achieving your personal goals for the year? Open a file in which to write your reflections that can be used during the year as a Professional Development Journal. Your reflections (on all the above activities) could be logged in your Personal Development Journal to demonstrate your ongoing learning and contribute to your annual CPD requirement.
- If you are undertaking initial teacher training, your reflections provide evidence for LLUK standards AS4, AP4.2, AP5.2, AS7 and elements of Domains B and C.

The diversity of the teacher's role

Teachers' identities have traditionally been bound up in the activities of teaching and their subject knowledge. I am sure that most of you would agree that the popular image of teachers' work held by those outside of the profession is of activities, such as:

- presenting new material;
- giving instructions;
- providing explanations;
- asking questions;
- offering advice;
- checking behaviour;

- marking work;
- providing feedback.

You might often also hear your colleagues describing the 'real' work of teaching in the Lifelong Learning Sector as:

- preparing sessions;
- delivering them;
- assessing work or performance.

Although these activities are central to teachers' work – and face-to-face teaching, preparation and assessing tasks remain central to teachers' perception of what their job entails – if you are really serious about improving the quality and effectiveness of your teaching and learning, I would suggest that it is not just what you do in the classroom at present that needs investigating because what is now happening (or for many has already happened) is that core elements of professional practice are being eroded and additional non-teaching tasks are added to workloads. The teacher's role extends beyond the classroom into the organisational environment.

The concept of the 'extended professional' was introduced some time ago (Hoyle, 1969) but it is as relevant today as it has ever been. Hoyle describes the extended professional as someone with a perspective on their role that extends beyond the immediate demands of the classroom. This contrasts with Cooper and Macintyre's advice about focusing on classroom practice and resonates with my observations in Chapter 1 that a *wider understanding* of the role is required. To see what I mean, have a look at the extracts below to see how the teacher's role has been described by different authors over the years.

Brain (1994: 97) suggests that the teacher in further education is also a:

> learning facilitator/supporter, learning resource producer, information technology specialist, pastoral worker, marketer, course/programme manager, deliverer of integrated core skills, raiser of European awareness, team worker, tester, assessor, examiner, deliverer of open/flexible/distance learning, administrator and increasingly manager.

Gewirtz's (1996: 4) contention is that, as a consequence of more direct management control, the activities absorbing teachers' time are:
- balancing budgets;
- target setting;
- performance monitoring;
- quantifying results.

According to Armitage et al. (2007: 7) a teacher's role includes activities such as:
- serving on committees;
- undertaking quality audits;
- designing courses and distance learning packs;

- recruitment;
- marketing.

In their research on colleges, Huddleston and Unwin (2007: 25) cite an extract from an employment contract of a main-grade teacher in one of the largest FE Colleges in England and the range of duties that the teacher will be expected to undertake:

> Formal schedule teaching, tutorials, student assessment, management of learning programmes and curriculum development, student admissions, educational guidance, counselling, preparation of learning materials and student assignments, marking student work, marking examinations, management and supervision of student visit programmes, research and other forms of scholarly activity, marketing activities, consultancy, leadership, supervisory, administration and personal professional development.

Williams (2007: 43) intimates that it was the effect of FE Colleges being taken out of local education authority control in 1992, which meant colleges having to compete independently and teachers having to work under different contractual arrangements, that had a considerable impact on the teacher's role:

> The new contracts stated that teaching was only one aspect of the lecturer's role; this made the way clear for extra responsibilities relating to recruitment, retention, pastoral work, needs assessment and working with support and administrative staff, which would all be necessary parts of the inclusive learning agenda. Alongside new contracts came new forms of accountability, annual performance management appraisals, performance-related pay and a newly vigorous external inspection process under the control of the Further Education Funding Council (FEFC).

Butcher (2008: 253) states there is ever-increasing diversity within a teacher's role which includes organisation of classroom teaching and concern with each learner's individual progress, but there is a need to assimilate into practice:
- the effective management of the overall quality of the various systems;
- liaison with other professionals;
- effective communication;
- reviewing learning;
- working relationships;
- quality assurance.

The extracts above highlight the diversity of the teacher's role in the Lifelong Learning Sector and illustrate the wide range of duties expected of the role. From these perspectives, it can be seen that the role is certainly not limited to teaching but includes managerial and administrative work. The examples provided by the authors draw attention to the mix of teaching and non-teaching duties involved. It can also be clearly seen that Hoyle's concept of the extended professional could be applied to the role of the teacher and that the role has been more than face-to-face teaching, preparation and assessing for many years.

Check It Out   3.4

Identify teaching and non-teaching tasks
- From the lists of duties presented above, identify the tasks that you currently undertake as part of your day-to-day professional practice.
- If you are undertaking initial teacher training, share this activity with your mentor and discuss the tasks they undertake as part of their normal routine.
- Identify any different tasks that you undertake currently that are not included above and add to your list.
- Divide the tasks into two lists: 'Teaching Tasks' and 'Non-teaching Tasks' to identify the duties that make up your role as a teacher.

You will need these lists for the 3.5 Check It Out activity.

Professional compromise and the teacher's role

Even if you look at the totality of the teacher's role and take a view that you have a role to play beyond the classroom or training workshop as an extended professional, it would appear that non-teaching activities have taken on increasing importance in recent years in the Lifelong Learning Sector. However, they are often linked to a concern about the quality of education and training being provided because of the detrimental effect on teaching of a growing administrative workload. The paradox is that, although tasks are identified as managerial and administrative, they are required because of the *changing educational practices* in the sector. Tasks such as the ones in the following list are predominantly administrative, managerial and non-teaching – but they are all *teaching-related* activities:

- recording of individual learning plans and tutorials;
- quality assurance documentation;
- course team meetings;
- organising and/or evaluating work placements;
- organising and attending industrial/educational visits;
- writing submissions for new programmes;
- internal verification, tracking progress and achievement;
- preparing for external inspection.

These tasks, and similar administrative and managerial tasks, support the view that non-teaching tasks are increasingly becoming part of the teacher's professional role, but most of them are essential to support your learners.

There is no doubt that non-teaching tasks prove time-consuming and can cause work overload if they are 'bolted-on' to teachers' workloads as educational practices change. Not all the old teaching ways are changed by individuals in the sector or outdated administrative routines dropped by organisations. Initiatives which are designed to increase the relevance of what the sector provides to the world of work afford benefits to the learner but may result in you being overburdened if you don't reassess your workload.

At this point it will be informative to look at case-study research which illustrates the day-to-day realities of teachers' professional practice and provides evidence of perceived tensions within the role of teacher.

Case Study Research 3.1

Teachers' work as professional compromise

My own research with full-time and part-time teachers in colleges, Sixth-form Colleges and other training organisations carried out over the last few years has shown that tensions are prevalent at two points in the teacher's role. First, there are tensions between organisational systems which cause frustrations and which aggravate rather than support the changing conditions teachers now face. Second, there are tensions as teachers juggle competing demands and have to make choices about which tasks to prioritise.

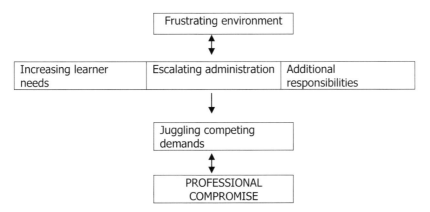

Figure 3.1 Teaching as professional compromise

- *A frustrating environment* – it is the physical environment of the workplace that places pressures on teachers as much as its organisational culture. Time wasted on accessing resources and finding source material or equipment means that jobs that should take only a few minutes seem to take forever. The frustrations are about everyday organisational procedures and often a lack of administrative support. Mundane frustrations, such as car-parking problems, room changes, missing or broken equipment and travelling between sites, seem to create as much pressure for teachers as lack of support from managers, internal inspection and/or supervision and evaluation of their performance by quality managers.
- *Increasing learner needs* – recruitment of learners with more diverse backgrounds is perceived as a reason for learners being more challenging and demanding and thus requiring more of the teacher's time. The learners' demands have an educational basis, such as dealing with large numbers in a group and the extra work this creates, or delivering several levels in one session because of the diversity of the group. Preparing flexible sessions to meet these requirements takes more time and assessing, marking and recording work is also more complex. Learners' needs can also be personal and teachers report feeling that they are now expected to deal with a wide range of personal problems which demand ever-increasing support for learners and guidance outside the classroom.
- *Escalating administration* – the feeling of not being able to keep up with administration and being able to plan and anticipate administrative demands causes tension for some teachers. Requests at short notice to assist with non-teaching duties, such as quality assurance data and meetings about preparing for inspection, are not only regarded as an additional burden but are cited as affecting the quality of teaching as they encroach on preparation and marking time.
- *Additional responsibilities* – teachers feel that their time outside the classroom or training workshop is no longer available for them to use as they wish, for example in preparing resources and researching for materials when developing new courses. Organising careers fairs, generating course advertising materials and giving talks in schools, although considered enjoyable, are all time-consuming. Teachers see such duties as additional responsibilities because they do not consider this work is part of a normal workload and yet it is compulsory.

- *Juggling competing demands* – the juggling of demands is perceived as twofold: first, between teaching quality and non-teaching demands, second, between work demands and home life. Having to leave the classroom or training workshop to deal with last-minute crises or scheduled meeting or events means trying to be in two places at once. Not only have teachers to prepare work for their learners to get on with, or set them work out of the allocated session which often generates more assessing later on, but they also have to deal with the work generated from attending meetings or events. Teachers point out that meetings are often related to quality assurance or raising standards, but attendance at such meetings threatens the quality of current provision. Alternatively, dealing with administration in class results in conflict for teachers who are concerned about their learners' progress. Problems are experienced by many teachers in juggling demands for extra work outside the organisation which have an impact on the quality of home life.
- *Professional compromise* – a lack of time for thorough research and preparation for sessions was identified as a way in which professional standards were compromised. Keeping materials up to date is described as difficult due to other demands outside the classroom or training workshop. There are many examples of this provided by teachers: not reviewing videos before use, not preparing worked examples, not devising up-to-date case studies, not marking to deadlines agreed with learners, not booking equipment or inviting expert speakers. When under pressure of time it is considered easier to use existing materials rather than develop new ones, but this can result in learner dissatisfaction. Teachers admit they find it difficult to meet learners' emotional needs when they are feeling under pressure from administrative tasks or additional managerial duties themselves. Ways to save time are found, e.g. by neglecting workplace visits to monitor students and liaise with employers, or not using new equipment because there is no time to try it out before a session. Teachers view this as letting standards drop and feel professional compromise means they are letting down their learners.

Case Study Research 3.1 reveals evidence of the tensions teachers participating in the research encounter in their everyday professional practice and Rogers identifies this, too:

> supposedly 'small' issues like flickering neon lights; doors that jam; inadequate furniture (ever had to 'scrounge' for chairs for a classroom?); poor staff toilets; poor organisational and communication processes are just some of the 'structural stressors' that staff face. Many of these structural/organisational stressors can (and should) be dealt with quickly. Letting them drag on (unattended) can be a daily irritant in an already stressful profession when we are seeking to teach (and manage) hard classes. (Rogers, 2006: 166)

One of the major ways that teachers cope with their frustrating environment and deal with increased workloads created by escalating administration and additional responsibilities is to try and juggle the conflicting priorities between teaching and non-teaching tasks, and the demands of home and work, by cutting corners and letting professional standards drop. In their view, this results in professional compromise.

Check It Out 3.6

How others see the role of the teacher and the teaching and learning environment

The notion of 'professional compromise' may be one that you recognise.
- Does Case Study Research 3.1 ring true with your experiences of your organisation and your approach to the role of teacher?
- If so, identify the similarities.
- If not, identify the differences and consider why you think this is the case.

Links To CPD

It is essential to be aware of your own practice on individuals and their learning. Review recent formal evaluations from your learners and reflect on whether there are signs of 'professional compromise' in your practice or whether the evaluations demonstrate your commitment to your role.

If you are undertaking teacher training, your responses to the above activity provide evidence for LLUK standards AS4, AK4.2, AP4.2 and elements of Domain B.

A compromise is generally achieved as a result of negotiations in which concessions are made and the parties meet halfway and come to some agreement. The teachers' accounts in Case Study Research 3.1 do not imply co-operation or any give and take within the organisation, but reveal that the teachers are very often weighed down and encumbered by organisational obligations which constrain what they want: quality teaching.

Tummons (2008) agrees that teachers have busy working lives and there may be barely time enough to carry out the day-to-day responsibilities of the teacher's role without attending training courses as well. However, despite their busy lives, if they want to achieve quality teaching, individual teachers must make CPD an important aspect of their professional life and Tummons provides a clear rationale of the reasons why it is so important.

A rationale for CPD: the teacher

1. To update subject-specialist knowledge
Subject specialism does not stand still. The things that are taught and learned change, perhaps because of new technologies, new ways of looking at older ideas or changing attitudes. Within different subject areas, what needs to be known and understood about that subject can and does change frequently.

2. To take account of changes to the curriculum
New technological advances or industrial standards invariably have an impact on the

courses that are offered within the sector. Curriculum documents are revised or even rewritten regularly: sometimes a course will be changed from one year to the next, often with little notice. Tutors and assessors need to keep abreast of these changes to the programmes that they are involved in, in addition to acquiring the new skills and knowledge that have driven these changes.

3. To update organisational and procedural knowledge
Changes to the curriculum may lead to changes in assessment procedures, or changes in the way that the course is run in the college or the workplace as a whole. CPD can involve learning about and taking on new workplace procedures as well as learning new subject knowledge.

4. To enhance employment prospects
It is quite common for a teacher to want to change jobs during the course of their career. Some teachers look to take on management responsibilities, sometimes in addition to maintaining a teaching role. Trainers and assessors working in industrial or commercial settings may decide to move to work in a college, and vice versa. In these, and other, circumstances, a strong CPD record can be a real asset when making applications and attending interviews.

5. To take account of technological changes
Changes in technology can have an impact on our teaching practice that goes beyond the confines of the subject specialism: we do not need to be teachers of a computing course to gain benefits from using technology in our workplaces.

6. To take account of legislative changes
Sometimes, the duties carried out by teachers change not because of changes to the course or to the subject matter, but due to broader changes in the world in which we live. The impact of the Disability Discrimination Act 2005 on FE Colleges is a good example.

7. To maintain a licence to practice
Since 2007 teachers in the Lifelong Learning Sector have been required to fulfil at the very least 30 hours of CPD a year, with a reduced amount for part-time teachers. Teachers have to maintain a portfolio of CPD that shows evidence of industrial/subject updating, including membership of appropriate professional bodies, development of skills in subject teaching, including the effective application of e-learning techniques, application of diversity and equal opportunity principles and use of learner feedback to improve performance.

8. To stay fresh and involved
Finally, it is worth remembering that staying involved and engaged with new ways of teaching and learning in a different subject specialism can keep teachers fresh, creative and inspiring.

(Adapted from Tummons, 2008: 34–6)

Tummons' framework confirms that CPD is essential for teachers to cope with their changing role and notes that it is not difficult for students to spot those teachers who are tired and jaded and lack enthusiasm for the subject they teach. One of the problems revealed in Case Study Research 3.1 appears to be the tension between teaching commitments and organisational issues which results in teachers becoming tired and jaded and then their enthusiasm wanes. CPD in Tummons' view enables teachers to be involved with their work through keeping up to date and staying fresh, creative and inspiring. Now that must surely be better for you than professional compromise!

Check It Out   3.7

Rationale for CPD

The framework provided by Tummons provides eight reasons for engaging in CPD.

- Identify which reasons may be particularly important for you to consider for your own personal and professional development.
- Prioritise the reasons and use the headings to record your subsequent activities in your professional development journal or portfolio.

Links To CPD

When you have identified your priorities for engaging in CPD and your own requirement to fulfil your hours of CPD for the current year, amend your Action Plan accordingly. Now you know your priorities, put some dates to the activities. Use your reflections from this activity to contribute to your Personal Development Journal or log on your IfL REFLECT account.

If you are undertaking initial teacher training, the above activity provides evidence for LLUK standards AS4, AK4.1, AP4.1 and elements of Domains B and C.

Looking at things from an organisational perspective, Tummons provides *A rationale for CPD: the college* which outlines reasons that organisations – rather than teachers – in the Lifelong Learning Sector have for encouraging CPD within the workforce – and not the least is to encourage quality teaching. However, before you consider Tummons' rationale for the organisation, a first step is to consider the organisation from managers' perspectives and evaluate the impact of these different perspectives on teachers' CPD.

Managers' perspectives on the role of the teacher and the teaching environment

It is not surprising that, in general, managers' individual actions and responses do not harmonise with the perceptions of organisational issues described by teachers in Case Study Research 3.1. However, the managers' accounts do highlight another apparent paradox. They reveal a dichotomy between *educational conditions* – such as new curricula requirements, classroom challenges and inadequate learner support – with *organisational conditions* – such as poor management systems, increased expectations and intensification of work through reduced hours for teaching or training. Their contention is that it is the *perception of these conditions* rather than the reality of the situation that can lead to conservative teaching rather than quality teaching – as the following case study reveals.

Case Study Research 3.2

Teachers' workloads and conservative teaching

My own research with middle managers in colleges, Sixth-form Colleges and other training organisations carried out over the last few years has shown that managers position themselves very differently from teachers regarding the reasons for the tensions in the teaching environment and their constructions of the workplace appear to be largely influenced by their attitude towards stress. Organisational elements such as poor management systems, increased expectations of the teacher's role and intensification of work are not in themselves problematic, according to the managers participating in the research, and only become so when teachers perceive them as stressful. Similarly, educational elements such as new curricula, classroom challenges and inadequate support for learners are not considered insurmountable and only become problematic if teachers are nostalgic for past ways of working. The combination of perceptions of stress and nostalgia for past practices leads to conservative teaching – just at a time when strategies to raise the standards of teaching and learning are put in place and creative responses are required.

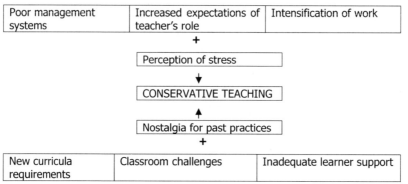

Figure 3.2 Workloads and conservative teaching

- At one end of the spectrum, there is an awareness of the endless, day-to-day pressures and the need to support teachers through support mechanisms in the form of democratic management and meetings with individual staff. This collaborative approach to managing staff is a strategy intended to provide an opportunity for involvement and ownership for teachers and an attempt to identify problems and alleviate stress. At the other end of the spectrum, there is ignorance of current departmental practice and individual teacher's performance and, perhaps one could infer, ignorance of the level of tension among teachers.

- One could speculate about the level of support provided for teachers when a manager considers it is the teachers themselves who generate the notion of being over-busy – it is in their minds not reality. Contrast this with a manager who recognises overload and increases the administrative team to relieve the burden on teachers as much as possible. Managers' perceptions of the teacher's role inevitably contribute to their management decisions.
- Intensification of work for teachers is attributed to changed expectations, organisational bureaucracy, monitoring of retention and achievement targets – or conversely as mentioned above, teachers' own practices. Quality assurance systems, the culture of continuous improvement and inspection regimes are variously seen as a cause of grief, a source of pressure or a culture that needs to be embedded into the organisation so that no one gets complacent. On the one hand, a management view is that 'good' teachers ignore bureaucratic systems and controls to prioritise teaching. On the other hand, flatter organisational structures require teachers to take on management roles and the managers' perception is that teachers are reluctant to be drawn into management functions, other than curriculum management.
- The majority of managers participating in the research regard teachers' contracts as problematic and a barrier to organisational progress and efficiency. Timetabling is deliberately used to bring financial savings, even though the pressure of reducing teaching hours is acknowledged. These managers' concerns are rooted in maintaining systems that provide evidence of meeting targets, adding value and keeping to budgets, seek to use teachers' time effectively and strive to introduce new approaches to teaching. They put a convincing case for learner-centred delivery, which generates teachers' concerns about losing work and being made redundant or replaced by non-qualified staff, rather than promoting the trust required for teachers to spend time on developing flexible modes of delivery which subsequently require less teaching.
- Managers attribute teachers' conservative approach to teaching to their nostalgia for past practices and managers' accounts tell of their efforts to reconstruct the teacher's role as facilitator, e.g. using central resource banks, which are hampered by teachers' desire to keep control of knowledge rather than manage learning. Managers' perceptions reveal a widely held view that many teachers cling to the centrality of content over learning and are unaware of the importance of the learning process, e.g. these teachers still see quality as face-to-face teaching, try to stick to traditional methods and are reluctant to work in different ways. The majority of managers consider that teachers' unwittingly contribute to their own overload and cannot envision the benefits new approaches to teaching and learning bring.

A complex picture emerges from Case Study Research 3.2 of managers' views of the role of the teacher and the teaching environment. On the one hand, there are managers adopting supportive strategies and, on the other, managers actively manipulating teachers' time, extending role boundaries and encroaching on the ambiguous area of non-teaching time. Both managers and teachers seek quality teaching, but there are conflicting notions about what this means. The marked differences between teachers' and managers' views suggest that elements in organisational systems, e.g. intensification of work, may not in practice lead to *intended* organisational outcomes. Have a look now at the organisational reasons for wanting to encourage CPD within the workforce that Tummons identifies and relate the reasons he gives to your own learning environment.

A rationale for CPD: the college

1. To improve the student experience
Students have all kinds of expectations about their teacher and fluent expertise in their subject area is just one of these. Others include punctuality in marking and returning assignments, an understanding of college procedures or even simply a sympathetic ear when things – not necessarily just studies – are not going well.

2. To maximise the effectiveness of staff
Employers often provide or encourage appropriate CPD activities to improve the student experience, which can at the same time help the teachers expand their professional knowledge. This might be procedural: organising learning support for students with disabilities, or making plans for teaching and learning. The college may use lesson observation to highlight areas for improvement in the classroom. Colleges are aware of the changing needs of the curriculum and of any employers with whom they work, and will make time for CPD that allows staff to stay up to date in their subject.

3. To improve staff experience
The majority of colleges do endeavour to provide a positive and worthwhile work environment for their staff. It makes sense for colleges to do so. By giving staff the opportunity to develop their practice, colleges can also foster the sense that staff feel valued by their employer.

4. To improve accountability
Providers of education and training are accountable to a variety of stakeholders: boards of governors, parents, students, funding bodies, government agencies, fee sponsors and employers. One of the areas in which the performance or effectiveness of a college is measured is the quality of the teaching provided. In this regard, CPD is important for colleges in helping to ensure that the teaching staff are working as well as they possibly can.

(Adapted from Tummons, 2008: 36–7)

Tummons' two frameworks, which provide one rationale for CPD for teachers and another for organisations, reinforce my own line of reasoning that both teachers and managers in organisations are seeking the same thing: *quality teaching*. To overcome different expectations by teachers and managers of the role of the teacher, what is required is the development of *social practices* that enable both managers and teachers in the organisation to become all that they are capable of being (Pollard and James, 2004: 1).

Senge identifies that it is the 'fifth discipline', i.e. systems thinking, that leads to an understanding of how complex organisations function and how they can be changed to work effectively. Senge's (1990: 303) theory is that the 'practice of organisational learning involves developing tangible activities; new governing ideas, innovations in infrastructure, and new management methods and tools for changing the way people conduct their work'. If you pursue Senge's theory, 'the manager who wants more commitment, flexibility and creativity from employees is advised to provide them with lots of learning opportunities' (Buchanan and Huczynski, 2004: 131).

Perhaps it is a matter of survival for teachers to cling to conservative teaching methods – not nostalgia – if it is perceived that engaging in CPD and changing your practice means you may well be doing yourself out of a job.

Check It Out   3.8

Reflect on your role as a teacher

It has been suggested in this chapter that educational practice *integrates* theory and practice and that your individual theory about teaching is developed through your reflection on your practice. The questions Case Study Research 3.1 and 3.2 raise are:

- New organisational structures demand different roles, but does this inevitably lead to professional compromise for teachers?
- Is it possible for teachers to retain their professional identity and meet quality requirements?
- Is curriculum development a way of doing oneself out of a job?
- Does your organisational environment inhibit development of your role as a teacher?

Reflect on these questions and come up with your own ideas (or personal theories) about your role as a teacher and developing good practice in learning and teaching.

Links To CPD

If you are already employed in the Lifelong Learning Sector, this activity could be recorded in a Professional Development Journal or logged on your IfL REFLECT account. Identify a project, e.g. planning for learning as a member of a team, that you could undertake during the current year and indicate ways in which you could overcome organisational difficulties and improve the quality of your practice. Include the details of the project in your Action Plan.

If you are undertaking initial teacher training, your responses to the above activity provide evidence for LLUK standards AS4, AK4.1, AP4.1 and elements of Domain D.

A professional identity

My professional experience is that the competing demands on the teacher are often manifest in the tension between classroom and non-classroom work. My contention would be that it is the way experienced teachers organise the totality of their workload that needs to inform your initial and CPD. It is not the separate elements of teachers' workloads that are problematic in my view – arguably it is the *combination* of them.

Furthermore, the teacher's role extends beyond these tasks and is identifiable in the *ethical practices* of teachers and the way they relate to students, colleagues and others. Such matters as values and principles are part and parcel of the teacher's concerns and must also be taken into account alongside teaching and non-teaching tasks when trying to develop understandings of how experienced teachers work and in your attempts to improve the quality and effectiveness of your own professional practice. Indeed, in Bloomer and James' (2003: 249) view, professional practice is not simply something that a teacher *does*, it is as much what the teacher *is*, for in their view professional practice is a constituent part of the identity of the practitioner. A holistic approach to your role as a teacher is, therefore, advocated as this enables exploration of all the factors that might be up for consideration for professional development.

Check It Out   3.9

Evaluate your contribution to your organisation's quality cycle
- Has the evidence in the chapter so far convinced you of the need to be aware of the organisational environment and issues outside the immediate classroom or training workshop if you want to be a successful teacher in the Lifelong Learning Sector?
- Has the range of duties teachers are expected to undertake raised your awareness of the need to consider both teaching and non-teaching tasks as potential opportunities for to improve the quality of your practice by evaluating your contribution to the organisation's quality cycle?

Links To CPD
- Collate any documents you use to contribute to your organisation's quality cycle, identify any improvements which could be made to them and make the improvements after collaboration with your colleagues. Use your reflections from this activity to contribute to your Professional Development Journal or log on your IfL REFLECT account.
- If you are undertaking initial teacher training, the above activity provides evidence for LLUK standards AS7, AK7.2, AP7.2 and elements of Domain B.

A study of teachers' learning in their workplace illustrates the inter-relationship between the individual and their organisation as an opportunity for continuing professional and personal development:

> It is not just that each person learns in a context, rather, that person is a reciprocal and constitutive part of the context. (Hodkinson and Hodkinson, 2001: 2)

In this view, the teacher and the context are connected. What the teacher does contributes to the organisational effectiveness. However, that connection between the individual and their organisation can be problematic: the individual and organisational influences can be either constraints or opportunities. Two things need to be in place. One is that the individual must want to improve and continue to learn, and the second is that the organisation must provide a supportive environment for CPD to take place.

A reframed perspective

This chapter has revealed the dynamic nature of the role of the teacher and the teaching environment and illustrates the implicit tension between organisational and individual expectations in the workplace. The stability afforded by traditional educational and organisational practices is being eroded by concurrent:

- curriculum changes;
- new delivery styles;
- different learner intake;
- increasing accountability.

As organisational practices are becoming more complex, the rate of change and speed of its impact has made the role of the teacher more complex.

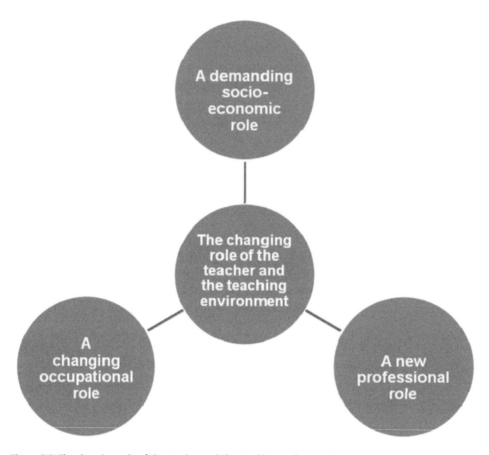

Figure 3.3 The changing role of the teacher and the teaching environment

New government policies cannot be implemented without developing new practices and Jarvis' (2002) view is that teaching in a changing world demands new skills. Many of the new techniques that have to be learnt by newcomers to teaching are ones that adult educators have used in teaching adults over the years, but he says that others are new for all teachers.

The changing occupational role means there is an opportunity for CPD through implementing new educational and organisational practices, for example through curriculum development projects, practitioner research to improve delivery or new course evaluation. In this way, innovation and improvement are built into the daily activities of teachers. Those of you who are undertaking initial teaching training are encouraged to use theories of learning to support the development of your occupational role in your placement. The individual teacher is at the centre of this change and your performance in the new role will depend on how you interact with the new teaching environment.

The development of lifelong learning policies has both social and economic strands. It is significant that compulsory teacher training emanated from these policies and the funding and impetus for raising quality in the sector is connected to the provision of resources for achieving these policies. The professional role of the teacher is being promoted by the introduction of the LLUK standards and simultaneously there is a need for teachers to take on a demanding socio-economic role. The shift in the last decade towards policies promoting social cohesion means there is an important role for teachers in providing vocational training to meet targets for economic renewal. New roles demanded by a changing world may challenge certainty in the workplace and a consistent self-concept and, although they may bring new opportunities, they also bring complexity and uncertainty. This is a view confirmed by Jarvis when he says that:

> Teaching is changing; it is being forced to change by the dominant globalizating forces of social change. Teachers are faced with playing new roles requiring many more and sometimes different skills. (Jarvis, 2002: 21)

As you respond to the changes and cope with the moves away from teaching and towards supporting learning, you are faced with increased observation and appraisal of your practice. A classic view is that the individual teacher's experience of educational change is overwhelmingly negative (Fullan, 1991). Fullan's famous studies reveal that in implementing change in educational settings there have been few successes and these have been short-lived. Interestingly, for Fullan the way ahead is through *melding* individual and organisational renewal: one cannot wait for the other but both must be pursued simultaneously. This implies a need to reconcile educational and organisational practices and suggests that individual teachers have to make positive changes to their own situations whilst organisations provide the support.

Success Story

Changing views of teaching and learning

I came into teaching years ago as a part-timer. At that time teaching was not anything like as serious as it is now. Some learners achieved, some didn't. As a teacher you tried your best. As we know, learning is a two-way process and not everyone wants to learn and years ago that wasn't considered a big deal. Yet now, not getting a high success rate is considered unacceptable and the fault is laid squarely with the teacher. Even though you can put everything in place for good teaching and learning experiences, you have to be realistic and recognise that student achievement will not necessarily be 100 per cent every time. Today, many teachers in the FE sector are beating themselves up about achievement targets, which, in my view, can be counter-productive and detract from a real quality learning experience. But the target-driven culture is not going to go away – we have to live with it now and into the future.

A diverse role

Although I've gained promotion and work in Quality Improvement now, I'm still teaching on teacher training. That means that there would seem to be a bit of a contradiction in my role; it's a bit like serving two masters. With my quality role, my remit is not just to raise the quality of teaching and learning in the college, but also processes, communications and data. However, the bottom line is that it's achievement statistics that have to improve. This appears to be at odds with the teacher-training aspect of my role, which requires a supportive, developmental process over time, not just a quick fix. However, teacher training involves encouraging everyone to be the best possible teacher they can be and this, of course, has a strong impact on quality improvement.

A new role for teachers

My plan is to bring the two roles together by refining college processes to make life more manageable for everyone and meld the supportive and quality improvement roles. At the moment I'm working on ways of improving teacher responsiveness to data systems. Traditionally, data systems have been the property of management and we've changed that around so that they become the property of course team leaders and teachers. They're encouraged to look at the data on a regular basis and check, e.g. retention and achievement statistics. A teacher knows a student has dropped out, but if they see that just one drop-out reduces the retention rate to 95 per cent the implications of retention become real and they can see what losing their student means for the whole college. You can't do anything about improving statistics if you don't have anything to do with them. We're encouraging teachers and course leaders to access and take ownership of the statistics on a regular basis. It's too soon to say whether it's made a significant difference yet, but we want students to be offered advice and guidance before dropping out and for teachers to see data systems in a different light. If problems with a particular course retention are identified, then support and guidance can be offered to teachers to improve this. In addition, individual support for new teachers, reviews of curriculum areas and action plans to improve teaching and learning and a full programme of CPD linked to identified development needs will help to improve the learning experience for all our students. Therefore, Quality Improvement extends the support mechanism to all teachers.

A professional identity

My teaching helps me to keep a grip on reality – if managers don't teach they lose that. I can really empathise with my teacher trainees who are studying and teaching 23+ hours a week – this is a big task when new to teaching. I think that to be successful, teachers today need, firstly, a genuine desire to make a difference to people's lives, stamina, high energy levels and good health. The teacher-training team try to model different teaching methods so that trainees are on the receiving end of different experiences. We encourage them to try out different methods in their own classroom and be innovative by attempting methods that they haven't tried before. We try to help them build their confidence, make changes and take responsibility for their personal and professional development from the outset. We've developed a strong relationship with our partner university and the quality of our teacher-training provision is well regarded and recognised – so that's a measure of success which is rewarding for all concerned and satisfying for me as it brings the different aspects of my role together.

If you asked me ...

When I observe teachers, the best ones:

- have the ability to engage a whole class of learners;
- ensure that *all* learners learn;
- demonstrate confidence in the classroom;
- display professional growth from the start;
- are flexible, innovative and try out new things;
- don't rely on whole-class teaching but use student-centred learning.

My advice for those starting out on a teaching career would be:

- know all about your role and think about where you want to go;
- be well prepared and organised as this enhances your teaching;
- be proactive – find out what's changing, look ahead to new developments, new qualifications;
- never stop learning – don't think that because you've got the qualification that's it;
- have empathy with your students – remember what it was like being a learner yourself and try and understand the mindset of 16 year-olds;
- be nice to your students – remember, the reason you are a teacher!

(Programme Leader for Teacher Training)

The two aspects of the Programme Leader's role, described in the above case study, enable them to 'meld' individual development through teacher training and organisational renewal through quality improvement as Fullan suggests. Through this joint role it is possible to reconcile educational and organisational practices and support individual teachers to make positive changes to their own situations whilst providing the organisational support. As a manager–teacher, this Programme Leader is in a particularly good position to offer guidance to teachers and they consider that managers who don't teach lack an understanding of what teaching is like today. Those whose job it is to assess quality teaching would be advised to take on board the guidance offered above and also note how it mirrors the professional view of someone who is head of a centre for professional learning at a university:

> Managers, inspectors and teacher trainers may well ask, 'How do we assess teachers then?' The answer is simply, 'Don't'. Don't *measure* them. They have knowledge. *Get to know* them and you will improve your understanding of what teaching in FE or any sector of education is about. (Hayes, D., 2007: 178)

Getting to know teachers is good advice and it is worth remembering that the role of the teacher and the teaching and learning environment is diverse. Hayes reminds you that good teachers relate well to their learners as they not only have the knowledge but also possess a love of their subject, which catches the imagination of learners: in his view quality teaching can't just be assessed using checklists.

> **Successful Strategies**
> Consider your role as a teacher and your teaching environment at three levels:
> - *Micro* – your occupational role is about your technical skills of teaching and CPD requires a problem-solving approach to which aspects of work-related practice to improve in the ever-changing teaching environment of the classroom.
> - *Meso* – your professional role is shaped by your values and CPD requires informed decision-making and evaluation about how to develop your role as a practitioner in the workforce of the organisation and take on new responsibilities, e.g. in your team, department or faculty.
> - *Macro* – your socio-economic role is a result of policies emanating from outside the organisation and classroom but which impact on both and CPD requires critically reviewing the way your role and environment are shaped and reshaped by the prevailing political context and demands of the world of work.

The two examples of Case Study Research in this chapter have illustrated that the role of the teacher in the Lifelong Learning Sector is diverse and dynamic and that the teaching environment is often an area of tension. The way teachers perceive their workload is reflected in their approach to their role and professional development. Ideas introduced above about the teacher role are developed and explored further in Chapter 6.

In Chapter 4 you will have an opportunity to consider your own approach to CPD as you check it out against research depicting four different approaches taken by teachers in the sector.

Part III Constructive Practice

4 Approaches to Continuing Professional Development

In this chapter you will find sections on:

- the conditions to support ongoing professional learning;
- the different goals of CPD;
- a holistic approach to teachers' personal learning;
- professional learning in the workplace;
- the importance of intentions for professional learning;
- key factors in approaches to CPD;
- personalisation of CPD.

The chapter addresses issues relating to Domain A: AS5 Collaboration with other individuals, groups and/or organisations with a legitimate interest in the progress and development of the learners.

For those undertaking initial teacher training, the chapter provides opportunities to generate evidence for LLUK standards AS4, AS5, AK5.1, AP5.1, AS7, AK7.2, AP7.2 and AP7.3.

The conditions to support ongoing professional learning

The following words by Hoban may make gloomy reading, especially if you make a real effort to reorganise your workload so that you can attend staff training sessions or travel to events in order to keep up to date and find out what's new, when perhaps you would really rather just be getting on with completing your paperwork or preparing material for next week's sessions:

In a conventional professional development programme, an innovation is usually presented to teachers in a workshop or a one-off professional development day with the expectation that it is implemented in a linear step-by-step process with little back-up support. However, this implementation process is usually short-lived because of the lack of conditions to support ongoing teacher learning. Often teachers are not reflective, ideas being presented are not in context with existing classroom practice, there is little collegial support [back in the workplace] and there is little time to modify relevant aspects of classroom practice. Because of the absence of conditions for learning, there is little chance of any support being generated to promote educational change. (Hoban, 2002: 71–2)

Hoban's opinion is that educational change is not straightforward and attendance at conventional staff development workshops or one-off events is not sufficient to ensure that any innovation is then implemented in the workplace. He admits that learning does occur in one-off workshops because teachers may gain a better understanding of what they already do, but he asserts that these events tend to reinforce existing practices rather than change them.

What you need to implement any innovations are conditions for professional learning that encourage long-term learning and support the process of changing educational practice for individuals within an organisation. If certain conditions to support ongoing teacher learning are essential for professional development leading to educational change, then focusing on the factors Hoban has identified is an important first step.

A theoretical framework for a professional learning system is based on a combination of the following conditions for teacher learning that need to complement each other to support educational change as a complex system:

- A *conception of teaching* as an art or profession, indicating a dynamic relationship among students, other teachers, [organisation], classroom, curriculum and context. Because of these interactions, there is always uncertainty and ambiguity in changing teaching practice.
- *Reflection* is important, as teachers need to become aware of why they teach the way they do and to focus on understanding the patterns of change resulting from the dynamic relationships in which they are involved.
- Teachers need a *purpose* for learning to foster a desire for change and so content should be negotiated.
- The *time frame* is long term, as changing teaching means adjusting the balance among many aspects of the existing classroom system.
- A sense of *community* is necessary so that teachers trust each other to share experiences such that topics for inquiry and debate may extend over several months or longer. As a result of this progressive discourse, teachers theorise and discussions are generative so that new ideas are always evolving.
- Teachers need to experiment with their ideas in *action* to test what works or does not work in their classrooms.

- A variety of knowledge sources are needed as *conceptual inputs* to extend the experiences of the participants.
- *Student feedback* is needed in response to the ideas being tried out in the classroom. (Hoban, 2004: 68–9)

Hoban's theoretical framework provides guidelines for supporting educational change rather than relying on common sense and 'the way we have always done it' which Hoban says is usually what happens. Each condition is unlikely to sustain teacher learning on its own, but it is the *combination of conditions* that establishes a framework to encourage long-term teacher learning. The connections between the conditions are likened to the numerous, unbroken threads of a spider's web and they are described as all being part of the web which in its entirety makes up the theoretical framework of a professional learning system. It is clear that teachers need to be reflective and new ideas need to be introduced in context with existing practice. However, alongside this there needs to be support in the workplace to encourage you to try out new ideas and time is required to modify relevant aspects of practice and evaluate them.

Check It Out 4.1

Identify conditions to support your professional learning

To benefit from your attendance at staff development events and for your professional development to be effective certain conditions are required (see Hoban's framework above). Your answers to the following questions will reveal whether the essential conditions to support your ongoing learning are in place.

- Do you find time to be reflective about the way you teach and the relationships encountered in your working day?
- What innovations can you identify that would enhance your learners' experience?
- Can you identify a colleague or manager (it may be your mentor if you are undertaking initial teacher training) who would listen to your ideas, discuss them with you and support your new learning through experimentation?
- Can you identify a time during the week to devote to collaborating with colleagues and/or others about the innovation?
- How would you evaluate whether your new ideas enhance learners' experience?

If all the conditions for professional learning are not yet in place, think about what you could to do to put them in place.

Links To CPD

- If you are already teaching in the Lifelong Learning Sector you could record your responses to the above question on your IfL RELECT account and share this with the colleague or manager you have been collaborating with. Perhaps you could negotiate a time for professional learning with them.
- If you are undertaking your initial teacher training, your responses to the above activity provide evidence for LLUK standards AS5, AK5.1 and AP5.1.

Making changes is not easy, even if you attend staff training days and get support in your organisation, as it involves the adjustment of many different aspects of professional practice in a back and forth, iterative way. Hoban says that if you make one change in the way that you work it inevitably influences other things. In Chapter 3 it was pointed out that organisations are complex systems and Hoban's view is that educational practice itself is a complex system. Hoban says that one change, for example a government policy introducing a new curriculum for 14–19 year-olds, may mean changing:

- the instructional strategies;
- assessment;
- class organisation.

It seems that you can't change one thing alone as there is always some impact on something else. No wonder changing practice to improve quality and enhance your learners' experience can often be so difficult and time-consuming!

Any way of working can be made more effective. What you do must be evaluated, which can be done with a mentor by sharing your experiences and taking your learners' views into account. Learning from these evaluations and making changes requires risk-taking, practice and taking control of the learning environment. Minton says that it is your responsibility to ensure that the environment supports what learners have to do in order to learn and take control:

> You can create your own environment with a little ingenuity. You are in charge.
> (Minton, 2005: 108)

But how easy is it to take control and create your own learning environment? How often do you wish there were more hours in the day as you rush around trying to get everything done? Time, or the lack of it, is an issue which pervades any consideration of the conditions for engaging in CPD. Dadds (2002) describes teachers as working in an overloaded, 'hurry-along' context where time has to be used wisely. Lack of time results in teachers engaging mostly in task-orientated work and little time is left for deeper thoughts about practice as teachers become overwhelmed and concerned how best to survive (Hillier, 2005). There is a contradictory view that time pressures are used as an excuse:

> Increased organisational demands, workload, norms of privacy, departmental membership, timetabling and the physical nature of the institution are often used as an excuse for not having time to collaborate. (Anderson, 2002: 21)

Anderson is referring to teachers' claim that there is a lack of time for formal collaboration in organisations, but in my view informal opportunities for collaboration are also dwindling. How often do you choose to use your lunch breaks for the short-term benefit of feeling prepared for your next teaching session, rather than choosing to spend it in mutual exchange of views about future professional practice with like-minded colleagues, which has long-term benefits?

Different views of time are generated by different experiences and interpretations. The inner duration of time varies from individual to individual, e.g. it can 'drag' or 'fly'. You may experience time 'flying' when you are trying to include all the relevant points in an important presentation but for an audience member who finds it all irrelevant to their particular circumstance the hour-long presentation seems to 'drag'. As a professional group, teachers' sense of time is not consistent but varies as it is also grounded in other aspects of their lives both at work and at home. Nevertheless, the way time is spent in the course of a working week illustrates considerable diversity in how teachers spend their time, a general feeling that more must be done in less time and evidence of the impact of localised employment relations in the Lifelong Learning Sector. What this does generate within organisations is a culture which says that 'you must work very long hours to appear committed'. If there is also little back-up support in the organisation, as Squires maintains, then opportunities for innovation are more difficult to fit in with day-to-day commitments.

> While teachers in schools and colleges are generally reckoned to be less autonomous than their counterparts in higher or adult education, recent changes in the latter sectors have led to an increase in external regulation in the name of accountability, consistency and the maintenance of standards. (Squires, 2003: 7)

Squires suggests that the degree of control you have over your own teaching may vary in terms of curriculum, materials, methods or assessment and there may be considerable differences between one organisation and the next, or even one department and the next.

Check It Out 4.2

Identify the level of control you have over your own work

Squires suggests you reflect on your own role in your organisation to find out the degree of control you have over your own teaching by responding to the following questions:

- Do you design your courses or follow a laid-down curriculum?
- Do you create your own materials or use prescribed textbooks?
- Do you have a say in who comes on your course?
- Are you free to teach as you want?

- Who sets and marks assignments or exams?
- Who inspects or evaluates your practice?
- How far are any of the above under your control, or subject to external – perhaps even national – regulations?

Links To CPD

Reflection on your responses to the above questions should provide insights into aspects of your teaching that you can control and help you identify goals for professional development that you can instigate and carry out individually, or ones that need collaboration from your departmental colleagues.

If you are undertaking initial teacher training, your reflection provides evidence for LLUK standard AS4.

Teaching is not just what goes on in the classroom, but encompasses everything you do to support learning. You need to consider what opportunities arise within your whole workload for your own professional learning and how much professional autonomy you have in your workplace.

Case Study Research   4.1

First key factor in approaches to professional development: level of control over workload

If the professional learning context is one in which lack of time and workplace pressures are inextricably connected this has a critical bearing on the *level of control* a teacher may be able to exert over their workload to create opportunities for their continuing personal and professional development.

The different goals of CPD

A common goal of professional development is taken to be improved practice but there are many different routes towards that goal. This chapter reveals that teachers in the Lifelong Learning Sector choose different routes, not just according to their career stage but also according to their individual mindset and working context. Tummons (2008) agrees that CPD can take many forms and have many purposes and suggests that some activities easily lend themselves to being identified as CPD, e.g. going on a training course in order to learn new teaching techniques.

Check It Out   4.3

Identify what constitutes CPD

Tummons (2008: 34) poses questions about what CPD consists of, how it should be carried out and how it should be prepared for and justified.

Other activities are a little less clear-cut: is reading (to take one example) a form of CPD or simply something that tutors should be doing anyway? Do activities organised by official institutions always count as CPD? Do activities carried out on an unofficial basis count as CPD? Who gets to 'set' the CPD curriculum?

Tummons' questions are designed to make you think a bit more about what constitutes CPD and how you would justify activities that you have chosen.

Links To CPD

Examine your action plan for CPD and identify who sets the agenda – you or your organisation. Up-date your action plan in light of your response and add justifications for any activities chosen.

If you are undertaking initial teacher training, your reflections on what constitutes CPD and your justification for activities provides evidence for LLUK standard AS4.

It seems that all too often improvements resulting from professional development activities are talked about as if they were something that we could all recognise without difficulty. On the contrary, strategies to improve practice raise the issues of value conflicts and dilemmas. You have to think carefully why you are doing them and who will benefit from the improvements.

What seems good for some situations and teachers may be inappropriate for others. As professional practice means different things to different people, it is difficult to achieve a consensus. What you think is important to improve and how you choose to spend your valuable time is influenced by your personal values about education, even if you are responding to an innovation identified as an organisational priority or a new government policy. Your level of commitment to implementing change is most likely to be influenced by how worthwhile you think the change will be and more than likely you weigh up whether all the effort will be beneficial to your learners in terms of what you value.

The routes available for a teacher to take on their professional journey towards improving practice are well documented:

- through reflective practice (Ghaye and Ghaye, 1998; Hillier, 2005; Moon, 2005; Pollard, 2008);
- through action research (Jameson and Hillier, 2003; Coles, 2004; Petty, 2006; Campbell and Norton, 2007);
- through up-dating technical competence (Brookes and Hughes, 2001);
- through developing social skills (Rogers, 2002; Reece and Walker, 2007; Armitage et al., 2007);
- through acquisition of knowledge and gaining formal qualifications (Denby et al., 2008; Tummons, 2008).

With their knowledge of college-focused, staff development policies, Oldroyd and Hall (1991) tackle the question of professional values by suggesting that the goal of professional development is not just one thing but a cluster of activities that develop *informed professional judgement*. This is a concept that has stood the test of time and which fits well with the LLUK standards. They describe it as a blend of professional experience informed by the results of formal evaluation and research studies. Indeed, it mirrors Eraut's (1998) proposal that the purpose of professional education and training should be to develop *professional capability*, which again is a blend of skills which includes competence in a range of tasks, roles and jobs but goes beyond these. He proposes professional learning and development must be ongoing and take account of changing individual and social contexts. This involves being able to develop or transform your practice over time, to construct new knowledge through your experience of practice as well as learning from others. In turn, Eraut's ideas complement the conditions to support the ongoing teacher learning that Hoban (2002) advocated (see page 86).

For Ramsden (2000) the goal is *educational effectiveness*. His evidence from research in improving teaching and learning in Sixth-form Colleges and the Higher Education Sector is that there are no certain prescriptions for good practice, there are only *teachers*. Educational effectiveness depends on:

- *teachers'* professionalism;
- *teachers'* experience;
- *teachers'* commitment.

From a learner's point of view, too, a teacher's personal attributes are important. Research into what constitutes good practice in the eyes of learners can be summarised in two ways:

1 Relating to the *qualities* that teachers should demonstrate:
- be enthusiastic;
- warm;
- approachable.

2 Relating to the *teaching attributes* that are required:
- clear aims and objectives;
- be a subject expert;
- be open to others' views. (Reece and Walker, 2007: 17)

It is evident that professional identity, personal attributes and the individual teacher's commitment are considered by experts in professional development as critical to improve practice. The perspectives explored in this section reveal that the goal of improved practice is broad and can encompass a wide range of activities involving differing knowledge, skills and attributes which can be technical, social or personal. Definitions of CPD vary depending on the perspective of the person putting them forward and the ones reviewed here are all-embracing concepts such as:

- informed professional judgement;
- professional capability;
- educational effectiveness;
- qualities and teaching attributes.

These open-ended concepts of CPD have advantages in that they can embrace all the further learning that is carried out by teachers in the Lifelong Learning Sector which contributes to how a qualified professional thinks and acts at work. However, they also suggest a potential disadvantage in that the breadth of activity that counts as CPD may be difficult to recognise, especially for teachers who are relative newcomers to the Lifelong Learning Sector.

- How does someone new to teaching know what constitutes professional judgement, capability and effectiveness?
- How does someone at the outset of their career in the sector know what activities to engage in to achieve the loosely defined and rather vague ideas that are encompassed by the above concepts?

Tummons confirms that CPD is an important aspect of the teacher's role and that there are different notions about what professionalisation entails. Therefore, CPD can take many forms and have many purposes.

To be successful and achieve the goals you set, you need to understand the concepts discussed in this section and be aware of how you are developing these personal attributes through your professional learning from day-to-day experiences in the workplace and other activities and training opportunities.

A holistic approach to teachers' personal learning

The theoretical basis for much adult learning is provided by the humanist school and was arrived at as a reaction against behaviourism and is concerned with the *process* of learning. This view is summarised as:

> Learning is a total personality process; life is a learning experience; true education is individual and about personal growth. (Armitage et al., 2008: 75)

This holistic theory emphasising experiential learning is particularly relevant in relation to professional development as it incorporates the notions of:

- personal growth;
- increased autonomy;
- competence;
- the active search for meaning.

These are all goals of successful personal learning that are worth seeking. Humanistic theories stress the active nature of the learner: the learner's actions largely create the learning situation. According to Jarvis (2002) the active learner is someone who is self-directing, intrinsically curious and motivated to learn. The emphasis in the humanist school of learning is on the drive of the personality and movement towards the fulfilment of goals which learners set for themselves. The theory is that learning comes largely from drawing upon:

- all your personal experiences, e.g. in your workplace;
- the resources of the wider community, e.g. your learners' feedback, your colleagues' experience, your manager's knowledge, your mentor's expertise and local employers' vocational skills and knowledge.

Reece and Walker (2007) claim that the key to effective, long-term learning is based on experiential learning, the features of which are:

- personal involvement;
- stimulation of feelings and thinking;
- self-initiation;
- self-evaluation.

Again, the features of experiential learning demonstrate a holistic approach to learning connecting your thoughts and feelings and involving personal responsibility for your actions. The main issue surrounding what Reece and Walker call 'self-initiation' and others call 'autonomy', 'self-direction' or 'independent learning' is that although they are seen by some as the *traits* of adult learning, they are considered by others as the *goals* of adult learning rather than the traits or characteristics that adult learners already possess (Moran, 2001). One of the reasons for this latter view is that new situations may challenge adult learners' assumptions, beliefs and understandings about themselves as well as what they are learning. According to Hanson (1996: 101) one of the reasons why adult learners act in this way is that new situations may challenge their assumptions, beliefs and understanding about *themselves*, as well as what they are learning and that adults *suspend their adulthood* as learners.

When you embark on something new and there is uncertainty about whether you will be successful or not, this may be perceived as a threat or result in personal stress. You may be worried about how others will judge you: to overcome your fears you probably need your colleagues' support rather than their criticism. There is an assumption that teacher learning for CPD will be self-directed but my experience suggests that collaboration with the wider community of learners, colleagues, managers, mentors or local employers is a more fruitful route.

In Boud's view independence from an authority figure is a stage through which learners need to pass to reach a more mature form of relationship and to be a part of the wider community of professionals.

> Even with independence as the goal there is an unavoidable dependence at one level on authorities for information and guidance. *Inter*dependence is therefore an essential component of autonomy in action. (Boud, 1988: 29)

Initially, you may depend on the support of your line manager and rely on them for information about what to do next, or you may seek assistance from colleagues and need their reassurance that you are on the right lines. Obviously it is the professional development activities that you choose to achieve your own goal(s) that are the key to future success. What is worth seeking is that you become an *interdependent learner* – working with others and helping each other. You'll learn lots from colleagues, but they'll also learn a lot from you and you gain experience and develop professional autonomy. Successful CPD benefits from an active engagement with your environment and a constructivist approach to knowledge – a fuller discussion of this appears in Chapters 5 and 7.

Professional learning in the workplace

There is considerable evidence that learning takes place through work (Eraut, 2000; Billett, 2001; Engestrom, 2001; Evans et al., 2002) but there is no single theory of learning in the workplace. Rather, it is argued that a range of theories and empirical findings may be applied to this area. The term 'workplace learning' can encompass many things. It can relate to work placements, on-the-job training or informal learning experiences. The recognition that the workplace is a major site for learning is not new, but has gained prominence through changing workplace conditions, demands for a multi-skilled and flexible workforce, support for lifelong learning, the emergence of the notions of learning organisations and the knowledge society. As demands in the workplace change, people have to drop old practices and take up new ones, and teachers in the Lifelong Learning Sector are no exception. To make this happen it is recognised that there is a need for continuous training and for support and development of learning in the workplace.

Learning in the workplace is often described as either formal or informal but it is difficult to make a clear distinction between the two as there is often a crossover between them. Informal learning in the workplace has often been thought of as being embedded in the demands of the workplace and absorbed as a natural consequence of actually doing the work, without conscious effort or explicit awareness. However, Hicks (2002) suggests that learning occurs at many levels and in many ways and that, while the values and attitudes of the trainer and organisation may be *implicitly* communicated, information and skills may be imparted quite *explicitly*. Her observations of organisational approaches to learning are relevant to teachers in the Lifelong Learning Sector:

> It is surprising to observe that in some organisations learning is left to chance. The individual employee is expected to 'pick-up' behaviour, attitudes and skills. The process could be likened to training and development by osmosis.(Hicks, 2002: 345)

The importance of intentions for professional learning

Thinking about formal and informal dimensions of learning as separate entities has been questioned and accounts of informal learning tend to derive from what it is not, i.e. it is not *formal* learning, rather than from what it is. The evidence is that learning is predominantly determined by the complex social practices of any learning setting. The extent to which learning is formal or informal is not really the issue:

> in all or nearly all situations where learning takes place, elements of both formal and informal learning are present. But the most significant issue is not the boundaries between these types of learning, but the inter-relationships between the *dimensions* of formality/informality, in particular situations. Colley et al., 2002: 39)

Colley et al.'s view is that social practices and the learning setting *integrate* what are sometimes termed formal and informal components. For example, some things you just pick up, whereas with other tasks you might ask someone else how to do them or someone might give you explicit instructions when they give you a job to do. Considering learning in this way avoids the over-simplification that only formal learning happens in formal settings, e.g. undertaking qualifications while enrolled on a programme of study in an educational institution, and only informal learning happens in informal ones, e.g. through workplace practices.

What is most relevant for you when considering your CPD as a teacher is, as Billett (2001) maintains, that there are *intentions for work practice* and there are goal-directed activities that are central to the organisation and continuity of practice. However, you may find that there is a tension between the need for continuity of work practice and for organisational goals and your need to realise your own personal, vocational or professional goals. It is inevitable that organisations will require compulsory participation in activities to improve the effectiveness of the organisation and achieve organisational goals. However, part of the attendance at mandatory events will almost certainly involve personal learning and self-development for teachers. Just because you are made to attend some staff-training event, which you are not particularly enthusiastic about and would not choose for yourself, does not mean that you will gain nothing from it. If you are open to the possibility of learning and attend mandatory sessions with the *intention of learning* something from them because of the time you are investing in attending, you may be surprised about how much you gain.

> **Case Study Research   4.2**
>
> ***Second key factor in approaches to professional development: intention to continue to learn***
> If the professional learning context is one in which notions of improved practice are not clearly defined by experts and fully understood by teachers, this has a critical bearing on teachers' *intention to continue to learn* and their awareness of engaging in continuing personal and professional development through, e.g. staff discussion and student feedback.

Key factors in approaches to CPD

In this chapter, I identify two key factors in approaches to CPD which are relevant to teachers' personal and professional learning in the Lifelong Learning Sector:

1. control over workloads;
2. intention to continue to learn.

These two factors are ones that authors have theorised about when considering workplace learning, whether of a formal or informal nature. Also, whether it is in different organisations or in the same organisation, the level of control over their workloads and their intention to continue to learn are in evidence in the way individual teachers talk about their approach to CPD (Steward, 2004). If you take these two factors together, you can look at approaches to CPD in a multi-dimensional way and, by plotting teachers' views on their workloads and personal and professional learning, it is possible to represent different approaches diagrammatically, which provides simplicity and makes it easier to work out.

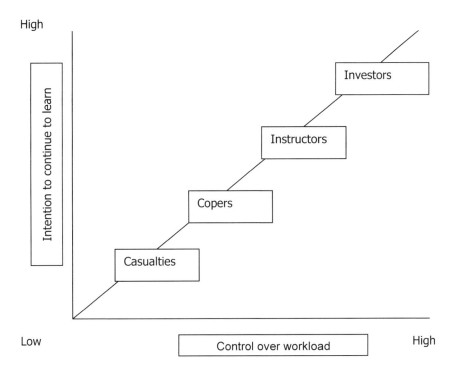

Figure 4.1 Teachers' approaches to CPD

Below are the key factors that I have discovered which distinguish how each group of teachers approaches CPD, which you need to think about when you look at Figure 4.1.

Teacher approaches	Teacher response to CPD
Casualties	The first group of teachers feels their workload is unmanageable and they are too stressed to contemplate personal and professional learning and are unaware of opportunities to learn in the workplace.
Copers	The second group of teachers feels their workload is demanding and although aware of the need for improvement consider there is not enough time to undertake intentional personal and professional learning.

Instructors	The third group of teachers feels their non-teaching workload is an obstacle to their teaching commitment and their intentional learning focuses on developing resources to improve their teaching.
Investors	The fourth group of teachers feels workload is organised and focused and they always have an intention to continue to learn and are constantly looking for new ways of improving their work.

Does the typology in Figure 4.1 strike a chord? Do you recognise the categories I have identified? Does it make sense to you?

But a word of warning. You might find yourself uncomfortable with the 'type' of teacher you associate yourself with. You don't have to stick at one fixed point on what should be a continuum. I admit that I am advocating that there is the notion of a 'ladder' in the model and that successful teachers appear to have climbed to the top and are 'investors' – but even here I am not advocating that there is any prescriptive way of working as the critical thing is that 'investors' make their role their own. The whole point of the framework is for you to develop your understanding that there are alternative ways of working and different approaches to professional development; it is not a matter of accepting that you are one type or another or labelling your colleagues as such. That is something you should avoid as, as Bannister and Fransella warn, it just reinforces our prejudices and assumptions:

> It is as if we type-cast ourselves in a general way as *either* Cavalier or Roundhead, *either* tender-minded or tough-minded, *either* romantic or classic ... The orderly and materialist and practical look with contempt on lives they see as half-baked and self-indulgent. The sensitive and lyrical and passionate are appalled by those they see as rule-bound and mercenary. (Bannister and Fransella, 1971: 189)

Don't categorise yourself (or, indeed, a colleague) as either a 'good' or 'bad' teacher. However, it may prove interesting for you to find out more about the different approaches to CPD and for a bit of fun see where you might fit in! As you read the case studies, reflect on the experiences that the teachers recount and, even if they are working in a different setting from you, try to relate it to your own context.

Teachers as 'casualties'

Teachers, whom I conceptualise as 'casualties', describe feelings of working to the limit of their capacity, of falling apart or being thrown in at the deep end. They can be described as *casualties of the system*.

> 'Looking back I realised that I was starting to fall apart. I started to find it very difficult to get into work and even harder to do the training sessions that had been allocated to me. I was working to the best of my ability but often I would "dry up" in sessions and lose track of what I was saying or supposed to be doing and I could feel the groups losing patience and just staring and waiting for me to get on. I didn't really have enough time to prepare the training sessions and felt I had been thrown into the deep end. If anyone asked me a

Teacher as 'casualty'

> question about something that I hadn't thought about before I just couldn't think straight or get out a sensible reply. The group members were all paying a lot for the training and I knew they weren't getting their money's worth. They did start complaining and each time I made out to my manager that they were "demanding customers" or a "difficult group".

> I didn't want to admit how bad things were as I thought he'd get rid of me. Sometimes I do just want to walk out. I'm so stressed out after some sessions that I can't work properly for the rest of the day. I come in early to try and sort things out for the day and often I'm here very late as well but often I still don't get things done, and I certainly haven't got time to take on any professional development projects that my manager has suggested.'

> (Trainer in a private training organisation)

At times everyone works under pressure, but when the pressure becomes too much this may result in stress. 'Casualties' display behaviour that is not customary in the workplace, such as bursting into tears or losing their temper for no apparent reason and storming out of meetings, which are symptoms of stress. But despite feeling inadequate and exhausted, these teachers keep working and manage that stress in some way or other. The fact that they remain in the workplace is a credit to their powers of survival – but that is achieved at a cost.

Working long hours results in constant tiredness for 'casualties'. Even by working evenings, weekends and through holidays, preparation does not get done satisfactorily and consequently 'casualties' suffer when they go to a session feeling unprepared. During sessions concentration lapses and learners respond negatively to what they see as a 'bad mood'. This instant feedback reinforces feelings of inadequacy in 'casualties'. Criticism from colleagues exacerbates these feelings, whereas lack of any positive feedback from managers also contributes to stress as 'casualties' feel their efforts and commitment are not noticed or appreciated and their professional development requirements are not supported.

One response is to blame themselves for mistiming activities, getting into a muddle when teaching or struggling with regulations as a new assessor. Another is to blame others, particularly learners who are challenging and difficult. Resentment builds up when managers expect routine administration to be completed which takes time from teaching or preparation. What is not recognised is that there may well be more work to do than can be done to an acceptable standard in the time available and 'casualties' who are stressed do not want to expose their weaknesses and may be reluctant to discuss work overload or negotiate about it with managers.

Working conditions are held responsible for feeling stressed, such as excessive workloads at particular points in the year. Working harder does not improve quality, as quality erodes when people are under pressure. When the pressure eases you would think 'casualties' should be able to improve quality, but 'casualties' do not suddenly become efficient and effective when the crises are over. When stressed, feeling tired, trying to catch up and working against deadlines, the only way to survive is by lowering quality. If managers push for administration, 'casualties' do the only thing they can, i.e. spend less time on other things, and their preparation suffers. The result is that lower quality in teaching gradually becomes the norm for them.

Administration, which is required by the organisation to demonstrate efficiency and effectiveness, results in 'casualties' having extra work to do. They experience stress in the form of role overload and perceive themselves as glorified clerks, administrators, assessors and verifiers as well as teachers. All these tasks compete for their time and attention. 'Casualties' see their role as fragmented and differentiate between roles. They describe this as having to switch on and off and play more and more roles and regard themselves as a *casualty of the system* because of the stress of moving from one role to another.

When 'casualties' fear going into the classroom or training workshop through lack of confidence in their skills as a teacher, individual stress is no longer a private concern as it affects learners and colleagues. There may well be individual personal traits which influence the way 'casualties' approach their workloads, but environmental conditions contribute to their stress. Kelly's (1955) famous 'personal constructs' theory suggests that we make sense of the world in order to achieve what we prefer within that world. Teachers as 'casualties' appear to construct the world as being out of control: disordered, with constant interruptions, conflicting demands and role overload. When lurching from one crisis to another, 'casualties' are struggling to survive from day to day and it becomes impossible to look beyond tomorrow – let alone the distant future.

These teachers do not seem to be aware of the learning opportunities that their workloads offer. They are aware of problems, reflect on them, evaluate them and even avoid them. What they appear to do is think about problems but fail to learn from experience and turn them into new and improved actions. Experience is not accompanied by alterations in practice. What they do not do when under considerable pressure is anticipate ways of *developing the capacity to increase control over their workloads*.

'Casualties' define the problems they face as *their* problem. They make the assumption that to be a work hero they have to do everything themselves and place emphasis on solving problems rather than on preventing them from arising in the first place. This assumption results in inefficient practices and 'casualties' are aware of overload, survive by making compromises, but this does not solve the problem. Thus 'casualties' make more compromises and feel manipulated and vulnerable. The tension gets worse, the problem is still there, they blame themselves and they suffer and feel unable to take responsibility for their own CPD.

Check It Out 4.6

Teachers as 'casualties'
- Do you ever experience the situations that teachers as 'casualties' describe?
- If so, do you deal with them in the same way as 'casualties'?
- What conditions for Hoban's personal learning scheme seem to be missing here?
- Are any reasons from Tummon's rationale for CPD present in this account?

Teachers as 'copers'

Teachers whom I conceptualise as 'copers' work under pressure but adopt strategies that help to release that pressure. Although extra work is done to avoid being stressed at work, there is still a feeling the work is never-ending and incessant – rather like being on a treadmill.

Teacher as 'coper'

'Most of the time I feel there is never a moment when I can stop. I'm working all the time. It's like a bad dream – I feel as if I'm running really hard but am still in the same place and not any further forward. I take an awful lot of work home, especially at weekends and I try to get everything ready for the following week, but more often than not there's so much to do at home that my preparation and paperwork doesn't all get done. The students I teach are very bright and often get through a lot more than I plan for. I don't want them to know that I'm not organised so during break I often go to a colleague and ask them if they've got anything I can use to complete the lesson.

I wouldn't go to anyone else as I don't want people to think that I'm not coping, but I know that I can trust that particular colleague and she is a great support and listens to me and sorts me out when I get in a state about difficult students. I did say I would collaborate on a project with her that would count as our professional development but, to be honest, she has done most of it as I never seem to have time to get round to doing the extra work. There's never enough time.'

(Teacher in a Sixth-form College)

One way 'copers' manage is to work harder. Some stay at their desk and work through breaks, but for others the office or workroom is not conducive to getting on with work because of all the hustle and bustle and this is a source of frustration. They cope by taking work home and spend hours in the evening and at weekends doing it. 'Copers' are fearful that they could be seen as failing, and working at home enables them to manage and put up a front of being organised at work.

When working long hours, aspects of workloads which cannot be controlled become a threat. The administrative burden increases time pressures and to manage 'copers' complete administrative tasks in sessions. Less time is spent on teaching and learning – and learners notice. A way that learners can complain is through formal evaluation and 'copers' fear such evaluations and learner criticism and dread having to deal with disgruntled learners. A downward spiral is almost inevitable: 'copers' have to deal with challenging learners and spend even less time on teaching. 'Copers' are defensive about evaluations and criticisms and can feel learners are deliberately antagonistic. Their way of coping is to blame lack of resources or distance themselves so they are not so emotionally vulnerable.

Avoidance strategies are used in a variety of situations. It could be a matter of ignoring paperwork in the hope that it would not be noticed, taking on less work so that it could be done satisfactorily or, more radically, reducing contract hours from full-time to part-time. Avoidance strategies, such as the latter, may alleviate stress and allow 'copers' to manage, but they rob the organisation of experienced staff.

Monitoring what works and reusing session plans and materials sounds efficient and is a popular coping strategy. Reusing materials may save time and effort but this is at the cost of creative teaching and opportunities for development. 'Copers' feel they do the best they can in the time available, but feel there is insufficient time to develop as a teacher. They perceive their role as multi-tasking and trying to juggle different roles. It is a balancing act which is difficult to master.

Teachers as 'copers' engage in short-term planning, time management, unburdening to colleagues, being selective about paperwork and distancing themselves from learners. These strategies enable them to survive and manage, but do not allow for development of practice. One of the most difficult aspects of the workload to control is covering for staff absences or illness. It seems to be the last straw when everyone is so busy and even deters 'copers' from going to staff development sessions themselves if they need cover. 'Copers' learn to manage, but when unexpected or extra tasks turn up pressure builds and things fall apart. In a rapidly changing environment coping strategies are a limited way of practising.

'Copers' define the problems they face in the workplace as too much work. To cope they either ignore work or work harder. They feel guilty about the work they ignore and feel tired and stressed due to the increased effort of working harder. However, the problem is still there, there is still too much to do so they use the coping strategies more: ignore more or work harder. Some ignore work by reducing hours and working part-time or leaving the workplace altogether. Others work longer and harder and put up a front of coping in the workplace. Anxiety builds as there is so much work to do to keep up with changes and the perception that there is too little time to get it done.

Case Study Research   4.5

Teachers as 'instructors'

Teachers whom I conceptualise as 'instructors' find their rewards in teaching and are convinced that learners like them to teach in a traditional way. Their self-esteem and professional image is bound up in their subject knowledge and expertise as an instructor.

Teacher as 'instructor'

'In my appraisal I was told that I needed to work as a team member more, but I find that you can't rely on other people to do things to the standard that you would like. I prefer to organise my resources myself and then when I'm doing my workshop sessions I feel I'm in charge. I like that. I know that one or two people in my department think that my ideas about teaching are a bit old-fashioned but I say why change things if they work. All this talk about listening to learners doesn't get the work covered. There's a lot to cover and I've got to get it done before they go off on work placement. I've got a bit of a reputation for not standing any nonsense and young people today do need a lot of disciplining, they don't seem to have learnt how to behave in college. I've had a lot of experience and I don't think it helps anyone if someone's messing around and not letting the others get on so I do send people out of the class – which I know my colleagues think is an easy way out, but I don't think I should have to spend my time sorting them out when I should be in my workshop teaching those who want to learn.

I'm going to use some materials I've developed for my workshop sessions as evidence for my professional development. I've made a really useful booklet out of loads of handouts that I've used in the past with lots of diagrams and activities in it that can be worked through. I did it because the apprentices we get nowadays don't seem to have the skills in the '3Rs' that they used to. If any of the others in the section want to use it they can. I don't mind putting in the work for this new idea about having to do so many hours of professional development, but I'm not doing it for everyone else's benefit in the team, it's for me.'

(Teacher of Technology in an FE college)

'Instructors'' practice may be underpinned by a belief that learners are not capable of taking control of their own learning. Developing resources, acquiring new materials and researching take up a considerable amount of time and 'instructors' look after resources by methodically filing them, updating them and reusing them. This results in efficiency but not creativity. Getting a file and organising tasks will enable 'instructors' to put their house in order, but it is a cosmetic strategy and does not encourage real curriculum development or consideration of new ways of working. The focus is on subject content, its acquisition and organisation which is admirable. However, the assumption is that the teacher possesses the knowledge and skills and imparts them to the learner who is in need of input: an outdated concept of teaching in which teaching is viewed as a programme of instruction which is teacher-centred, with predicted outcomes and structured processes to achieve them and which depends on lectures and exam questions in sessions – all of which 'instructors' can control. in this view there is an attitude towards teaching as a one-way process which is dependency-creating, rather than learner-centred and encouraging independence and interdependence.

Images of teaching and subject matter formed during their own education may provide a basis for practice for 'instructors'. These taken-for-granted beliefs may mislead 'instructors' into thinking that they know more about teaching than they actually do when they start out as teachers, and make it harder for them to form new ideas about methods of delivery as their career progresses.

Professional satisfaction is gained by preparing learners for employment, but the problem is that 'instructors' find learners lacking in basic skills, or that their vocational area is not recruiting learners of the same calibre as in the past. Their construct of learners is one of learners who keep up in class, behave themselves and do not cause extra work. This springs from a deep-rooted set of attitudes towards learners, again arising perhaps from their own experience of school. Learners with problems are viewed as disruptive to classroom teaching and their exclusion is regarded as beneficial to the rest of the class. 'Instructors' are committed and caring, firm disciplinarians and demand respect from learners.

The aspects of teaching that concern them are those that they cannot control, such as the learner's background, personal problems or social issues. 'Instructors' have a traditional view of the learner–teacher relationship, whereas learners nowadays may need individual help, require extra tuition and want emotional support. 'Instructors' recommend that learners go and get extra help from a centralised, learning-support facility and separate the supporting role from their role as a teacher.

'Instructors' reflect on their practice, chat about professional problems and seek advice from managers and colleagues. Their model of teaching is one of efficiency and organisation and a concern to impart subject knowledge that would help them into employment. Through experience, 'instructors' are learning techniques that enable them to deal effectively in class, but are not broadening their outlook and exploring alternative methods and approaches. Reflection is not necessarily accompanied by alterations in ways of thinking about practice.

'Instructors' are well aware of learning from their work and focused on acquisition of skills and teacher competence. The use of IT for teaching, as well as preparation, is considered important and a source of intentional learning. Learning from direct experience is identified and this leads to an understanding of learners' needs. Monitoring and evaluation of session plans and materials is a way of learning about what works, but in a changing educational environment reusing materials only serves to maintain the *status quo*. Time management is a strategy used to get marking done and cope with the workload. Teachers as 'instructors' are not immune from workload pressures but have control over them and a firm model in their head of their role as a teacher who also exerts control in the classroom through the teaching methods chosen.

'Instructors' define workplace problems as intrusions on teaching. Curriculum meetings are welcomed as beneficial, but meetings about organisational matters mean less time for preparation and are seen as an obstacle to teaching. They focus on the teaching role, organise their resources and develop their subject expertise. They even provide managers with the data they need, but they don't necessarily feel all this is appreciated. 'Instructors' claim managers do not recognise what they regard as exemplary work; they do not pat them on the back and say 'Well done!'. Instead managers want them to change the way they teach. What is more, the learners do not recognise their good teaching either; they can't keep up and want more help. This means focusing more on teaching, resulting in entrenched views about teaching and non-teaching tasks.

Check It Out   4.8

Teachers as 'instructors'
- Do you ever experience the situations that teachers as 'instructors' describe?
- If so, do you deal with them in the same way as 'instructors'?
- What conditions for Hoban's personal learning scheme seem to be present here?
- Are any reasons from Tummon's rationale for CPD present in this account?

Case Study Research 4.6

Teachers as 'investors'

Teachers whom I conceptualise as 'investors' put great store by their relationship with learners and in getting to know them, and they display empathy with learners. They express a love of their job, a passion for supporting learners and the effort is seen as an investment for the future.

Teacher as 'investor'

'I love what I'm doing. I feel I'm making progress all the time. I have loads of ideas for change – but things don't always go fast enough for me. I do plan and prepare before taking the next step and put a lot of effort into making sure things are properly developed. Rather than rush in, I like to make sure before I start anything and before I share my ideas with colleagues or tell everyone else that it's going to be an improvement. I think I'm one of those people who is always picking up new ideas and looking for new things all the time, and I'm still thinking how I can improve things and make things better for myself and my learners and colleagues even after teaching for 18 years.

One of the reasons why I'm always learning is that the job has changed so much. For example, the 14–19 initiative has made teaching really challenging. You have to know how to handle younger learners, get them engaged and focused. There are increasing behavioural issues in classes around the college and some of the younger learners are difficult to handle, but I would say to colleagues that if learners are not focused and not on task, then you are likely to get misbehaviour from them, which changes the dynamics of the classroom.

Some teachers seem to think that active learning is just doing activities and keeping learners busy and have forgotten about the value of deep learning. You have to make things relevant to learners and embed literacy, maths and IT into what you do and make it part of their vocational work, and encompass lots of good practice into what they're really interested in. I try to make the learning environment as much like the workplace as I can and encourage certain standards.

I do think that learning should be interesting and fun for learners, but I have read a research study which says that when the learners have *exceptional* fun they show *moderate* learning and when they have *moderate* fun then learning had a *bigger impact*. This makes real sense to me and I think learning must come first and foremost, but that doesn't mean that you can't give learners a voice and have enjoyable sessions.

I feel that my professional development is continuing. My vocational qualifications and expertise have always had to be up to date and 30 hours CPD recorded and checked by the External Verifier, so I always felt vocationally up to date. Now there is a requirement for the same for my teaching and I welcome this. It does mean another 30 hours of CPD but, although I cannot use my teaching activities for my vocational CPD, I can use my vocational updating for part of my CPD for teaching. It is extra work, but when you incorporate new ideas into your teaching you feel enthusiastic and that motivates everyone. For example, the other day I went to an event where they used balloons for the icebreaker which worked brilliantly and immediately my mind was racing and I was thinking about how I could use balloons and I got really excited about trying it out when I next have a new group!'

(Teacher of Beauty Therapy in an FE College)

'Investors' are happy to invest time in extra tutorials and preparation, and care and respect for learners underpins their practice. Watching learners progress and grow in confidence is a source of satisfaction. 'Investors' take a long-term view of their role in supporting learning and watching learners' development in the hope that their learning experience might be a life-changing one. Their aim is to plan creative and interesting sessions which provide opportunities for learners to achieve, and their priority is to know what learners are going to get out of sessions. Learning is not just learner-centred but is learner-goal-oriented and encourages independent learning. They feel a need to understand learners, recognise their needs and respond to them as individual learners. 'Investors' enjoy taking risks in their approach to teaching as learners' needs change.

'Investors' also develop good relationships with colleagues. They enjoy team teaching, sharing views and supporting each other. They broaden their knowledge of teaching by watching each other and comparing strategies, which enables them to develop images of quality teaching. There is a notion that an organisation is created every morning and built up by everyone working together. This image of a mutually supportive and collaborative environment is a vision that 'investors' subscribe to. Developing relationships with employers and supervisors is a way of finding out about learners' vocational needs and building links between classroom or training workshop and workplace. As well as networking with colleagues and employers, 'investors' develop good relationships with their managers and make them aware of what they are doing and discuss issues with them.

'Investors' enjoy being organised and feel it is important to use time well. They do not feel they are being compelled by others to do extra work or put in extra hours; it is something they want to do for their own satisfaction and for the benefit of their learners.

By having a purpose and providing learners with an overall sense of structure and attainable goals and gradually moving from dependent to independent and inter-dependent learning, 'investors' have the satisfaction of identifying progression. In creating a learning environment for their learners they control their own environment and are aware of the positive learning opportunities for themselves. Through controlling their workloads in this way, their new experience is positive. A forward-looking momentum ensures experience, reflection, experimenting and evaluating become a way of working. 'Investors' develop their skills, and the positive outcomes increase their confidence to try things out, be flexible and adaptable. 'Investors' are ambitious, take on new responsibilities and build up a repertoire of skills. They reflect about the nature of learners, the qualities of good teachers and the skills required.

Critical reflection on their experience enables them to develop their own strategies, and they intentionally set out to learn from new experiences. They evaluate the need to build up relationships with learners. Through self-evaluation they become aware of the benefits of taking risks with their approach to teaching and how this develops their confidence as professionals. Purposeful conversations with colleagues about their workloads develop their awareness of team teaching, collaboration and having a common vision. In this way, 'investors'' learning is interactive: engaging directly with teaching and learning by observing colleagues in the classroom, engaging with ways of handling the subject matter and participating in discussions with others about their experiences. There is a determination to set goals for themselves and reflection about how they could be achieved – and they encourage learners to do the same. This is a process of sharing what is valued. What is driving them is providing opportunities for learners to do well and to do this they are focused and engage with others to broaden opportunities and effect change in their lives.

'Investors' struggle with the reality of the workplace just as other teachers do, but they set out intentionally to improve poor practice. They identify ways to make improvements, carry them out and the improvements bring rewards. This makes them make more changes, take more risks and the results increase their confidence. They have evidence that what they are doing works well. They surmount their problems by their care for their learners, they respect them and do not make compromises, the rewards are there and their tension is overcome.

Check It Out 4.9

Teachers as 'investors'
- Do you ever experience the situations that teachers as 'investors' describe?
- If so, do you deal with them in the same way as 'investors'?
- What conditions for Hoban's personal learning scheme seem to be at work here?
- Are any reasons from Tummon's rationale for CPD present in this account?

Personalisation of CPD

Previous research has identified the importance of informal learning for teachers despite their different organisational contexts. Of relevance here is Marsick and Watkins' (2001) definition of informal learning as not classroom-based but intentional and learner-controlled.

When considering the question of whether CPD achieves the goal of improved practice, it also has to be recognised that teachers come in different guises and that every situation is unique. The four approaches to CPD you have read about in this chapter illustrate that teachers are not a homogeneous group; there are significant differences with regard to biographies, experiences and perceptions in the four situations described and the way that 'casualties', 'copers', 'instructors' and 'investors' respond to educational change and personal and professional learning. Nevertheless, two key factors have been identified as playing an important part in teachers' approach to CPD: *control of workload* and *intention to continue to learn*.

Creating the typology and identifying categories of different approaches to CPD is certainly not an attempt to *label* teachers and put them squarely in one category or another and say that's where they belong. To be more precise, it is a way of making the information about all the different approaches taken by teachers accessible to other teachers and to allow you to view my interpretation and judge its applicability to yourself. Although the typology accommodates all features that I consider important, there are certainly other ways of looking at the situation that would satisfy these needs. It is up to you to decide whether it illustrates different ways of working in the Lifelong Learning Sector.

Check It Out 4.10

In this chapter, teachers are identified as 'casualties', 'copers', 'instructors' and 'investors'.

- Do you feel that the way you approach CPD relates more to the experiences recounted in one particular category rather than another?
- Do you recognise yourself as one particular type of teacher?
- Do you seem to fit into more than one category?
- Do you think that at different times you would put yourself in different categories? Remember, at different times of the year you may feel differently about the amount of control you have over your workload, e.g. you may feel under pressure at the start of a new programme, or your intention to learn may fluctuate, e.g. when you have a load of assessments to mark or records to complete.

It is clear from the typology that different expectations and approaches to learning must be considered. In the introduction, I stated that Peeke (2008) reports that the personalisation for *learners* within organisations is well recognised, but has yet to be widely accepted as a concept to approaches to CPD for *teachers*. The evidence presented in this chapter suggests that because of the different situations teachers find themselves in, and the different approaches they take, personalisation of CPD is essential as a way of enabling all teachers to engage in learning that has an immediate impact on improving their day-to-day professional practice.

But how do you evaluate what makes CPD successful? Martinez (1999) considers context, current practice and priorities and perspectives are limiting because judgements about the success of CPD activities are made with reference to improvements in *teachers' inputs* rather than improvements in *learner outcomes*. Improvements in learner outcomes must surely be the goal, but:

> Human beings are not like jugs to be filled with knowledge from their teachers; they are not like plants dependent for growth on inputs which are controlled by outsiders. They can decide and take the initiative in their own learning. (Rogers, 2002: 106)

I would agree with Rogers that learners can make decisions about their own learning and are not dependent on teacher control, but take an oppositional view to Martinez: I consider *teacher inputs*, i.e. not as information that is pushed into learners, but rather what teachers bring to the learning environment through their personal skills and attributes that support learning, have the *potential to improve learner outcomes*. The way 'investors' work is an example of this and is demonstrated by the way they control their workload to provide opportunities for development and have an intention to engage in personal learning which enhances learner outcomes.

Successful Strategies
- Research with teachers in the Lifelong Learning Sector indicates that two key dimensions are consequential for approaches to CPD: their control over their workload and their intention to continue to learn. Successful teachers demonstrate a degree of professional autonomy in their work and are always ready to learn.
- What teachers bring to the classroom to support learning has the potential to improve learner outcomes. Successful teachers focus on developing their personal skills and attributes.

In Chapter 5 you will have an opportunity to learn just how one type of teacher, i.e. 'investors', go about their CPD successfully.

5 Professional Development as Constructive Practice

> In this chapter you will find sections on:
> - CPD as encompassing all work-enhancing activities;
> - constructive practice
>   1. constructing a professional role;
>   2. constructing professional knowledge;
>   3. construsting professional relationships;
>   4. construsting a repertoire of intellectual skills;
> - constructive practice in use.
>
> The chapter addresses issues relating to Domain A: AS2 Learning, its potential to benefit people emotionally, intellectually, socially and economically, and its contribution to community sustainability.
>
> For those undertaking initial teacher training, the chapter provides opportunities to generate evidence for LLUK standards AS2, AK2.1, AP2.1, AS4, AK4.3, AS7 and elements of Domains B, C, D and F.

CPD as encompassing all work-enhancing activities

All teachers in the Lifelong Learning Sector now have to provide evidence of post-qualification professional development to maintain a licence to practise, and you may be wondering what counts as professional development. Day and Sachs provide a definition, which may hold the answer:

> Continuing professional development (CPD) is a term used to describe all the activities in which teachers engage during the course of a career which are designed to enhance their work. ... Moreover, because teachers, like the students they teach, think and feel, are influenced also by their biographies, social histories and working contexts, peer groups, teaching preferences, identities, phase of development and broader socio-political cultures, the purposes, design and processes of CPD will need to mirror these if it is to result in effective outcomes. (Day and Sachs, 2004: 1)

The description of CPD as encompassing all the work-enhancing activities that a teacher may engage in during their career, as Day and Sachs maintain, means that it can encompass a massive range of activities undertaken by teachers who bring different experiences and attributes to them. If you relate this to the Lifelong Learning Sector, this is not surprising when you consider the range of organisations within the sector and the diversity of the workforce. The complexity of CPD, therefore, generates varied approaches and presents considerable challenges to individuals in the sector today who are making decisions about choosing activities that result in the most effective outcomes for themselves and their organisation.

My professional experience mirrors Day and Sachs's view that recognising individual differences is vital and my own research reveals that teachers in the Lifelong Learning Sector are in no way an homogenous group and approach CPD in very different ways. The argument I presented in Chapter 4 is that the way teachers *control their workloads* and their *intention to continue to learn* are two constituent elements of their approach to CPD. The categories of 'casualties', 'copers', 'instructors' and 'investors' I introduced to you in the last chapter enable you to take a multi-dimensional view of approaches to CPD, and this fits very well with the mix of biographies, social histories, identities, etc. that Day and Sachs talk about. They illustrate that teachers have certain characteristics, hold particular views and behave in different ways. My evidence mirrors their view in that the actions and motivations of teachers vary from one category to another and illustrate a range of attitudes.

It is clear from comparing the approaches that individual teachers take to CPD that not all teachers' activities are *work-enhancing*. A striking example of this is the evidence from Case Study Research 4.3 and 4.4, which confirms that teachers' activities do not necessarily improve their practice, help their professional development or boost their confidence. 'Casualties' do not manifest the personal or professional change which is incorporated within effective outcomes for CPD and their workplace activities do not lead to improvement in practice. They are clearly affected in a *negative* way by the changes in their organisations. It is questionable whether they make any *positive* changes themselves.

However, it is the *difference* between the ways that 'casualties' and 'investors' (see Case Study Research 4.3 and 4.6) approach CPD that is significant here. 'Casualties' do not seem to have time for professional learning, whereas it is approached most effectively in the way 'investors' practise. Bearing in mind the differences in approach, the most useful way ahead is to:

- look at how 'investors' successfully approach CPD;
- translate my research findings into a model that practitioners could use;
- ensure that the model identifies which approach results in effective outcomes.

The practical relevance of the model I have developed is that it is based on what individual teachers in the sector do daily in their organisation and, as such, provides workable ideas that can be taken on board and could be implemented by you in your workplace.

Before you go on to look at the way 'investors' approach CPD, it would be a good idea to remind yourself of some alternative explanations about what constitutes successful professional learning. First, in Chapter 4 it was seen that Hoban's professional learning system provided guidelines for a supportive framework which is required if work-enhancing activities are to be implemented successfully. He asserts it is the combination of an eclectic set of conditions which make up the system that is required to encourage professional learning:

- a conception of teaching;
- reflection;
- a purpose;
- a time frame;
- a sense of community;
- action;
- conceptual inputs;
- student feedback.

Likewise, Tummons provided a second approach in the form of a rationale for CPD which comprised a range of reasons:

- to update subject-specialist knowledge;
- to take account of changes to the curriculum;
- to update organisational and procedural knowledge;
- to enhance employment prospects;
- to take account of technological changes;
- to take account of legislative changes;
- to maintain a licence to practise;
- to stay fresh and involved.

A third approach is identified by Feiman-Nemser (2001) which focuses on the central tasks of learning to teach. She sees preparing, inducting and developing teachers as a professional learning continuum and considers induction and initial teacher training at one end of a continuum with CPD at the other end to strengthen and sustain teaching. Feiman-Nemser suggests that the professional learning undertaken in initial teacher training can be extended through a teacher's career and become part of a larger vision and plan for professional development. She identifies four tasks for CPD that turn the idea of a professional learning continuum into a reality:

- extend and deepen subject-matter knowledge for teaching;
- extend and refine repertoire in curriculum, instruction and assessment;
- strengthen skills and dispositions to study and improve teaching;
- expand responsibilities and develop leadership skills.

The three approaches presented above make it clear that complex relationships, such as the one between teachers' practice and their professional learning, depend on many things and, if you understand CPD as encompassing *all work-enhancing activities* as Day and Sachs did, then it follows that the approach of 'investors' is not a single activity. Bearing in mind this identified need for a *mix of conditions and reasons*, in this chapter I explain how 'investors' engage in work-enhancing activities and provide my own guidelines to inform your future practice. My view is that there are four discrete clusters of features which make a difference to the way 'investors' approach professional learning:

- role;
- knowledge;
- relationships;
- skills.

The perception of these four features underpins the way 'investors' practise and influences the intention of 'investors' to engage in personal and professional learning over time. Importantly, 'investors' are recognised by their colleagues as *successful* and achieve effective outcomes for their learners through work-enhancing activities.

Check It Out 5.1

Recognising success!
Bring to mind a colleague who is considered successful by you, your colleagues or the organisation and then ask yourself:
- What makes them a successful teacher in the Lifelong Learning Sector?
- What aspects of their practice can you identify in your own practice?

- How do they structure teaching and learning to benefit learners emotionally, intellectually, socially and economically?

Remember the old adage – 'success breeds success'. What are the 'star' qualities that make that particular person a top teacher or the most accomplished expert?

Links To CPD
- Evaluate ways of using this information to develop your own practice.
- Evaluate your own successful approaches and plan ways of incorporating more aspects of it into your day-to-day practice.
- Share your ideas with your colleagues and/or mentor.
- Implement your ideas and record the impact doing so has on your professional development.
- If you are undertaking initial teacher training, your responses to the above activities provide evidence for LLUK standards AS4 and AK4.3.

Constructive practice

In this section, I take the recurring themes that are identified in the way 'investors' practise and frame them within the concept of construction. The thesaurus provides three meanings associated with the concept of construction:

- building;
- creation;
- interpretation.

The way 'investors' practise fits these notions: they build, create and interpret their role, their knowledge, their relationships and their skills. They approach their practice in a constructive way: it is positive, beneficial to themselves and others and productive and practical. The four strands of constructive practice are:

1. constructing a professional role;
2. constructing professional knowledge;
3. constructing professional relationships;
4. constructing a repertoire of intellectual skills.

The four strands are contained within an overall model of practice: constructive practice.

Constructive practice is an optimistic image of professional practice in which the expectations of the individual and the organisation converge. It represents the way successful teachers as 'investors' overcome problems in the workplace, clearly envision their purpose and take responsibility for their future direction. Successful teachers build their own professional and subject knowledge, create positive pro-fessional relationships with others and have clear expectations about their role and the ways they interpret it.

Constructive practice is underpinned by constructivism as a learning theory, which has both intellectual and social connotations:

> *Constructivism* is based on the idea that learning is a result of mental construction whereby new information is connected to what we already know and our mental frameworks adapt and develop. ... (Note the frequent use of construction meta-phors in this theory – building, scaffolding, framework.) (Scales, 2008: 61)

The use of constructive metaphors is particularly apt for CPD. In the next sec-tions I look at each of the four strands in turn and indicate the *work-enhancing* activities undertaken under each one. The strands are separated so that they can be examined, but the secret of success is that they are all *integrated* in successful practice!

1. Constructing a professional role

Constructing a role combines ways of perceiving role congruity, vision and purpose and personal skills and attributes.

- *Role congruity* – 'Investors' perceive all aspects of their role as in harmony with one another. 'Investors' to not see diverse activities such as developing training programmes, verifying assessments, visiting other organisations and liaising with employers, marketing, recruiting and completing administrative tasks as pulling them in different directions; they regard them as part and parcel of the job and congruous with their role as teacher. The different responsibilities are not considered to be at odds with each other as they identify a distinct role for themselves as *supporting learners*, which means that all their day-to-day workplace activities are undertaken for that one purpose. This reflects Miner's (1971) classic notion of a self-established role which contrasts to the prescribed, formal role expectations and expectations imposed by others that they work with, whether within the organisation or outside it. 'Investors' do not experience the role ambiguity and role conflict that emanate from role overload, which many teachers in the Lifelong Learning Sector experience, as they create their own role. In this sense they are role-makers. Working hard and working extra hours are perceived as long-term investments (not a source of stress or an imposition) that bring rewards as learners progress. 'Investors' determine their own expectations and these are discussed and negotiated with managers.

- *Vision and purpose* – 'Investors' have a clear idea of what they want to achieve, know how to achieve it and why it is important. Their vision is of creating learning opportunities for all their learners which are life-changing. They are ambitious and identify goals and set clear objectives for themselves, but are driven by their purpose of realising learners' achievements, rather than just by meeting organisational targets. Their orientation to work provides a close fit between the everyday reality of their workload and their purpose, and affords them enjoyment in their role. They construct a role that is consistent with their vision of good practice and yet are responsive to the realities of their workload.

- *Personal skills and attributes* – The attributes that 'investors' regard highly and bring to their role are enthusiasm, respect for learners, caring for learners, creativity and risk-taking. They demonstrate self-confidence, flexibility and adaptability. The personal skills valued are good communication, working with others, being organised, analysis and evaluation. They draw on these skills and attributes to meet the expectations of their role. 'Investors' concentrate on developing the repertoire of skills that their vision of good practice demands and this enables them to move towards that vision. Building up the repertoire of skills has positive outcomes: they are happy in their role and recognise their achievements. It is this self-awareness that is a feature of their practice and enables them to surmount work overload and role overload, develop confidence and take control of their learning.

Success Story

Role-maker

I consider that I've been successful in my career because I have achieved something I never thought I would. I've gained qualifications, become a teacher and now support other teachers. I'm a subject support coordinator in Adult Education for those teaching and assessing NVQ qualifications for teaching assistants. The job is a responsible one and has grown a great deal since I started. There are some aspects of it which I'm not too keen on, just as there are with any job, but I love teaching and so I've made sure that I can still manage to fit in some teaching – even though the job is developing and expanding all the time.

From teaching assistant to teacher

Some years ago I was working as a teaching assistant in a primary school. It was before inclusion policies were implemented and I wasn't working in the classroom alongside a teacher but had my own room so children, e.g. those with Special Educational needs (SEN), came to see me. I helped them and supported them and the system worked really well. I took my Advanced Certificate in Teaching Support and when I had completed it the tutor asked me if I was interested in teaching for Adult and Community Learning (ACL) as they were expanding their provision and needed people to teach. The idea of teaching hadn't occurred to me before.

I taught one group as a sessional tutor and loved it. Inclusion policies were now in place and the qualification had become an NVQ by then and, although I was not keen on working in the evenings, I loved the job. So, I left my job as a teaching assistant in the primary school and then became a full-time tutor in Adult Education.

Role development

When I started, there were six people in the whole curriculum area. I became interested in developing a course for the new NVQ and wrote a Level 3 course, which soon built up as funding streams became available, and before long we had lots of people enrolling.

I've developed other courses since then and eventually part of my job involved supporting the new qualifications. Eventually, that part of the job was advertised as a full-time post as subject support coordinator. I filled in my application for it but was undecided about applying as I was not sure I wanted it really. By then there were 20 tutors to support and they were all asking me whether I was going to apply. What made me decide to take the plunge was that one tutor contacted me and said 'It won't matter who gets the job, I'll still contact you'. It took others to have confidence in me before I recognised that I had been doing the job successfully part-time and had the experience to do the job advertised!

Now we have 47 tutors and we are responsible for the whole provision for the County Council's Children's Services and have upwards of 1,500 trainee Teaching Assistants on the programme. Due to the Lifelong Learning changes in 2007, there was a requirement for all assessors to be qualified. Most of the tutors are schoolteachers so needed their A1 qualification to assess. I did my A1 and my IV qualifications so that I could teach the assessor qualification as well. Currently, we just offer the assessor qualification in-house to our own assessors, but we are contemplating opening it up to outsiders because there is a demand and we have the experience and expertise.

Developing skills and attributes

One of the great things about being in this job is working in partnership with a colleague who started out in very much the same way as me. We manage together. She is the one who sees the bigger picture and drives the next initiative, whereas I am more feet on the ground, I focus on the detail and am the one to say 'Wait a minute'. We complement each other really well as we have differing skills, but we think alike and both have a commitment and desire to succeed.

I'm doing more professional development currently as I'm taking my Diploma in Teaching in the Lifelong Learning Sector (DTLLS). I've learned a lot. I know when I joined the course I already knew a lot and had a lot of experience, but I've developed my approach to teaching and learning through doing the course and gained a great deal of confidence. I would really love to have more time to spend on my coursework and deepen my knowledge even more, but it's not so easy when you're working full-time and studying part-time.

I've also had the opportunity for professional development through observing others. When you observe very experienced teachers you can help them and give them ideas as their tutor, but you also gain a lot and learn yourself from watching them and discussing with them what they do. You can get complacent when you've been in a job for a while and it's really important to keep on learning and develop your ideas.

If you asked me ...

If I was talking about professional development to someone who was starting out on their training or beginning their teaching career, I think I would do the following to encourage them to be successful:

- First, I would help them to develop their own learning plans. In a large organisation, especially in a curriculum area with an accredited vocational qualification with rigid standards where tutors have written a Scheme of Learning and Learning Plans, everything you need is in place. But, I feel strongly that individuals should develop their own learning plans for teaching sessions. I've observed people using plans I've developed and they don't appreciate the different inferences intended – where I might emphasise something or bring in humour, etc. I don't think it works if you use a Learning Plan that someone else has developed – it usually falls flat.

- Second, I would encourage them to develop their own resources. I know that it's common practice to use prepared resources and materials, but I think that individuals need to use their own ideas, use their imagination and think of activities and be a bit creative.
- Third, I would without question encourage them to undertake their Preparing to teach in the Lifelong Learning Sector (PTLLS) or DTLLS. Not only will they gain a qualification, but they will gain in experience and confidence too. I would say you need to keep up to date and renew your enthusiasm and commitment to the job through professional development.

(Subject Support Coordinator – Adult Education)

Although this subject coordinator didn't start off with the idea of teaching as a career, they responded to the opportunities presented to them and have shown ambition and purpose in their job and commitment to developing their role. This is illustrated by the way they have gradually taken on more responsibility, gained more qualifications and moved into new areas, e.g. managing and assessing. They are realistic about the importance of partnership working and recognise their colleague's skills as complementary to their own. There is no doubt that they have made the job their own and know what they want to achieve, what is more they are enthusiastic about creating learning opportunities for all their tutors and supporting them in their own CPD. The subject coordinator in the Case Study exhibits the qualities of success; they are an 'investor' in a real sense.

Check It Out   5.2

Define what success means to you

The concept of 'success' is a very subjective and personal one and is likely to be different for each individual. I don't think I've met anyone who deliberately sets out to be a failure, but I have met many teachers who haven't consciously set out to be a success and wouldn't know if or when they've achieved it. It's important to work out your own definition of what success means to you.

- Complete the following sentence: Success for me would mean that I …

Links To CPD

Now you have thought about what success would mean for you, set yourself realistic targets for achieving that success and incorporate them into your Action Plan. Use your definition to evaluate how well you have achieved your personal targets.

If you are undertaking initial teacher training, your responses to the above activities provide evidence for LLUK standards AS4 and AS7.

2. Constructing professional knowledge

Constructing knowledge combines a constructivist approach to specialist area knowledge and knowledge and knowledge of teaching and learning.

- *Constructivist approach to knowledge* – 'Investors' take a constructivist approach to knowledge and create their own knowledge. Through reflection of their experience they discover and build their interpretations from their ideas, evaluations and feelings about learners, colleagues, their practice and their subject and in this way their learning experiences influence subsequent learning. Thus, 'investors' make sense of their professional world and can change it, rather than just respond to it. Their knowledge is, therefore, provisional and contested. Learning is initiated by the 'investor' as they seek to understand conflicts or problems. Knowledge is not about acquiring more and more information, but constructing new perceptions. It is an active engagement with the environment and with themselves. This may increase tension as 'investors' struggle with the realities of their workload in the search for something better and closer to their vision of their role. Constructing knowledge is very often achieved through learning that is initiated by the investor's sense of disquiet with present practices and through the search to do things better and improve their practice.

- *Specialist area knowledge* – Learning includes goals, purposes, intentions, choices and decisions and most teachers – unlike 'investors' – are unclear how they fit into learner-initiated learning. The 'investor's' preparation starts with learners' needs and seeks to strengthen, not weaken, the different experiences brought to learning by sharing and valuing them. Information-gathering is in the hands of the learners not the teacher; they are doing the work. Investors' expertise is in how to access that knowledge, familiarity with materials and how they relate, e.g. how learners can successfully complete a module. They understand what the learners find confusing and difficult and view subject knowledge from the learner's point of view. 'Investors' view learning as strengthening learners' capacity for growth, e.g. how they can raise standards from pass to distinction level. Confidence in their vocational expertise and control over their subject knowledge enables them to respond to learners' requests for information and transfer control to the learners.

- *Knowledge of teaching and learning* – The 'investor's' view of knowledge is very different from the traditional one often associated with teaching, i.e. direct transfer of information from teacher to learner. The kind of role they play in the process of learning is radically different as 'investors' view learning as the active construction of knowledge by the learner through interaction with subject knowledge or the teacher. Unlike other 'types' of teacher who do too much in the classroom, or work too much on their own and exclude students from part of the task, they take the view that learning is not finding out what other people already know, but solving their own problems for their own purposes, i.e. learners set their own goals. Knowledge is gained by questioning, thinking and testing until the solution is part of learners' life. 'Investors' transfer the task of searching out material and trying to make sense of experiences to learners, and let learners take the initiative in their own learning. 'Investors' seek to promote independence and self-reliance, and put stress on creative learning. They also develop their professional knowledge by purposeful conversations with colleagues. Control of their professional knowledge enables them to relinquish control over learners.

> **Success Story**
>
> ### Knowledge development for personal and job fulfilment
> At the moment I'm a Customer Services Trainer in an international company which does business all around the world and with offices in both the north and south of England. In the past I had done training as part of my role, but during a low point in the demand for training in my organisation I drifted into other things and had done progressively less and less training. While I was doing professional examinations in my field, which is part of the financial services industry, I noticed that colleagues were all involved in doing loads of professional development and it was this that got me interested in my own professional development. I felt I had strong technical knowledge but was less strong on the training side. What I learned during my professional development over a period of time helped me during my interview for promotion to my current role as a full-time trainer.
>
> ### Gaining formal qualifications to open up career opportunities
> Some years ago, I did a Certificate in Education. I had thought that teaching in a college might be a possibility for me, but when I was doing the teacher training course I found that those already employed in colleges all seemed so cynical, for example about inspections, etc., and there didn't seem to be any job security. I didn't have a master plan for career progression then, but felt that formal qualifications could open up opportunities in the future. I did a first degree after that in Post-compulsory Education and found that the more I did the more I wanted to learn. There just wasn't the time to learn about things you were really interested in in depth, though, and explore things such as philosophy. I discovered that I liked studying and, although my qualifications are not recognised formally by my employers and I'm not sponsored by them, they definitely make me more effective at work. I also find that studying provides me with rewards that my work doesn't.
>
> The idea of teaching was planted in my mind by the manager of the course at the college where I was studying. We discussed a possible career option might be to teach and what opportunities there might be in the future. At the time I felt that it would be too much to take on a part-time teaching post on top of a full-time job and family commitments, and I was really focused on my studies and getting good results. Although, as I said, I don't have a professional development plan, since then I have been thinking seriously about moving in that direction and, say, getting part-time work outside my organisation and reducing my hours in it. Studying has given me more confidence to think like this about my future.
>
> ### Enhancing professional practice through formal studying
> Things are going really well at work and this is down to ongoing professional development and helped by my studying. The way that it has really benefited me in my job as a trainer is it has helped me become less of a 'bog standard' trainer and I bring more to the workplace than I used to, and this is noticed. Most of the training I do is classroom-based and the majority of the work is systems-based. I feel that the

other side of the business, i.e. the people development side, is neglected at the moment and there is a plan for the systems-based side to reduce and for the soft-skills side to be picked up. Of course, the need for efficiency and costs determines the way ahead in my organisation, but I am now taking a Masters degree which I hope to use to either help me become more valuable in my present organisation or to open up opportunities outside work. I realise that, more and more, I am thinking of my career path and the reason I applied for my current job was to progress on to Masters level.

If you asked me ...

The qualities that one would need to bring to the role of trainer in a large commercial organisation in my opinion are:

- knowledge of your industry, e.g. finance, insurance, pensions etc.;
- knowledge of current training practice;
- the ability to learn;
- good communication and ICT skills;
- a strong sense of caring for people, e.g. helping them to progress, and an interest in others' development.

(Customer Services Trainer – International Company)

The case study above illustrates that developing both knowledge about teaching and learning and specialist subject knowledge have contributed to this trainer's progression and recognition in the workplace. The gaining of confidence and the emergence of a career plan could perhaps be attributable to two kinds of knowledge which Rogers (2003) discusses in relation to adult learning:

- The first is 'actionable knowledge', which is practical knowledge that is implemented in the workplace – such as technical training skills which are observable and, if appreciated by trainees and the employer, increase self-assurance.

- The second is 'applicable knowledge', which is relevant knowledge, but abstract rather than functional and not necessarily usable – such as the theoretical knowledge gained from formal studying, which requires the development of critical thinking, and this means being able to take more control over your own learning and professional development.

Formal studying is an excellent way of continuing your professional development, particularly if the programme on which you choose to study utilises inputs from learners such as their experience, insights, capability and competence and doesn't rely on inputs provided by the teacher alone.

3. Constructing professional relationships

Constructing relationships combines relationships with learners, relationships with colleagues and relationship with other stakeholders.

- **Relationships with learners** – Abandoning the notion of information transfer for helping the learners to engage in a series of learning activities, means 'investors' change teaching methods. This in turn changes the relationship between teacher and learner. They see their role in the learners' search for and discovery of knowledge as a supportive one, and acknowledge that they may enhance learners' motivation but cannot teach them in the conventional manner, only facilitate learning by creating an environment for learning. What investors do is support the learner, not just transmit the subject, and allow learners to assimilate new knowledge into their experience through self-discovery and self-appropriation. They recognise learners' capacity for discovery and constructive learning and trust learners to work things out for themselves. Handy (1993) asserts that increased trust and respect for colleagues follows if role ambiguity and role conflict are reduced, and this benefits the learners. Control is returned to the student as they become active in the learning process which 'investors' consider is essential to the learning process.

- **Relationships with colleagues** – 'Investors' develop relationships with colleagues through team teaching and other collaborative activities. They seek out opportunities to work cooperatively and build supportive networks. This supports Handy's (1993) contention that there is good evidence that close and positive interpersonal relationships with members of one's role set can mitigate substantially the effects of role problems. Handy asserts that unilateral solutions to workplace problems tend to be self-defeating and so it is no good trying to solve problems on your own as improvement strategies need to be collaborative and cooperative.

- **Relationships with others** – 'Investors' have positive relationships with managers and they extend the boundaries of their role to develop relationships with employers and familiarise themselves with learners' workplace colleagues. If there are positive relations with others, then role differences and problems are reduced and there is the potential to build trust and respect.

Success Story

Relating to learners in a different environment

I am from the north-east of England originally and have done different jobs and worked in different places. One thing that had a big impact on how I now think about my role and the way I currently work was the time I spent in Romania. I was based in Bucharest and it was a really challenging environment in which to teach. There were no resources and even the paper we used was very thin and poor quality and so you had to utilise anything you had and improvise, which taught me to be flexible and adaptable. The students all called me 'Professor' and everything was very formal in contrast to this country, but everyone was so keen to learn and even the other teachers themselves came into my sessions so that they could practise their English. My experiences of teaching in another country made me think about the relationship between me and my students – the formality in Romania and the more informal one in my present job – and what makes a good learning environment.

Encouraging learners to think about their relationship with others

Currently I'm working in an FE College on Child Care and Early Years Courses and in contrast to Romania things seem quite luxurious. I'm not saying that there's no shortage of resources in college, or that the students don't experience deprivation, because the college is in a designated area of social deprivation. But it's a different sort of deprivation – I feel the area has been left behind and we haven't moved into the twenty-first century. I think that the area suffers more from neglect than deprivation. I like to bring new ideas into the classroom and get students to think 'out of the box' but lots of them find this difficult because they have no experience outside their immediate circumstances and locality. For example, when you're talking about equal opportunities to young people, they appear to have no concept of racial issues and why young black children might be vulnerable, because they have no experience of black issues in the local area. Even the more mature students find it difficult to empathise with issues of equal opportunities, which is a concern on Child Care and Early Years courses. I often wish everyone could experience life outside their close-knit community, as I did when I worked abroad, as it does broaden your outlook on life and opens up your ideas about your relationships with other people.

Working collaboratively with others

The current curriculum development project I am working on is a joint venture between four colleges to develop and implement a Foundation Degree in Child Care, which was successfully validated this year by two universities. We have regular meetings with colleagues from the other institutions and I find working in this way very supportive. Working with colleagues from outside your own college helps expand your horizons and provides a network of people who have the same professional interests, who care about the same things as you do and whom you can ask about issues that crop up. I've really benefited from working with others and enjoyed developing the Foundation Degree for use in my college in collaboration with colleagues from other institutions and working cooperatively means that you don't have to solve all the problems on your own and you don't feel you're working in isolation. It's been a good professional development opportunity for me.

If you asked me ...

I remember what it was like when I started out in teaching, and I was very shaky at the beginning. At university in Wales when I was doing my teacher training, we did learning theory but it didn't mean much to me at that point. I knew all about andragogy and pedagogy but I didn't know the basics, like how to mark and would have benefited from studying, say, criteria used to assess and how they differed for different levels, which would have been of real practical help. Based on my own experience I would say that to be successful a teacher needs to:

- be organised, e.g. with paperwork, planning etc.;
- get their priorities right from day one;
- be aware of the boundaries and establish what is acceptable or not between teacher and student in the classroom;
- separate work and home and don't let work intrude on home life;
- be friendly and approachable, but professional;
- not be afraid to ask for help from colleagues;
- acknowledge their weaknesses;
- be realistic about what they can achieve.

(Teacher on FdD in Child Care – FE College)

The advice from the teacher in the case study above reveals their awareness of relationships between teacher and learner, between teacher and colleagues and between work and home. Are issues of equality, diversity and inclusion in relation to learners and the local community problematic in your setting? The significance here is that the issues are all viewed through the teacher's personal experience, so remember that your ideas of what a teacher needs to do to ensure equality and be successful may be different and warrant comparison with those identified in the case study. What the case study does reveal is that this teacher has a commitment to enable learners to contribute to community sustainability.

4. Constructing a repertoire of intellectual skills

Constructing a repertoire of intellectual skills enables teachers to engage in CPD.

- *Tools for constructive practice* – Building the flexibility and depth of understanding that 'investors' demonstrate entails developing the skills of critical reflection, analysis, evaluation, research and inquiry. 'Investors' use data gathered from observation of colleagues, working with like-minded teachers and serious conversations about teaching and learning with colleagues. They broaden their professional and subject knowledge through working in teams, networking and undertaking new roles. They control their practice by continually developing what they are doing, not just by thinking alone but organising their own knowledge about themselves, their subject, their learners and their colleagues.

> **Viewpoint**
>
> ### *Developing teaching skills through the teacher's specialist subject*
> I welcome the fact that the new LLUK standards require reflection and evaluation of a teacher's own practice and entail the need for CPD. I admit that in improving the quality of their practice teachers could either focus on teaching skills or keeping up to date with current knowledge in respect of their own specialist subject area. But I don't think one thing precludes the other.
>
> I think that improving practice involves developing teaching skills through the teacher's specialist subject. I know there is a movement towards CPD for subject-specific updating and I'm sure this is welcomed by teachers from a vocational background. Such teachers need to use their expertise in their teaching: they need to continue to feel abreast of their subject area not just for their own benefit for their future career but also for credibility with students.
>
> The current importance placed on meeting the requirements of industry and employers means that it's understandable that vocational updating becomes a priority, but in my view this should not be at the expense of pedagogical understanding as I think this needs to move forward in an innovative way.
>
> The ideal scenario would be that organisations provide opportunities for teachers so that they meet both requirements. One problem as I see it, though, is that because of

Ofsted much of the development that occurs is targeted towards specific things, e.g. questioning techniques and schemes of learning. My concern is that this tends to atomise the process of teaching and learning rather than making it holistic. Critical reflection on why these technical skills are being targeted would enable teachers to evaluate vocational and pedagogical aspects and develop understandings of the complexity of the teaching role.

(Teacher of FE in HE)

Check It Out 5.3

Targeting technical skills
- Have you experienced an internal organisation observation recently, or an external observation by an Ofsted inspector? What did you target in your preparation for the inspection?
- Critically reflect on the observation and inspection process and evaluate any feedback you received.
- Write a reflective account of your views on measuring quality in education and in your organisation in particular.

Links To CPD
- Pick one target to improve technical skills, e.g. to set objectives. Check objectives in your session plans, course outlines, specifications and assessments briefs. Drawing on theory where possible, write a reflective account of how you improved your objectives and why, and evaluate how this benefited your learners intellectually.
- If you are undertaking initial teacher training the account provides evidence for LLUK standard AS7 and elements of Domains B, C and D.

Using constructive practice

Teachers, whom I conceptualise as 'investors', reconcile the tension in workloads by perceiving their role differently. They view their workload as the way of meeting both the expectations they set themselves and their learners' expectations. Such teachers see *learners' needs* as *their needs* and the more effort the teacher (or the learner) puts in and tries to achieve what they want, the more their expectations seem to converge. Organisational issues, which could be defined as a problem by many teachers, are surmounted by 'investors' perceiving their role as providing opportunities for learners to achieve their own goals.

But how do they meet their managers' expectations? If the tasks required are seen to support learners there is not a problem, but if initially they are not, then this is regarded as a matter for discussion with their managers about the validity of the tasks. Constructive practice does not, therefore, mean eliminating all tasks that do not seem directly related to teaching and learning, stipulate measurement or demand accountability, as in the long run these tasks affect the quality of teaching and learning. What it does mean is asking managers for clarification and resolution of conflicting expectations. If you have discussions with managers about role ambiguity it will:

- open your mind to another viewpoint;
- broaden your awareness of the wider environment;
- make you alert to the consequences of implementing policies.

There may still be differences of opinion between you and your managers, but you are able to make a more informed choice and a more realistic assessment of the situation. Managers may have different expectations of you in regard to particular tasks, but this is not to say that they do not recognise quality provision and have a desire to support teachers or have the learners' best interests at heart.

The use of constructive practice means that as a teacher you need to look at quality in education in a different way. It is not a process of passing on information, or passing down culture from one generation to another. It is not a matter of content or control over learners and getting them to conform. The provision of learning opportunities allows learners to take what is required so that they can grow and develop in the way they want and achieve their own goals. The control is passed to the learners. They take as much responsibility for their own learning as they can, which illogically allows the majority of learners freedom. If this takes place, the relationship between learner and teacher changes radically: the teacher becomes a co-constructor of knowledge (Barth, 2000). The paradox is that the more teachers control their workload, and the more they have an intention to learn, the less control they exert over learners and the more they achieve. You have to remember that for some of you expecting particular groups of learners, e.g. at Foundation level, to take control of their own learning would be like abandoning them to their own fate and in this case you must use your professional judgement and try and share control with them as much as you possibly can.

Check It Out 5.4

Working more constructively
- Consider ways in which learning has the potential to change lives.
- How do you create opportunities to highlight the potential for learning to positively transform lives?
- What actions do you take in your teaching and learning to enable learners to benefit emotionally, intellectually and socially and to prepare them for their future employment and become effective citizens in their community?

Links To CPD

- Read educational textbooks and/or do a search of academic journals on the internet on what 'transformative learning' means. Use this information in tutorials to get to know learners' views. Write up a theoretical account of transformative learning and how it applies to your learners for your Professional Development Journal.
- If you are undertaking initial teacher training, your responses to the above activities provide evidence for LLUK standards AS2, AK2.1, AP2.1 and elements of Domain F.

Constructive practice represents the way successful teachers in the Lifelong Learning Sector take responsibility for their future direction.

STRATEGIES FOR SUCCESS

- Remember that success means different things to different people so you must identify what CPD would contribute to your success as a teacher.
- Developing relationships with others means setting boundaries and you have to make different choices for different contexts, e.g. with learners, colleagues or employers.
- Viewing your role holistically as one of supporting learners enables you to undertake routine or additional tasks without resentment or stress as they contribute to your learners' achievement.
- Using knowledge gained from undertaking formal study contributes to success and recognition in the workplace.
- Improving practice involves developing teaching skills through your specialist subject.

In Chapters 6, 7, 8 and 9 you will find further examples of constructive practice and tasks that successful teachers use in their professional development, together with guidelines and advice I have gleaned from them, to help you with your own approach to professional learning for your own future practice.

6 Constructing a Professional Role

In this chapter you will find sections on:

- the teacher's role compared to an actor's part;
- the teacher as a competent practitioner;
- the reflective practitioner and the reflexive teacher;
- role congruity;
- vision and purpose;
- teacher as strategist;
- personal skills and attributes.

The chapter addresses issues relating to Domain A: AS1 Learners, their progress and development, their learning goals and aspirations and the experience they bring to their learning.

For those undertaking initial teacher training, the chapter provides opportunities to generate evidence for LLUK standards AS1, AK1.1, AP1.1, AS3, AK3.1, AP3.1, AS4, AK4.2, AS7, AP7.1, AK7.2, AP7.2, AS7.3, AP7.3 and elements of Domains B, C, D and F.

The teacher's role compared to an actor's part

Before you can start to consider what it means to construct a professional role as a teacher, you have to be sure you know what 'role' means:

> What do we mean by 'role'? The dictionary definition is '*role*: an actor's part ... a person's or thing's characteristic or expected function'. This is a useful way of

thinking about 'role' because of the emphasis on playing a part, on interacting in a particular way with others, as well as on functions to be performed. It also highlights the concept of dynamism. Every actor differs in his or her interpretation of a given part, and makes of it something unique, as well as fulfilling its formal requirements. (Harrison, 2002: 153)

The related ideas of a 'formal role' that is functional and given and a 'unique role' that is interpreted and developed are identified by Harrison when she compares the idea of a professional role with an actor's part. If we use the analogy of an actor in a stage production, then an actor has a specific part to play and a particular function to perform in the theatre when interacting with other cast members, which is a formal and functional role. However, in playing that part each actor delivers the given lines but interprets the part differently in an attempt to make the role their own and, hence, their performance unique. In fact, the unique interpretation becomes an important aspect of an actor's performance and one that the critics highlight and the audience appreciates. It is what a particular actor brings to the role that is admired. I would say that this is pretty true of teaching, too, and an actor's part has a lot of similarities with the teacher's role – but they are definitely not the same!

If you are asked to remember good teachers from your own schooldays it is likely that you will have no difficulty at all in recalling at least one and perhaps more, but what do you recall?

While it is not uncommon ... to recite the 'personal qualities' of fondly-remembered teachers, such as a sense of humour, a commitment to fairness, good communication skills or infectious enthusiasm for the subject, these are often expressed in the very vaguest of terms. (Moore, 2000: 120)

Moore suggests that what you remember in a hazy way from the past are personal qualities and aspects of personality rather than the technical skills related to teaching such as planning, management or assessment of work and progress. It is not the expert teaching skills that make an impact on you as a learner and which you later remember, but the personal qualities which make the teacher *charismatic*.

Check It Out   6.1

Characteristics of good teachers
- Think back to your own schooldays and recall which teachers made an impact on you.
- What was it about them that made them memorable?
- Check whether you identified personal qualities as Moore predicted.
- Analyse why you responded to the qualities so positively.

- Looking back, do you think you attributed charisma to the teacher – rather than them being really charismatic?
- What personal qualities do you think your learners attribute to you?

Links To CPD
- Write up your responses to the above statements and questions as a reflective account.
- Review learners' evaluations of your sessions or programmes and identify the personal qualities that your learners attribute to you.
- During informal conversations with learners, or during tutorials, ask them what personal qualities in teachers they respond to best.
- If you are undertaking initial teaching training, your responses to the above activities provide evidence for LLUK standard AK4.2.

Although you tend to remember the personal qualities of teachers, which are recollected as charismatic, what really makes them successful according to Moore is that they have the ability to communicate clearly to their audience. The teacher's audience is generally made up of groups of learners who are individuals with very different personalities, experiences and backgrounds – probably very much like an audience in the theatre. He considers that thinking of a teacher as *communicative* is probably a better idea as communication is a two-way process and the teacher has to listen to the learners and respond to their needs in the classroom. Nevertheless, in a similar way to an actor, a teacher also has to think about how they present themselves in the classroom. For example, they have to decide when to talk and when to listen, where to stand and how to respond and show interest and enthusiasm. But, just like an actor, this could lead to a teacher being more concerned about their own performance than that of the audience (which for the teacher is that learners are learning) and relying on personal style rather than the skills of planning and preparation. So, here's a warning if you're thinking that your teaching needs to be all singing and dancing to succeed:

> But does a lecturer have to turn himself into a clown and his classroom into a funfair in order to motivate students? ... if students had to go from class to class singing and dancing and playing bingo, the novelty would wear off pretty quickly. (Hayes, P., 2007: 76)

In this day and age, the teacher's performance, however charismatic, may begin to wear thin if learners don't feel they are getting on well and making progress and the organisation won't be happy if it doesn't achieve the targets it sets. As a teacher in the Lifelong Learning Sector you need to be enthusiastic and perform well – but enthusiasm and a convincing performance are not enough on their own. You also need to be an expert in your subject and well prepared. In other words, you also need to be competent.

The teacher as a competent practitioner

Moore suggests that although the model of good teaching that is popularly held by most people is that of the charismatic/communicative teacher, the model that predominates on initial teacher training courses is that of the competent practitioner. I am sure that if you are undertaking initial teacher training (or you cast your mind back to when you were) you are aware that your tutors and mentors are trying to ensure that you have a confident start in teaching. I expect they are making sure you understand learning theories and acquire the practical skills to impart your subject knowledge, such as planning interesting sessions, delivering them in a positive way, recording assessments and managing learners' progress effectively. Sufficient knowledge, good organisation and adequate preparation are requirements of good teaching and your tutors' and mentors' main objective is to ensure that you are competent to work effectively with learners. Also, learners, employers and the general public need to be confident that the quality of teaching in the Lifelong Learning Sector is consistent. Minton maintains that developing your role in this way is quite complex:

> Competence in the use of any methodology involves being able to choose intelligently, with the knowledge, experience and skill to make chosen methods work effectively. This can only be acquired by experience. It also requires confidence, risk-taking and reflection on what actually happens, and the will to learn from that experience. (Minton, 2005: 152)

Minton points out that competence involves making professional choices about the way to do things, implementing your choices effectively and having the will to learn from that experience. As he says, this requires knowledge, experience and skill and reflection on what happens. Working effectively involves performing to the expected standard in all aspects of what the role requires, including taking risks when implementing new ways of working or coping with non-routine work. Competence in a role, therefore, requires *personal* confidence.

Fawbert (2008) states that competence is the standard expected within an occupation which defines any role and against which performance is assessed, i.e. it is the formal, functional or given role that Harrison identified which is made explicit in the standards rather than the unique, interpreted or developed role. The LLUK standards ensure that those undertaking initial teacher training cover the same content across the six domains, address the scope, knowledge and practice within each and are assessed against the same criteria, regardless of where they are taking their qualification. However, there are points for and against competence-based assessment, as Table 6.1 shows.

Table 6.1 An analysis of the strengths and weaknesses of competence-based assessment

For – Competences provide the learner with:	Against – Competences create situations where:
explicit, predetermined outcomes.	creative, divergent and critical thinking is limited.
individualised, student-centred instruction.	assessment-centred, group processes are subverted.
the means of demonstrating skills and understandings.	there is a lack of encouragement to synthesise and generate knowledge.
a teacher who is a facilitator (humanist theory).	the measurable, observable imperative creates a positivist approach to learning (behaviourist theory).
a flexible, modularised delivery.	the reductionist, disaggregation of learning can severely limit a more holistic view.
continuous assessment.	the overconcern with assessment and the necessary level of administration is restricting for teachers and learners.
a forum to demonstrate the mastery of specific performance objectives.	the demonstration of learning only through behaviour restricts the development of higher-level learning outcomes.
a process where achievements are recorded in details.	some professional diagnostic activities cannot be expressed adequately enough.

Source: Auerbach in Fawbert (2008: 209)

Table 6.1 shows that a key strength of the competent practitioner model of the teacher role is that outcomes are made clear, which encourages learner-centred teaching with the teacher acting as a facilitator. The LLUK standards make the purpose of teaching and learning abundantly clear and allow for the use of a wide range of strategies and, as the criteria are frequently related to a vocational area, there is a need for the teacher to keep up to date with vocational practices and not just rely on their own previous experience of training.

Whilst all these factors enhance the quality of teaching and learning, the need for consistency in content and assessment has to be balanced against the need for flexibility to accommodate the widely varying roles of teachers within the Lifelong Learning Sector. Moore identifies three particular difficulties with the competent practitioner model which reflect some of Auerbach's comparisons:

- the list-like nature of competences give the impression that the identified competences provide the entire knowledge and skills required of a teacher but his evidence is that despite achieving the criteria many student-teachers or newly qualified teachers still have difficulties in the classroom and often cannot understand why;
- it is difficult to answer the question: 'What makes an effective teacher?' and provide everything that has been identified in the criteria and then phrase the criteria using words that exactly convey this image;
- the attempt to isolate and define skills and kinds of knowledge that all teachers need regardless of the kind of person they are or the circumstances in which they work is problematic and misleading.

Check It Out   6.2

Competent practitioner model
- Do you see the LLUK standards as a list that has to be gone through and ticked off?
- How do you think achieving the LLUK standards (in Domain A relating to professional values and practice) have contributed to your development as a teacher?
- How do you think the LLUK standards help learners to progress and develop?

Links To CPD
- If you are already a qualified and experienced teacher, take the opportunity to bring yourself up to date with the current LLUK standards so you are aware of the baseline competence required for newly qualified teachers. The complete set of standards is to be found in Chapter 2.
- Identify areas in the standards that would develop your competence.
- If you are undertaking initial teacher training, the information generated from the questions above provides evidence for LLUK standards AS1 and AS4 and elements of Domains A–F.

The reflective practitioner and the reflexive teacher

I am sure that you are familiar with the growing popularity of the notion of the reflective practitioner. Indeed, reflection and evaluation of practice and CPD are integrated into the LLUK standards. Moore identifies what teachers need to reflect constructively:

the discourse of the reflective practitioner emphasises not so much the *acquisition* or development *per se* of the skills and areas of knowledge required for successful teaching, but rather the particular skills needed to *reflect constructively* upon ongoing experience as a way of developing those skills and knowledge and improving the quality and effectiveness of one's work. (Moore, 2000: 128)

Moore seems to suggest that competence and reflection complement one another in many ways rather than being completely contradictory: reflection addresses the particular circumstances relating to a given problem arising from trying to achieve competent teaching and learning. Its strength is that, unlike the competence model which breaks down activities, the model of reflective practice encourages teachers to take into account the 'whole picture'. But an important consideration is what techniques do teachers – and particularly student-teachers – have to acquire and develop to reflect constructively? Teachers are encouraged to reflect on their practice using diaries, journals and evaluations but Moore says that it is not so much these solitary activities that are important but *dialogues about practice* held between student-teachers, teachers, tutors and mentors. These dialogues enable:

- questions to be asked about problematic practice;
- alternative actions to be discussed and devised;
- new ways of working to be tried out;
- experimentation to be evaluated through further dialogue.

This collaborative process is favoured rather than relying on individual reflection as this can lead to teachers blaming themselves for problems in their workplace and in their own performance – the cause of which, in many cases, may be out of their control.

Whilst the concept of the reflective practitioner has become a bit of a slogan, Moore asserts that reflection which does not challenge an individual's assumptions just reinforces the *status quo*, and dearly held views, attitudes or prejudices are unchanged. What this means is that it is not enough to reflect on practice, you need to reflect upon the *ways in which you reflect*, i.e. become reflexive. The outcome of this is that, whilst reflection focuses on practice, being reflexive focuses on the *practitioner*. However, he warns that this needs to be done with care and common sense but, if it is part and parcel of being a competent and reflective practitioner, being reflexive can bring benefits in that it develops awareness of practice and the wider environment in which it takes place and 'handled appropriately may offer the teacher the best opportunity for genuine development and change' (Moore, 2000: 146).

Reflexivity provides an opportunity, e.g. to examine learners' behaviour but rather than focus on the way learners are disruptive or demotivated and don't engage with the sessions you prepare, it may bring to the fore considerations about *your* fear of losing control in the classroom or *your* fear of failure. It might seem hard to look at things from this point of view, but in the long run reflexivity provides you with a more critical engagement when addressing problems experienced in the classroom and in the organisation. Reflexivity encourages a deliberate attempt to make improvements, preferably in dialogue with others, and requires you to become both a theorist about your teaching and learning and a researcher of your practice.

Teacher as a strategist

To summarise, Moore identifies the teacher as a:

- communicative subject;
- competent subject;
- reflective subject;
- reflexive subject;
- theorist and researcher.

He suggests that no single model describes a good teacher as there are many different kinds of good teacher, but he does contend that teachers need high levels of expertise across the models and need to be *strategic* in the way that they work. He urges teachers to borrow freely from the models of good teaching and sees teaching as a strategic activity which needs to be:

- eclectic;
- flexible;
- organised;
- structured;
- responsive;
- contingent;
- personal;
- informed by and contributing to theory and debate.

You may well have come across the same ideas within the LLUK standards, but Moore's ideas are quite a list for you to consider when constructing your role! My conclusion is that the actions of successful teachers are intentional, planned and considered: pointers for the way you approach your own professional development.

Role congruity

A role comprises a set of expected activities and duties associated with a particular position within an organisation in order that the organisation can achieve its targets. The need to single out the activities and duties identified as the responsibility of an individual member of the workforce is important so that the organisation functions successfully and all the activities that the organisation requires to be performed to be successful can be coordinated and covered. Therefore, role differentiation becomes important to organisations and each employee has a distinctive role to play. Your organisation identifies your formal role as a teacher and sets out your individual function within a department or group.

However, successful teachers in organisations perform their formal role but, in doing so, interpret their role and develop it. Just like actors in the theatre, they make the role their own. Focusing on what they really want to achieve means teachers as 'investors' construct their own role to make their job worthwhile. It may well be that you had a favourite teacher when at school who influenced your decision to become a teacher yourself and who may have even inspired your interest in your subject specialism. However good a role model that favourite teacher was, now that you are a teacher, or training to be one, you need to acknowledge their influence but use it to make your teaching role *your own*, and not try to be someone else or something that you are not.

To do this you need to be aware of what will make your job worthwhile; you need to identify your purpose and vision. The factor that distinguishes the way that successful teachers practise, whom I identify in my research as 'investors', is that they see their role in a holistic way – not as an unmanageable load of different activities and duties pulling them in several different directions at once.

Although you have been encouraged to compare the role of the teacher with that of an actor playing a part, and teaching does require a performance, what goes without saying is that you remain true to who you are as:

> It is axiomatic that, in the end, though teaching may always be something of an 'act', the successful teacher has to remain true to 'who they are'. (Moore, 2000: 121)

The teacher's role is about *being you*, not about becoming lots of different characters with every new task or every new group of learners. This involves long-term self-development to enable you to make the role your own – and that is worth investing in. The following case study provides an excellent example of these ideas in practice.

Success Story

Being true to myself

I know you want me to talk about my current role, but I want to tell you about my background because nobody knows how I think and how I was driven to overcome difficult situations in my life and how I got to where I am today. My experience gives me my strength – working with people – and helps me relate to their difficulties.

My schooling and first jobs

I did OK at school, I got a bunch of O levels but didn't stay on to do A levels. Although my father won a scholarship and had a good education, my parents thought it would be a good idea for me to train as a hairdresser, which is what I did. I went along with their ideas for my future and I feel my own schooling was a bit like that – education was something that was done to me and I accepted what I was told. At that age I was very timid, quiet and shy, but I had a couple of interesting jobs in the beauty industry. I married very young and developed an interest in holistic beauty therapies which I loved and worked in a famous spa – but I became bored with the work and there was an opportunity to do some teaching at the spa's private college. When I was doing this full-time, I enrolled at an FE College on a City and Guilds Teaching Certificate 7307. In fact, I remember I had to have a 'special dispensation' to take the examination as I was under their minimum age! Anyway, I was offered two evening classes at the college and achieved my Teacher's Certificate and was still teaching full-time at the private college. So, what with a young child and the demands of family life, it was tough.

Achieving a work–life balance

We then moved away and I did get work in a Tertiary College, which was a different working environment to both the private and FE Colleges, but at that time my marriage broke up so I returned nearer to my home area and found myself back teaching in the private college. The only house I could afford was miles away and what with living in an isolated area, the travelling, paying childminders, etc., this was not the happiest time of my life. I felt I needed to spend more time with my daughter and after several attempts I eventually got a full-time job in an FE College – so I had regular hours and holidays. I had been absolutely determined to get that job and make a good life for my daughter and myself and made several attempts at it and was not put off by the original rejection. Having got the job I got the opportunity to do a Cert. Ed. teaching qualification. The whole experience was life changing and I made myself a five-year plan, part of which was my ambition that I would be a head of department within five years. I'm happy to say I achieved this.

Widening my experience

My life took a turn for the better, I remarried, had two children and later we made a move to a new part of the country. The deal was that I would work part-time, which I did for a while, but gradually I felt this wasn't enough. I had taught for so many years and, although the job was interesting, I was looking for something more. I applied to be an Additional Inspector for Ofsted as a subject specialist and undertook and passed the training. As a part-time AI, I was involved in five full inspections and one rein-spection. I found the inspection work quite stressful but really enjoyed the survey work I was engaged in. When the inspection regimes were restructured I didn't really feel enthusiastic and committed enough to continue with another organisation, but I recognise the whole experience has given me a much wider understanding of education, quality improvement and observation processes, etc., which has been invaluable.

Changing my role

About 18 months ago I got the offer of a part-time post in my college as a quality manager. The new role was for seven sessions (0.7 fte) a week and I continued with some teaching in my curriculum area. I had a really tough first year with lots of strategic and corporate changes and it was a really steep learning curve for me, but I enjoyed the demands of the role. When I was appointed as quality manager, my line manager was the Vice-Principal for Curriculum but, in response to changes in funding structures, etc., the role changed and my new line manager is Vice-Principal for Finance and Resources. After a year in post, the good news is that I was successful in being appointed full-time, but with the additional responsibility of Staff Development. Staff Development has been an area that I felt I wanted to work in so as to provide solutions to improving the quality of teaching and learning.

My current duties involve lots of mundane things: keeping corporate documents up to date, ensuring safe storage and retrieval when required and managing internal audits some of which are mandatory and others optional. I manage a rolling programme for

Corporate Services and act as a 'bridge' between auditors and staff and do all the chasing up. I try to keep a handle on things so when Ofsted visit it's not hideous. I see my job as helping staff to get things ready and provide support and guidance so that things don't get on top of them.

Investing in my role and recognising achievements

I had a very successful first year in post and now we have a small team. I support heads of department in quality issues and address organisational problems about staff development and appraisals. A part-timer does the auditing aspects, which she is brilliant at and an administrator looks after all the Staff Development admin and she's really efficient at that. I've developed an electronic system for lesson observation that not only captures all the narrative and quantitative data but links everything together. I can prepare a confidential report that draws together data from individual observations and collates it so that I can produce a strengths/weaknesses profile for departments, which is invaluable for the heads. A case in point is it highlighted that in one department the internal observations revealed constant lateness which was out of line with other departments so we were able to formulate a strategy to address this after discussions with a head where the timekeeping was excellent. Our system supports quality-driven action and we wouldn't have had such clear comparative information in the past. The system is obviously only as good as the Ofsted criteria it captures, but it does allow us to see exactly what we need to change or check up on and enables best-fit matching, e.g. a teacher was identified as outstanding at differentiation and we initiated an informal 'buddying-up' with someone who was struggling. The information is confidential, personal and not published so we are making quiet inroads and not making under-achievement public.

Constructing my own role

What really drives me is quality improvement: supporting staff who have difficulties identified through observations. I can be understanding, but at the same time something has to happen though, it has to get better. I'd like all new staff to have mentors but in a cash-strapped college the senior management aren't yet convinced of this. I mentor two Beauty students doing teacher training and I do some delivery on the course myself – so I'm known around college and staff see me as very firmly in the curriculum, which is good as they tend to stop and ask me things or drop in for a chat about their concerns, but this also brings pressures!

I don't want to appear to be blowing my own trumpet, but I am self-confident now. When I first became a manager there was an element of 'they tell me what to do and I do it'. Now I have the confidence to put my own edge on it, change the agenda, broaden my role. I'm not driven by processes but accept and understand them. My ambition is to improve people's performances. I am still ambitious and discussed this in appraisal and it was suggested that I take an academic route to progress. I've enrolled on a Masters degree to prepare for senior management eventually.

If you asked me ...

My advice to others who seek success is to:

- be aware of how you are with people and stay open-minded;

- be willing to learn as it takes time and experience to feel confident to know what you're talking about;
- take good care of yourself and do what is right for you;
- develop a professional relationship with someone where there is mutual respect and with whom you can really talk about issues at work;
- accept that you can achieve some of your targets and ambitions and not others and that you may still worry and be self-critical but if you identify what you want and you're determined, you can get there.

(Quality Manager – FE College)

The case study above reveals that this manager has control over their workload, has an intention to continue learning and that they have developed their role and made it their own: they have adopted Moore's model of a teacher as strategist. Evidence of this in the case study is that the boundaries of the formal role are blurred: they are carrying out their management function but have chosen to incorporate a teaching role into their workload – a role which has a direct relevance in contributing to quality improvement in the organisation through introducing best practice to student-teachers in their initial teacher training programme. This manager attributes their success to overcoming the ups and downs of life, which many of us face. Instead of giving up, as many of us would when things don't turn out as we plan or hope, they were determined to overcome them by their own efforts. Jarvis explains that it is really our life history that makes the difference:

> Perception of the situation is largely determined by individual biography and it is, therefore, subjective and individual. Learning ... is the process of transforming that present experience into knowledge, skills, attitudes, values, emotions, etc.; it is a matter, therefore, of modifying the individual biography, which in its turn will affect the manner by which future situations are experienced. (Jarvis, 1995: 67)

If your own life story, your life plan and your current experience are not in harmony, then questions arise about what your life means. You may ask yourself:

- 'What am I doing here?'
- 'Where am I going?'
- 'What's it all for?'

Your individual biography and your understanding of your present circumstances are related, but if you want things to improve and get better, then you have to consciously want to change. You have to have an intention to continue to learn.

It is often in times of difficulty that opportunities for learning occur – but you
have to acknowledge the current difficulties, understand how they arise from past
experience and consider how they might impact on your future. You have to get
things into perspective. Insights about the way ahead may seem to come out of the
blue but they are more likely to come from reflecting on your experiences and then
planning for the future in a more positive way. It may sound trite advice if you've
been going through a bad time, but try to do as the popular song says – pick yourself
up, brush yourself down and start all over again!

Vision and purpose

When considering your vision and purpose in your role, it is worth bearing in mind
that Jarvis (1997: 7–8) claims that education has only three basic criteria:

- institutional provision;
- subject matter;
- learners.

He suggests that education can be provided by any institution for any purpose.
However, at a practical level, i.e. at every point of your professional practice, there
are values involved. These values are not actually inherent in your actions or your
behaviour but are actually ascribed to them by others – just as learners tend to ascribe
characteristics to their teachers. For example, providing vocational education for 14–

16 year-olds is generally regarded by most people as a worthwhile thing to do but for a minority it is dubious whether education should be so narrowly focused on preparing young people for the workplace rather than spending time on broadening their minds while they are still at school. The values ascribed to vocational education will be different for apprentices, employers, parents, college teachers and university admissions officers. The value of education is in the experience of the individual. Jarvis points out that those values are learned by individuals as a result of living in society and in this sense are cultural, so they are open to debate and different interpretations.

If you compare your approach to teaching and learning with those of your colleagues, do you always see eye to eye? I suspect that on most occasions there is a lot of agreement about how you see your role, even if an outside observer watching you all teach might find a wide variation in your performances. Within a professional group, such as teachers like you and your colleagues, there can be a considerable amount of agreement, but that is not surprising as you've all undergone comparable training and have had to meet the same standards to gain your professional qualification. Inevitably, there are similarities in the way you see your role, and, for the most part, in day-to-day practice your judgements about what to do or how to behave tend to converge.

Nevertheless, there are events in everyday practice that seem to highlight the differences between teachers. A good example would be if you are required to undertake 'blind marking'. Some examination boards or professional bodies require two people to each mark one piece of work, then compare and agree a joint final mark. If you've been in this position, you will know that it's most unlikely that both of you will give exactly the same mark or grade – particularly if you are assessing, e.g. one of the following:

- a presentation – Business Studies;
- an artefact – Creative Arts;
- a collaborative project – Education Studies;
- an essay – Humanities;
- a dance performance – Media Studies;
- a practical project – Construction Industries.

You may well have been party to intense discussions about the way the marking was carried out and grades given, or even called in an external assessor to arbitrate when things couldn't be resolved. If you haven't been directly involved, you are probably aware from colleagues' experience that the process of internal verification of marks and grades for vocational qualifications may also raise contentious issues when a judgement that a learner is competent is challenged, e.g. on the grounds of the validity or sufficiency of the evidence. If the assessor and the verifier have conflicting opinions about the quality of the portfolio, these need to be resolved.

Most likely, what is happening on these occasions is that colleagues are placing *their own values* on the assessment process and outcome and they perceive things differently from you or the other assessor. The last thing you want is for teachers to be regimented and all think and act alike, but if there is a great deal of difference between assessment decisions then you have to recognise that individual teachers are clearly reflecting their own preferences and perceptions; they are basing their decision on *their own values*. That's what makes us individuals. We are free to think and act differently.

Individual differences are celebrated in life and as teachers you are encouraged to be creative and meet the needs of your learners and support them in the process of becoming independent. So, as a teacher, you need to be very aware of what it is that makes you an individual and different from your colleagues and also what you and your colleagues have in common as professionals. In other words, you need to be aware of *your own values* and how these impact on teaching and learning.

In life, individuals are constantly being assessed and evaluated and indeed you and I assess those around us both at home and at work all the time. We are always placing our values on others and the way they do things. We comment on others' behaviour, their dress, what they eat, where they go on holiday and the sort of house they live in or the car they drive. At work we remark on the attitude of learners, the commitment of team members, the wisdom of strategic decisions by managers – even the dress code of colleagues is up for discussion. We judge others by our own standards and values.

But as an assessor with the power to pass or fail learners, which may affect their progression or future employment opportunities, you have to question whether your judgement is fair. Issues of fairness are, of course, important in life generally but I would say they are vital part of your professional identity as a teacher because you are in a position of authority. This is not just a philosophical argument or an idealist viewpoint – it is a practical issue, too, as values 'provide the motive force for many things that we do' (Petty, 2004: 476).

As a teacher you may think that many decisions are made by others, both inside and outside your organisation, and that you have little influence on the way your organisation functions. But Petty points out that in practical terms you influence your learners in many ways and your values constitute the motivating force driving your actions which underpin your vision and purpose in your role. He provides plenty of examples, such as when you:

- guide learners in their choice of subjects;

- recruit learners onto a particular programme;
- decide what support learners need to succeed;
- monitor the progress of learners;
- design a learning programme to maximise learner success;
- make improvements and adapt them to learners' needs.

You encourage the development and progression of learners by valuing and responding to their individual experiences:

> If we want the promotion of equality and diversity to underpin everything we do, it's helpful if we take some time to focus on it, both in terms of how it fits with our personal and professional values, and of what it means in practical terms for our professional practice. What does the promotion of equality and diversity *look* like? What strategies and attitudes does it require in our classrooms or workshops, and in our organisation as a whole, in order to succeed? (Wallace, 2007: 42)

The answer to Wallace's question is that in order to succeed, whether you are conscious of this or not, everything you do is underpinned by your values when you:

- decide your priorities in the workplace;
- select particular strategies to adopt;
- choose specific teaching methods;
- evaluate your learning programmes;
- reflect on your vision and purpose.

Petty suggests that a good way of making your values more transparent is by asking yourself fundamental questions about your role.

Check It Out 6.5

Find out what's important to you and become more aware of the values underpinning the way you carry out your role as a teacher by responding to questions adapted from Petty (2004: 475).

- Why do you teach?
- What are your ultimate professional purposes and expectations?
- Why do you plan and prepare in the way you do?
- Why do you want to improve the way you carry out your role?

CPD LINKS

- Analyse how you put your values into practice. Evaluate your role and identify how you promote inclusiveness, diversity issues and equality. Identify actions in your sessions that would indicate how you value your learners and the experience they bring to their learning.

- If you are undertaking initial teacher training, your responses to the questions and evaluations from the above activity provide evidence for LLUK standards AS1, AS3, AK3.1, AP3.1 and elements of Domain F.

There is a view that the most successful organisations are 'vision-guided' and 'values-driven' (Barrett, 2006: 1). If you want to sustain high performance in your organisation and achieve your organisational objectives, for example the ones set by the organisations which are inspected by Ofsted, you have to measure and monitor indicators of performance, i.e. values and behaviour, and respond to what they tell you. There are four aspects which Barrett identifies for consideration:

- **individual personality** – personal values and beliefs, which are internal and non-observable by others;
- **individual character** – personal actions and behaviours, which are external and observable by others in individuals;
- **collective culture** – group values and beliefs, which are internal and non-observable in collaborative working and shared decision-making;
- **social structure** – group actions and behaviours, which are external and observable in systems and processes. (Barrett, 2006: 3)

To sustain high performance and for change to be successfully implemented, the culture of the organisation has to be continually adjusted. Vision has to 'guide' and values have to 'drive' all aspects of decision-making and be reflected in every system and process within the organisation, i.e. demonstrated in social practices within the organisation. Not only that, the *behaviour of individuals* in the organisation has to reflect the organisation's *collective vision and values* because as Barrett (2006: 4) puts it: 'Organizations don't transform. People do!'

You need to be aware of your internal values and beliefs so that your personal actions and behaviours can be observed by others, e.g. your learners, your colleagues, your managers and internal and external inspectors demonstrate them. Bennett illustrates how he did this:

> I was determined that I would try to make the students in my charge not only learn but grow in confidence. The happiest moments for me are when I see a group leave my class smiling because they know that hour they spent with me was worth it. ... My work in the college with my students means I can pass on the most important gift – confidence to change things. The confidence that doesn't just simply say 'Yes we can'. Rather the confidence that says 'If they [prominent people in black history] did it so can I today'. Being a black educator, with a particular background, has helped me find creative ways to help young people do that. That's what matters most to me. (Bennett, 2009: 20)

As an individual, just like Bennett, you have a crucial role to play in sustaining the high performance of your organisation. If you want to be seen to be working in an outstanding organisation, you have to play your part.

Success Story

Professional development for a purpose

When I think about my professional development, there hasn't been a year that I haven't done anything. Currently I'm doing Cognitive Behaviour Therapy (CBT) training. I don't intend to use it in a therapeutic sense, but my interest in CBT is that it models the skills that are beneficial to coaching, which is very relevant to me as I'm a management consultant specialising in professional development. Before setting up my own company, I held a variety of posts in industry and education and have many years of experience in working with clients from a range of local, national and international companies. I have specialised in how people and teams work within organisations and have gained a strong reputation for coaching others in challenging issues.

Reviewing practice

Although I've been coaching for some time, I recently did the Certificate in Coaching which I found was an opportunity to refresh my knowledge and also re-examine why I'm doing what I'm doing. For example, when I was reviewing my practice I realised I was slipping into an 'advice-giving' mode, so doing the course became a self-monitoring opportunity for me. I've done most of my training in 'bite-sized chunks' and have probably done three coaching courses in this way and now completed four on CBT training.

I've had to travel to London for a lot of my professional development so I've been meeting new people and this has helped me build networks of like-minded people. An unexpected outcome of all the visits to London has enabled me to see more of my family and catch up with old friends. As well as learning I've enjoyed myself – which is the best way of learning!

For my professional development before that, I did a Neuro-Linguistic programming (NLP) course. I'm not critical of the course I did, but the models used and the lack of robustness. I learned that what I needed was models that had some empirical basis – so it did make me think and question. The people I work with need to look at worst case scenarios, whereas NLP models don't look at that. I was invited to do an observation of a teaching session following my critique – so the course leaders were certainly open to being critically assessed.

Role exploration

Another professional development opportunity I really enjoyed was becoming a Belbin Associate. That involved on-line 360 degree feedback sent electronically about your team role and role contribution – which was fascinating, but not always what I expected and which created challenging conversations because of others' perceptual differences. That was some of the best professional development! To become a Belbin Associate I spent three days in Cambridge and it was a privilege being taught by

---

Belbin himself. Every year I get invited back to Cambridge for two days of seminars and discussions between brilliant practitioners from across the world about how the tool can be used – it's amazing the differences in approaches and it's a real opportunity for people to share differences and difficulties and build networks.

Professional vision

I've also qualified to use the Myers-Briggs Trait Inventory. The HR world has loads of tools and techniques available but they need to be applied only where there is evidence, with supervision and they require evaluation. In my consultancy I do use these tools, but I help others apply them. Professional development offers opportunities which need following up and putting into practice – you have to think 'What difference will it make'? Some organisations seem to take a superficial approach to professional development and on occasions I have lost out on work because I proposed to take a deep approach. I have been presented with lists of outcomes which don't seem to connect – but could be ticked off one by one. I have a model in my head that professional development is multi-dimensional and needs to draw on aspects that are valuable to people to deal with the realities of the workplace and each aspect reinforces another.

Personal values

I would say that professional development is not a fast, quick fix. It is more of a painful, agonising journey in which challenging conversations can make you uncomfortable. My personal circumstances mean that I've had loads of treatments for MS, which is unusual in the world of business and management consultancy. But, if you look around most people have something wrong, or know someone who has, and this helps me empathise and be patient.

If you asked me ...

What I would say if you want a successful career is that you need the following:

- Trust. The ability to trust your instincts, trust other people and trust your knowledge is crucial. For me there's an ethical aspect to this as clients have to trust me and I have to trust them.
- Connections. It's only through connections that you'll be successful. I know I have lots of faults – but I do have the ability to connect with people.
- Resilience. A degree of toughness, self-assurance and stamina is required to be successful in any career. If you aspire to setting up on your own like me, then you have to be prepared for the fact that there is no protection, there's no-one else but you.
- Self-belief. You have to believe that you can make a difference as, if you don't feel that you can make a difference, what is the point? Personally, I only want to work if I can make a difference – I won't be drawn into the rhetoric of professional development, but its practice.

(Professional Development Consultant)

The case study above exemplifies someone with a clear idea of what they want to achieve, who knows how to achieve it and why it is important. This consultant has constructed a role which is consistent with their vision of good practice and yet they are responsive to the realities of their personal circumstances, role and workload. Their values are evident in the creation of learning opportunities which are life-changing. The excellent guidance for a successful career offered here is well worth emulating: it is vision-guided and values-driven.

Organisations in the Lifelong Learning Sector measure and monitor the performance of teachers but often fail to respond to the values driving teachers' performance. If, as Barrett (2006) asserts, values-driven organisations are successful organisations, then to maintain quality teaching, organisations in the sector need to be aware how values are reflected in systems and processes. Petty applied the notion of building a values-driven organisation to teaching and learning and provides an effective and useful framework for those working in Sixth-form Colleges and FE Colleges, which is well worth relating to your own organisational context if it is different.

Values-driven behaviour

Your approach to teaching is underpinned by your **values**, e.g.:

- To value students as individuals;
- To improve students' life chances;
- To create an interest and curiosity in [subject].

Your values are put into action by your chosen **strategy**, e.g.:

- Course organisation;
- Scheme of work;
- Tutorial system, etc.

Your strategy is supported by your chosen **tactics**, e.g.:

- Lesson plan;
- Teaching method used;
- Timetable, etc.

Your tactics are manifest in your chosen **behaviour**, e.g.:

- Your teaching;
- Your attitudes to students in the classroom and in the corridor.

(Adapted from Petty, 2004: 476)

It is clear that values-driven behaviour can be translated into practice.

Check It Out   6.6

Professional values

- Using the guidelines provided by Petty, express your own values as personal aims or objectives.
- Identify group or team values and express them as collective aims or objectives.

Links To CPD

- Have a look at your course documentation and examine how your personal values are incorporated in it.

- Identify and discuss group values with your team (or mentor).
- Rewrite course documentation, such as a handbook or training materials, and incorporate personal and/or collective group values.
- If you are undertaking initial teacher training, preparing documentation for the above activity provides evidence for LLUK standards AS7, AK7.3,AP7.3 and elements of Domain D.

Personal skills and attributes

There is an assumption that as a teacher you are an independent, self-directed professional. There is an expectation that you are an expert in your subject, up to date and innovative in your teaching. As a teacher you are urged to contribute to the achievements of your organisation and the prosperity of the future workforce. At the same time, as a teacher it is probable that you are constantly being told what to do in order to support learners more effectively, how to work more efficiently and adapt your practice to conform to an organisational view of what is considered to be best practice. To cap it all, you are now to be responsible for your own CPD! So you may wonder, what are the skills and attributes you need to develop to meet these often conflicting demands?

Identifying assumptions and expectations can best be done by engaging in critical self-questioning of your individual practice. It does not have to be a solitary activity, but it does need to be initiated and controlled *by you* rather than others. The quandary is that in order to improve and modify your individual practice you need to be open about things that are often kept private and participate in dialogue with others so you can check out your assumptions and expectations against theirs. It is only when you are aware of your assumptions and where they originated that you can critically question those assumptions because:

> no other person can 'teach' someone self-awareness, although another person can challenge, question, support, and otherwise foster the process. (Cranton, 1996: 59)

Self-awareness is essentially a developmental process and is more successful if you can find someone to foster that process. Townley notably developed the concept of self-formation in the workplace and distinguished it from self-awareness. The notion of self-formation, which is currently relevant to the concept of professional formation required to achieve Qualified Teacher Learning and Skills, is defined as:

> being aware of the details of what one does, one's daily routine, what one thinks and feels, not as indices of hidden aspects of self but as an act of memory ... self-formation is an act of noticing. (Townley, 1994: 275)

The act of noticing what you do is more than just being aware of your daily practice and requires recalling from memory the details of what you did and how you felt and bringing them to the forefront of your mind so that you can develop a new way of constructing your role. The *act of noticing* appears to be a critical factor in making sense of your practice and enabling self-formation. Self-awareness in itself will not bring change; you also need an intention to develop and the ability to behave in a different manner (Moon, 2000). Self-formation has to be self-initiated if it is to further professional formation. You have to take responsibility not only for identifying developmental needs but also for taking action to recognise opportunities for learning.

Check It Out   6.7

SWOT analysis

A commonly used management tool is a SWOT analysis which spotlights the Strengths, Weaknesses, Opportunities and Threats facing an organisation. Analysis using the four labels provides information that can be used as the basis for making decisions and solving problems.

I have adapted the general idea here so that you may apply it not to your organisation – but to yourself!

- **S**trengths – distinctive attributes you bring to your role and which you can develop to your advantage.
- **W**eaknesses – traits that limit your effectiveness in your role and which need modifying to improve your chances of success.
- **O**pportunities – knowing about potential changes or new policies that are arising and being responsive to chances to develop your role.
- **T**hreats – being aware of situations that might jeopardise your current role, future prospects or security and be prepared to meet them.

Sometimes the SWOT analysis is referred to as 'WOTS up'! You may find that carrying out the SWOT analysis helps you identify 'What's up' in developing your role.

Links To CPD

- To be successful, you need to be ready to take advantage of your Strengths and Opportunities and be aware of the drawbacks of your Weaknesses and Threats.
- Your Action Plan for CPD needs to be designed to take SWOT into account. Refine your Action Plan after completing the analysis.
- The SWOT analysis is good preparation for an appraisal interview and providers pointers for discussion.
- If you are undertaking initial teacher training, your SWOT analysis provides evidence for LLUK standards AS7, AK7.2, AP7.2 and elements of Domain F.

One of the positive aspects of the LLUK standards is the emphasis placed on the role of teachers in supporting learners to progress and develop and achieve their goals and aspirations. The standards promote a focus on learning and its potential to benefit people emotionally, intellectually, socially and economically and incorporate an inclusive learning agenda. These aspects of the standards mean that there is a need for teachers to provide tutorial support and feedback for all learners and work with colleagues to provide guidance and support for learners, all of which requires good interpersonal skills as well as technical knowledge.

The LLUK standards do not provide a prescriptive list of required skills and attributes for teachers (for which you may be extremely thankful!) so you are invited to identify the relevant skills and attributes required in your current role and context. My own research reveals a short list of the skills and attributes demonstrated by successful teachers to meet role expectations and move towards their vision and purpose in their professional role which are displayed below.

Check It Out   6.8

Personal skills and attributes

Use the table to compare with the skills and attributes you identified.

Personal skills	Personal attributes
<ul><li>good communication</li><li>working with others</li><li>being organised</li><li>analysis and evaluation</li></ul>	<ul><li>enthusiasm</li><li>respect for learners</li><li>caring for learners</li><li>creativity</li><li>risk-taking</li><li>self-confidence</li><li>flexibility</li><li>adaptability</li></ul>

Source: Steward (2004: 280)

Links To CPD

- Use programme evaluations from learners to identify what skills and attributes your learners identify as contributing to their progress and development.
- Identify skills and attributes that can be developed to improve the effectiveness of your role.
- If you are undertaking initial teacher training, your responses to the above activities provide evidence for LLUK standards AS1 and AS7.

Did you have difficulty in identifying your skills and attributes? In the hurly-burly of the workplace you don't often have time to stop and think on a day-to-day basis about how you are performing, and so the way you do things often becomes second nature. However, when you are thinking about how your learners perceive you and how you might improve aspects of your teaching and learning, you have to stop for a moment and consider what you bring to your role and how others view your teaching. You may well have identified different skills and attributes, and may value different teacher characteristics. That is all to the good because you work in different organisations with a diverse range of students. Nevertheless, although there is no way that I want to encourage uniformity, it is useful to be aware of the core of skills and attributes demonstrated by teachers who are considered successful.

Successful Strategies
- Although your teaching role may require you to perform in the classroom, successful teachers remain true to who they are. You need to bring authenticity to your role.
- No single way of teaching is considered best practice and you need to employ a range of strategies and achieve a balance between flexibility and structure in your role.
- Don't be beaten by life's ups and downs. Most people experience some personal hardships or professional setbacks. It's dealing with them constructively that counts.
- Work out how you would like to see your role in five years' time and think about planning how you can achieve your career aims.
- Personal skills and attributes contribute to your individuality and you must not be complacent about your role but try to learn from feedback and evaluations about possible ways to improve.
- Make inclusion and equality practices explicit as you carry out your day-to-day role.

In Chapter 7 there is a focus on ways of developing knowledge which contributes to the development of dual professionalism – a model of the teaching role being promoted by the Institute for Learning. The chapter advocates taking a constructivist approach to developing knowledge, which is an approach I have found to be effective and favour, particularly in vocational and professional education and training. When you read the chapter, see if you agree with me!

7 Constructing Professional Knowledge

In this chapter you will find sections on:

- dual professionalism;
- a constructivist approach to knowledge;
- a pathway into your specialist subject;
- specialist area knowledge;
- knowledge of teaching and learning;
- maximising learning.

The chapter addresses issues relating to Domain A: AS2 Learning, its potential to benefit people emotionally, intellectually, socially and economically, and its contribution to community sustainability.

For those undertaking initial teacher training, the chapter provides opportunities to generate evidence for LLUK standards AS1, AK1.1, AP1.1, AS2, AS4, AK4.3, AP4.1, AP4.3, AS5 and elements of Domains A–F.

Dual professionalism

As a teacher in the Lifelong Learning Sector, Hitching points out that you have 'dual professionalism':

> There are very few generalist practitioners in this sector. The majority of you have developed expertise in one or more distinct and specialist areas. These areas range across the academic, business, commercial and industrial worlds and deliver learning at many different levels of ability. Given that your teaching will potentially produce the national wealth of tomorrow, your professional expertise needs to

remain current; no easy undertaking when technologies are developing so rapidly. Furthermore, in order to pass those skills on to others effectively, training how to teach is now considered to have an equal priority with subject specialism. (Hitching, 2008: 1)

Whatever your background, Hitching declares you play a critical role in shaping the current and future workforce and you bring to that role a high level of specialist vocational skills, a wealth of industrial experience and/or academic qualifications. Not only do you have to keep your expertise in your subject and your specialist skills current in a rapidly developing environment, but you also have to pass those skills on to your learners through your professional skills as a teacher. You, therefore, have a dual professional role: as a subject specialist and as a qualified teacher.

Figure 7.1 IfL's model of dual professionalism

For many years, industrial experience was considered a priority for appointment in post-school teaching and training and candidates were selected on the basis of their specialist knowledge and qualifications, i.e. their experience in the 'real world' rather than in the 'educational world' was paramount. Since 2007, however, there has been a compulsory requirement for those teaching in the sector to have completed an approved teacher training course and hold a teaching qualification. Your role, in Hitching's words, is to train the workforce in the latest skills but you must also be several steps ahead of rapidly changing government priorities and at the same time be aware of the demands of your own organisation. This is a tough commitment. Davies (2008) asserts that, as a teacher, CPD is the only way you can manage this commitment and maintain the currency of your professional practice – thus ensuring that you are:

- the best *subject specialist* you can be;
- fully equipped in terms of the skills and knowledge that you need as *a teacher* in your particular organisational setting.

But the questions that may well be coming into the minds of many of you as you think about this idea of dual professionalism could be:

- How do you go about developing your professional knowledge for this dual role?
- What is the nature of the knowledge you need both in your role as a subject specialist and as a teacher?
- How do you apply new knowledge to your current workplace practices in the dual roles of a subject specialist and a teacher?

More significant questions in my view would be whether the way you think about knowledge really matters, or whether the views you hold are important, and if any of it makes a difference to the quality of your day-to-day work. My answer would have to be that it does as:

> CPD means maintaining, improving and broadening relevant knowledge and skills in your subject specialism and your teaching so that it has a positive impact on practice and the learner experience. (Institute for Learning, 2008: 18)

Your day-to-day work concerns teaching and learning and the reason why the way you think about knowledge really matters is that your views about the nature of knowledge have an important bearing on your approach to teaching and learning – whether you are really aware of this or not. Your views have a direct bearing on what you do, and how you do it, in your day-to-day workplace practices. Indeed, in his discussion on teacher training, Hayes encapsulates this way of thinking in one question:

> The single criterion or standard that is necessary for good teaching is 'Does this person know their stuff?' If a lecturer knows a subject, whether academic or practical, it can be passed on in many ways. (Hayes, D., 2007: 177)

I am sure that this is a question you asked about your teachers and, I am sure it is one that your learners will ask about you. Do you know your stuff?

Success Story

Developing professional knowledge

I always wanted to do teacher-education, but I never really thought in terms of becoming a manager when I was doing my own teaching qualification. As soon as I got into teaching, I thought teacher-education is what I would like to do. So, first I did a Masters degree in education which broadened my horizons and then later on I did an EdD. Both these prepared me well for the job of teacher-educator; they gave me an overview of teaching and training and enabled me to develop in an area I know about.

Developing management expertise

I have to say, though, that my higher degrees weren't such good preparation for a management role. My current role is managing teacher-education courses, but I still do a little bit of teaching which I really enjoy. As I become more experienced as a manager, I am beginning to see myself more in that role and enjoy it, too.

I think the difference between teaching and management is that as a teacher you become experienced at managing students' learning, but as a manager you're managing people and it's not the same process. You manage what they do and the role becomes more complex and broad. Contracts change, conditions change and managing that change is the difficulty. Nothing seems to settle. You dream that next year will be different and everything will settle down and you'll know what you're doing – but it hasn't been like that! I think as I've become more experienced, I've become more confident at dealing with the difficulties change brings.

Exchanging ideas about developing professional knowledge

One of my jobs is to do appraisals and I take this very seriously indeed. I see it as an opportunity for people to talk about what they want to do – which is very important in a sector where there seems to be little time for thinking about yourself and your future. I suppose because there's no history of ongoing professional development, no real culture established, some people are resistant to appraisal. They see it as another form-filling process, which is a real pity. To my mind, the introduction of CPD in the sector has enabled appraisal to become more sophisticated and enabled people to take ownership of their professional development. Now, it's not something that's done to them.

During appraisal I usually ask people what they've thought about for their own CPD, and we have a conversation in which an exchange takes place: they identify their strengths, their interests and we discuss the opportunities. I try to support most people in most things that they identify. It's their choice but sometimes there's a mix of being a bit directive and leaving them to choose. There are plenty of opportunities for in-house CPD for people to do, e.g. e-lab technology workshops. But I also encourage people to do things outside the college because it's an opportunity for networking and broadening their experience. If people want to do higher level qualifications I try and get the funding for them and have been successful at this, e.g. one

---

person is doing an EdD and another Masters level mentor training. We also bid for funded projects, such as an e-learning one, which is an opportunity to release people to do some research, e.g. action research projects with our partners in the regional CETT, keep up to date and develop in this way. There's also a Postgraduate Certificate for teacher-trainers that I'm interested in and which I'm currently exploring.

IfL REFLECT

In my view, the new CPD requirement enables people to have a better overview of the professional development process and better recording helps this. I encourage people to use the IfL REFLECT as a collecting point. It is new and for some people has been a bit of a challenge, but recording things does validate what people do and does provide evidence of what's been done.

If you asked me ...

From experience, my advice to those starting out in teaching would be that to be successful you need not just nebulous things such as charisma, the 'star' quality everyone talks about. Teaching and learning can be fun, and should be enjoyable for everyone, but it's not entertainment. You also need:

- sound knowledge;
- real passion;
- a high level of teaching skills;
- to be quick to pick things up;
- to enjoy what you're doing;
- to be good at learning.

I think that what's really important for success in the sector is for people to continue to learn. You have to stop now and again and pause for thought, think about what you're doing, what you get out of your job, what it all means – that's what counts.

(Manager and Teacher-Educator)

The case study above is an excellent example of someone who 'practises what they preach'. They have taken their professional learning seriously and engaged in developing their professional knowledge, both through formal learning opportunities and through informal learning in the workplace. As a manager, they now encourage members of the team to develop dual professionalism as experts in both their specialist subject area and in teaching, and also support them in meeting personal and organisational goals. The case study epitomises the Institute for Learning's personalised model of professionalism in which teachers make critical judgements on the value and benefit of a range of developmental opportunities, formal and informal, that are appropriate for the updating of subject specialism or industrial expertise, teaching and learning approaches and the work context (IfL, 2008: 18).

A constructivist approach to knowledge

In the Introduction to this book, it was suggested that you developed an Action Plan of activities for your CPD requirement for the current year (see Check It Out 0.1). It was recommended that you identify problems and dilemmas in your professional practice that needed resolving and incorporated them into an Action Plan. You may well have already embarked on your CPD activities for the current year.

Check It Out   7.1

Developing knowledge through professional practice

Here are some typical examples that other teachers in the sector have chosen for their CPD activities:

- trying out new systems of recording information;
- testing new ways of assessing learners;
- experimenting with new ways of delivering sessions;
- trialling different ways of supporting learners.

Consider this scenario:

If you had undertaken any of these suggested examples above, the way you would assess the success of these activities would be through your own improved performance. You don't have to sit an examination or pass a written test to know if they worked, what you do is weigh up what you consider are the advantages of the changes you made through your own efforts and judge for yourself whether the time and energy you spent on the activities was worthwhile. Most likely, you talked to your colleagues about the changes you made or even collaborated with them in putting them into action and, hopefully, talked to your learners about the impact on them. You probably reflect on why things worked and even contemplate further refinements or improvements as you try out new ways of working. All these activities mean you end up with new ideas which bring benefits to the way you do things in future, both for you and your learners. In other words, you have new knowledge at your fingertips to help you develop your practice.

- Do you recognise this scenario as a way *you* engage in CPD – or are encouraged to do so by your mentor?
- The activities provide an overview of Domains A–F.

If you consider that you would have approached a professional development activity as it was described in the above scenario then, whether by intuition or by prior education or training, as you undertook such a learning process you would have adopted a constructivist approach to:

- how you learn;
- the nature of knowledge.

Gulati reveals why the constructivist discourse is being embraced by teachers in the Lifelong Learning Sector: it is based on the premise of a few overarching principles which seem particularly pertinent to young people, adults and work-based learners:

> The key points that the constructivist discourse suggests are the importance of learner-control, learning in real-life contexts, flexibility in learning, freedom to choose learning resources and openness in discussing issues. (Gulati, 2004: 2)

For example, in the Lifelong Learning Sector, learner control is encouraged through Individual Learning Plans, real-life contexts for learning are commonplace, as well as simulated work environments. Additionally, the constructivist discourse is manifest in flexible learning programmes and a personalised approach to learning, which create choice for the learner and an opportunity for one-to-one discussion. If you are aware of constructivist learning theory and constructivism applied to the nature of knowledge, then all well and good, but if not it would be a good idea to think about your professional practice in relation to this approach (or another learning theory if you so choose) so that you can develop insights that help your own professional learning – which ultimately will benefit your own learners.

Check It Out   7.2

Constructivist learning theory and CPD activities
Referring to the key points that Gulati identifies above, complete the following sentences to develop an awareness of how constructivist learning theory underpins your activities – or reveals that it doesn't!
- Learner-control is evident in my CPD activities because I ...
- Learning in real-life contexts is evident because I ...
- Flexibility in learning is evident because I ...
- Freedom to chose learning resources is evident because I ...
- Openness in discussing issues is evident because I ...

Links To CPD
- Identify one CPD activity that you have undertaken. Reflect on how theory and practice are linked in the activity.
- Prepare a statement which outlines how theoretical aspects of constructivism or another learning theory apply to the activity.
- If you are undertaking initial teacher training, your responses to the above activities provide evidence for LLUK standards AS2, AS4, AK4.3, AP4.1 and elements of Domain B.

Although constructivist learning theories have become popular in recent years and are steadily becoming an axiom for new ways of thinking about learning in the

Lifelong Learning Sector, there is nothing radically new in the idea of a constructivist approach to knowledge. Essentially, the ideas introduced by Dewey at the beginning of the last century have been backed by more recent findings from cognitive theories developed by Piaget, then added to by Vygotsky's research and promoted by Bruner. These ideas were mirrored in Kelly's personal construct theory, also developed by educationists such as von Glasersfeld, and are now gaining widespread acceptance among teachers. The melding of these ideas over the years has resulted in a body of work which is broadly known as constructivism:

> The central idea is that human learning is constructed, that learners build new knowledge upon previous learning and therefore learning involves constructing one's own knowledge from one's own experiences. Individuals engage in their own knowledge construction by integrating new information into their 'schemes' and negotiate meaning through a shared understanding. (Armitage et al., 2007: 75)

Armitage et al. suggest that social and political contexts are important influences in the way teaching and learning are approached and the way one theoretical perspective is valued over another. They note that over the past decade teaching has become more concerned with the promotion of learning than with the transmission of knowledge, i.e. the *process* of learning appears to be more important than the *content* that is learned. They assert that no one theory can supply a 'blueprint' for how individuals learn, but each theory can offer insights for effective learning. Maybe, this is why constructivism is becoming so widely accepted by teacher-trainers and teachers in the Lifelong Learning Sector as it acknowledges both the diversity in teaching and learning and the diversity of learners' needs: different contexts, different experiences and different perspectives. These are exemplified in teaching and learning in the sector by the value placed on:

- authentic settings for vocational learning;
- the importance of workplace experience;
- the prevalence of work-based learning and assessment;
- the encouragement of learners to set their own personal learning goals.

Constructivism views learners as complex individuals with different needs and backgrounds. Indeed, constructivism champions individuality and difference and puts the learner, rather than the teacher, at the centre of the learning process. In other words, it calls for a *personalised* approach to learning and teaching. This means that you need to be aware of the backgrounds of learners and their language and culture, i.e. what they have inherited and learned through life that makes them individuals, as all these factors influence their learning. It is a learner's background and experiences that help shape the knowledge that they acquire in the learning process. But not everyone agrees with this view, as the following rather lengthy quote reveals:

> At this point, I should perhaps mention what is commonly called the 'constructivist' position. This holds that we all construe the world about us, and that what is important is to understand people's constructions, rather than what might be the case. In view of what I have written about schemas, it might be thought that I would find this position congenial. I do not, and this is because, in the constructivist position, 'what might be the case' tends to be lost by default. People who favour this position often refer to the work of George Kelly in support of it, so it seems appropriate to quote this man as well. He typically wrote, 'We have long since committed ourselves to a point of view from which we see the world as being real, and man's psychological processes as being based upon personal versions of that reality'. (Sotto, 2007: 261)

Sotto explains that in the course of having experiences, schemas are formed in our brain, and that we respond to the subsequent events around us on the basis of those schemas. He agrees that as everybody has different schemas in their brain, their reaction to events will differ. Sotto provides an example as a case in point: 'if four people are present at the site of a traffic accident, their accounts of it are likely to differ. Or one could say that they construe the accident differently'. But at this point he diverts from a constructivist position as he asserts that in *principle* the accident can be described accurately, and that one person's account of that accident might be more accurate than another person's.

My view would be that Sotto's argument is logical, but that, as he agrees, the reality is that different views would be forthcoming. From a pragmatic, rather than a philosophical, position what is as important for you as a teacher to take into account is how learners construe the topic of a session differently from the way you present it and the way you intend, i.e. to identify their personal versions of reality. That is not to say that the teacher's version is the accurate one, but that if learners want to pass an examination or achieve a qualification, there is a version of the topic that is construed by examiners and assessors as more accurate than another. You don't just want your learners to regurgitate the information exactly as you presented it, but, in my view, learners do need to understand what other people are currently saying or doing (or have said or done in the past) before they can think for themselves what it all means – then either reject or accept it. You need to encourage them to question the information, pose problems and come up with their own answers. Barth (2000: 196) puts forward the idea that constructing knowledge is not a spontaneous act for learners and that, as a teacher, you can become a 'co-constructor' as you negotiate the meaning of knowledge with learners. These are all aspects of knowledge that you have to tussle with as a teacher, while learners struggle to understand what knowledge comes within the bounds of accuracy.

But Sotto asserts, and I agree, that good teaching is about much more than helping people to acquire knowledge and can convey to the learner that it is important to open their eyes and 'thereby escape the shackles of common sense, conventional wisdom and the garbage purveyed by the mass media' (Sotto, 2007: 255). Learners have to be aware how others construe knowledge and learn to question different versions, including their own.

Two important ideas are associated with constructivism:

- It must be 'hands on', i.e. active and social. It was Vygotsky who promoted the idea that social interaction and communication through language are constituent parts of learning. It is considered that learning is a social activity and you learn through your connections with other people, e.g. from your family, acquaintances, peers and teachers, and the language used and the nature of the communication influences your learning.
- It must be 'minds on', i.e. cognitive and reflective. Knowledge is considered the means of making sense of experience and is generated by each individual – rather than the representation of something. In this way, each individual is responsible for the world they are experiencing.

Some theorists argue that the two ideas reveal different strands of constructivism, but I would regard them as two integral parts of one approach to teaching and learning. In the Lifelong Learning Sector, young people and adults develop their thinking by interacting with other young people and adults and also the world around them; in simple terms, by talking to each other, reading notes and handouts and writing notes, posters or portfolios:

> Teaching is vastly facilitated by the medium of language, which ends by being not only the medium for exchange but the instrument that the learner can then use himself [sic] in bringing order into the environment. (Bruner, 1971: 6)

In this way, social and cognitive aspects of learning are seen to be dependent on each other. Bruner confirms that the nature of language and the function it serves in communication and exchange of ideas through conversations, discussions and dialogue enables the learner to understand what things are intended to mean and must, therefore, be part of any theory of cognitive development.

Specialist area knowledge

If you are a newcomer to the ideas of constructivism, it is probable that there seem to be anomalies in the increasing popularity of this humanistic approach to teaching and learning and the focus on measurable and visible learning behaviours and outcomes in the Lifelong Learning Sector, where the majority of learners are enrolled on formal courses with a structured learning programme and/or pre-defined curriculum which are very likely allied to a vocational outcome. Key ideas that constructivism advocates are:

- **content is not considered as important as the process of learning** – but as a teacher you are urged to keep up to date with your specialist area knowledge and skills and bring current knowledge to your teaching and learning;
- **individuals construct their own knowledge** – but as a teacher you have a set of criteria to cover and specific objectives for learners to achieve;
- **responsibility for learning with the learner** – but as a teacher you are answerable to your organisation for meeting retention and achievement targets.

Constructivism appeals to current views of teaching and learning but, particularly for those of you who have been teachers for any length of time, there may be conflict with the traditional approaches to teaching and learning that you acquired in your own initial teacher training and have adopted in your professional practice.

To bring your teaching and learning up to date and to overcome these long-established practices, you have to focus on the *learner* when planning for learning rather than on your specialist area or what you will do as a teacher. Current views of teaching and learning involve the learner at the centre of any session or training course – not the subject knowledge or content. This perspective on learning requires teachers to be interested in the process of learning and not just in the imaginative presentation of their subject. If you are highly skilled and enthusiastic about your specialist area, then this is not always as simple to do as it sounds, as the tendency is to focus on what you can *teach* your learners rather than on how they learn. This is natural, as you are employed for your confidence in your professional expertise and want your learners to gain as much knowledge from you about your specialist area as possible. When preparing learners for employment or progression you are urged to make your sessions relevant and it is natural to want to impart as much vocational knowledge or specialist information to your learners as you can. Indeed, Williams affirms that:

> concepts of lecturer professionalism are based upon subject knowledge and to deny we have such knowledge is both dishonest and a disservice to the students we teach. (Williams, 2007: 39)

The challenge of dual professionalism (which emerged with the obligation of a professional teaching qualification) is that although you have the 'academic subject knowledge' or the 'technical accomplishment of high-level skills in a trade' described by Williams, you also have to select suitable teaching and learning strategies which are appropriate for your specialist area – not just lecture or tell learners everything. Subject knowledge is still essential, but what is also considered essential nowadays is knowledge about ways of creating a learning environment. That is not to say that didactic and instructive strategies need be completely dismissed, but that you should aim to redress the balance between teacher-led activities and learner-led activities.

Petty (2006) says that many criticisms of constructivism are based on a mis-conception that because learners make their own meaning, teachers *mustn't tell them anything*, but they need to be told that specialist knowledge can be construed differently by people with different perspectives. Don't let your learners have to sec-ond-guess important issues such as how knowledge represents the way things are in your specialist area because:

> Students also need to know how knowledge is created in your subject, the methods of enquiry that are used, and how ideas, theories and principles are tested and improved. They need to know that science, experts, religious and other authorities all create their own meanings and that history shows that they have all made mistakes. This is called the 'epistemology' of your subject ... (Petty, 2006: 30)

According to Petty, the very best teachers put emphasis on epistemology, though it is rarely on the syllabus as such, and it is considered important to tell learners about the grounds for knowledge in your specialist area. Put simply, you need to tell learners the 'rules' in your subject, the basic theories, why some aspects are important and others considered out of date or of no consequence in the workplace and how new information in your specialist area is developed, e.g. through controlled experiments, testing new ideas or trialling different work practices. You do this by embedding the characteristics identified above by Petty, i.e. ideas, theories and principles, into your sessions and devising learning activities that draw on learners' prior knowledge and which support their approach to learning. You can develop theoretical ideas by using visual resources such as diagrams or charts, getting learners to make or handle materials or create card games to introduce new ideas and con-cepts – all these strategies complement your 'telling'.

One important consideration when developing good practice in teaching your own specialist area, however, is to keep in mind that you learn most readily when you already know enough to have what Armitage et al. describe as 'schemes' in your head about information from previous experiences and can link, or hook, new information to them. You need to make connections to help you understand the message intended by the new information. So, this means that you cannot learn without knowledge and your learners cannot assimilate new knowledge about your specialist area without having some scheme, structure or framework (Piaget called them 'schema' and Sotto refers to 'schemas') already in place from previous learning so that they can build on this. This notion of building is where the concept of constructing knowledge begins to make sense for teachers of a specialist area.

However, the new specialist area knowledge can only be given meaning *by the learner*: they must fit new learning into their scheme or framework by testing out ideas based on their prior knowledge and experience before they can apply the new knowledge to a new situation. What learners already know and can do exerts a considerable influence on the quality of what they achieve when they learn something new.

I find it helps to think about it as a bit like learners putting events and experiences into a kind of storage system in their head, which they can use to help them understand new information and develop their knowledge. Conversely, perhaps the events and experiences already stored away may hinder their learning or confuse them. Therefore, you do need to have an expert knowledge of your specialist area so that you can:

- assess how much your learners already know about the subject;
- appreciate the past experience they bring to their new learning;
- recognise any potential barriers to learning in your specialist area.

Activities and assignments are needed in order to discover what it is learners already know and believe, and reveal where their understanding might conflict with – or lead to misunderstandings with – the subject material they are required to learn. You need to take all of these points into account when planning learning activities so that they meet the needs of your learners.

Sotto (2007: 133) points out that it is only 'too much telling' that hinders learning and 'to really learn, one must experience. Too much telling gets in the way of experiencing'. Your knowledge of teaching helps you resist standing in front of the group and *talking at them at length* as too much telling is not only boring for learners so they tend to switch off but also does not allow them to actually do something or think for themselves, i.e. it gets in the way of experiencing. You may well have experienced this yourself as a learner and only realised that you'd stopped paying attention when you dropped your pen or your eyes started to close!

Your expert knowledge enables you to devise learning activities that help learners grasp for themselves what you are presenting to them and so experience it for themselves. Your expert knowledge also helps you to pitch the planned activities at an appropriate level, which a teacher without your specialist area expertise might find very difficult. The more expert you get at teaching, the more you will be able to effectively incorporate social interaction and cognitive opportunities into your learning plans by:

- not overwhelming learners with information and boring them with endless facts and figures;
- keeping learners busy and active, not just for the sake of keeping them occupied, but so they experience specialist area knowledge and skills for themselves;
- getting the right balance between teacher-telling and learner-doing.

A pathway into your specialist subject

Another important consideration is that you must provide a *pathway* into your specialist subject for the learner, which is based on that learner's previous knowledge. There is a widely held notion of learning as being a journey for the learner: learners start out on the pathway at one point and all hope to reach an identified destination and the achievement of their personal goals. If you pursue that image for a moment, your role becomes that of a facilitator who encourages them in this endeavour rather than a teacher telling them all you know. You are rather like a guide on that journey to ensure that learners join the pathway and manage to travel along it with your guidance and support. Before setting out, any experienced guide would make sure that the members of the group had the basic skills and equipment to proceed – such as the right clothing and perhaps basic map-reading skills if they were a party of walkers. No self-respecting guide would take a group of inexperienced beginners on a gruelling trek through a tropical jungle as their first venture or on an arduous mountain climb if they'd never even done hill walking. An experienced guide would most likely start with something well within the capabilities of the group and take a route they could manage.

It's perhaps easy to think that this is just common sense – but the question is whether you actually apply these common sense ideas to your own learners, not just when they are starting a new programme, but also when they are starting a new topic. It's not that easy and maybe you have an urge to say to your learners:

- 'Keep up!'
- 'Everyone else is nearly finished!'
- 'You're holding everybody up!'

When you are an expert in your specialist area, it may be difficult to imagine how strange and different it is for beginners and how difficult it is to grasp the new ideas and reach the standards expected of them. If learners seem disinterested or lack enthusiasm it can be disappointing and you may lose patience. Perhaps learners don't complete the activities you set them in the session or meet the deadlines you set for project completion or assessment and you start to get exasperated. All this may be understandable, but it is not very professional. If this happens, what you are doing is thinking too much about your specialist area and the subject content of the sessions rather than thinking about the learner and how they go about learning the topic that is new to them.

As the image of a guide on a learning journey illustrates, it is your responsibility as a teacher to provide a way into the subject for your learners and you need to base it on your learners' previous knowledge. So, the traditional role of the teacher (that some of you may have been trained for) is now considered inappropriate. Using a constructivist learning approach means that as a teacher you are a facilitator and guide, rather than an instructor. Your role is to choose activities that are relevant to your specialist subject and which trigger your learners' thinking and encourage them to join in. This is done initially by using approaches they are already familiar with, or information they already know, by posing:

- a series of straightforward questions;
- a series of simple problems to solve;
- a set of increasingly more difficult tasks;
- a problem that requires a practical investigation to answer it;
- questions and problems in the form of games.

Gradually, with further encouragement and questioning from you (or other learners), they can begin to integrate the new ideas for themselves and start to try them out as possible solutions to the questions and problems posed.

At the beginning of a programme, activities for learners have two purposes:

1. you need to devise innovative ways to enthuse learners;
2. you need to assess what they already know.

Your learners should be enabled to start out on their learning journey confidently with guidance from you and, as the beginning of any programme is a critical time for learners, you need to support them to carry on and not drop out after a few hours or days of a new programme.

When you have a new group of learners, it is not easy to immediately assess how much individuals know and pitch the initial activities at the right level. However, if you're just starting out on your career as a teacher, my advice would be that it's much better to be able to say 'Well, you know lots more than I thought you would', which is likely to make learners feel good. Surely, that's more positive than saying, 'I thought you'd already know all about this, I'm surprised you haven't done it before', which is a bit discouraging for learners at the outset of a new programme. Your formative assessment of your learners' prior knowledge and their response to your feedback will help you adjust your planning for subsequent sessions. Again, your judgement will rely on your specialist area knowledge and expertise.

Check It Out 7.4

Initial learning activities

An induction session may well be your learners' first contact with your specialist subject, or if they are familiar with your subject it may well be their first contact with it at a higher level. Consider the following questions about learning activities with an induction session at the start of a new programme in mind.

- How do you ensure that you enthuse and motivate learners in your own specialist area and not spend all the induction session on administrative chores and housekeeping jobs?
- How do you ensure that your specialist area knowledge is appropriately applied to activities for newcomers?
- How do you ensure that you identify individual learning needs and potential barriers to learning in your specialist area at the start of a new programme?
- How do you ensure that initial learning activities are good practice in teaching in your own specialist area?

Links To CPD

Reflect on an induction session for a specialist course or area that you've been involved in and use your responses to the above questions to evaluate whether it fulfils the two criteria of enthusing and motivating learners and enabling you to assess their prior knowledge. Consider how you could improve the design to meet these criteria fully – or design an induction session from scratch if you haven't previously been involved in one.

If you are undertaking initial teacher training, your responses to the above activities provide evidence for LLUK standards AS2, AS4 and elements of Domains B, C, D and E.

Pitching your specialist area sessions at the right level to engage learners is not easy, especially with a large group. Planning for learning develops with experience but collaborating with others enhances this development if you:

- include your learners in the planning process;
- plan with members of a team in your specialist area.

You do not need to wait for formal evaluations to know what your learners think about their learning and your teaching, you just have to talk to them and listen to them. The same goes for members of your specialist area team, you just have to talk to them about your planning ideas and problems and listen to their suggestions and be open to their assistance. Social interaction like this is really important for your CPD.

Learners benefit when they take part in activities with the help of a more expert person, which could be you as their teacher or another learner in the group. Vygotsky's research showed that people learn as they are stretched beyond their own knowledge but only within a range that is within their grasp and that takes into account the knowledge and skills they bring to an activity. He called the level of understanding that is possible when a learner engages in a task with the help of a more expert peer the *zone of proximal development*. It is the proximity of someone more expert being involved in the task that is important as the research showed that learners working on their own rarely did as well as when working in collaboration with an expert. So, you might think this means that it is passing on specialist-area information that enables learners to do better. But Vygotsky warns that it is not direct teaching, but *engagement with the expert* which enables learners to improve their thinking about a task or make their performance of a task more effective.

Your expertise in your specialist area may create a tension when you are involved in learning tasks between a desire to teach and tell the learner, and a desire to let learners construct their own world. You have to think carefully about the role you play when monitoring learning activities. The learner's progress through collaborating with you as an expert is achieved by you:

- posing questions to the learner about what you are observing;
- getting the learner to reflect on what's happening;
- speculating about what's gone well to promote a response;
- encouraging the learner to work things out and think logically;
- observing when things are not going well and facilitating resolution;
- getting learners to figure things out for themselves.

You are supporting your learners by using the traditional teaching tools of observing and assessing, but the critical element is that you do this whilst *the learner is undertaking the task* and you talk to them about it while they are doing it. What you are *doing* is taking on the role of co-constructor of knowledge. What you are *not doing* is taking the opportunity to get on with your marking or catching up on your paperwork whilst the learners get on with the activity! It is the interaction that is important and central to the learner's progress and achievement: the expression of ideas, the communication of meaning, the encouragement to try something out. In everyday terms, what seems to happen is that learners can do more with a more expert person nearby, even though that person is not telling them exactly what to do, than they are able to do on their own.

An important role for you as a teacher in a specialist area is to 'stretch' learners:

- observe what's going on within an activity;
- assess where the learner is at by questioning;
- engage in dialogue about what comes next;
- support learners as they try things out;
- encourage learners to reflect on new knowledge or performance.

This teacher role is very different from the traditional one of standing at the front of the class and giving instructions and passing on information whilst the group sit passively and listen. Traditional teaching isolates the learner from social interaction, for example, by:

- sitting alone;
- no talking to each other;
- working individually on tasks;
- getting information from one designated textbook;
- waiting quietly for the next instruction.

In contrast, constructivism encourages interaction with others. The use of conversation and the sharing of knowledge are considered integral to learning. Recognising the importance of social interaction to learning does not mean a 'free-for-all' in the classroom or everyone shouting across the room or all demanding attention at the same time. The design of activities that encourage learners to discuss, to share and to explore and find out new things together, needs careful planning if it is to be effective.

If you are planning a new programme or meeting new learners, you may confront the limits of your professional knowledge, which can be unsettling. However, a bonus is that, if you can work with colleagues, particularly members of your specialist area team who are more experienced, or a mentor, you will benefit from 'proximal development' through the collaboration. You will experience how more experienced teachers think through and solve problems, explore ideas and devise ways to involve the learners. Once you have had a chance to get the planning in place and work through the new programme, you can begin to consider how your learners think and respond. The most challenging thing is to focus on the learning process to develop professional knowledge and this will bring the deeper understanding necessary to develop your ability to improve future programmes. The shared understandings reached through working with more experienced colleagues reveal how knowledge is created in your subject and how it is tested and improved, i.e. you have developed an understanding of the *epistemology* of your subject, which Petty asserts is so important for you to talk about and share with your own learners.

Knowledge of teaching and learning

Whilst advising that there needs to be much more rigorous research in this area, Petty reveals that Hattie's studies on expert teachers already confirm that some teaching methods work better than others and that the way they are used makes a difference:

> Expert teachers have knowingly or intuitively adopted a constructivist approach ... such as challenging goals, interactive dialogue and students writing their own notes. (Petty, 2006: 312)

Whether it is by luck or judgement, expert teachers adopt a distinctive way of teaching. Interestingly, a constructivist approach is not so much about teaching but about learning and how it happens. However, there are certain teaching approaches associated with constructivism, all of which promote active learning or 'learning by doing'. The evidence suggests that three criteria set expert teachers apart from others because they:

- **set challenging goals** – achievement is enhanced to the degree that students and teachers set and communicate appropriate, specific and challenging goals.

- **provide quality feedback** – achievement is enhanced as a function of feedback.

- **have a deep understanding of their subject and teaching and learning** – increases in student learning involve a reconceptualisation of learning.

The importance of this knowledge for teachers in the Lifelong Learning Sector is that these three criteria are applicable to many settings and, therefore, relevant for the diversity of teaching and learning undertaken across the sector. Whatever subject you teach, no matter what level your learners are at or the type of organisation you work in, it is possible to assess the evidence in relation to your own setting.

Check It Out 7.6

Deepen your understanding of learning and teaching

To develop your knowledge of teaching and learning, a good place to begin would be with two questions to start you thinking about what sets expert teachers apart:
- How do you set challenging goals for your learners?
- How do you provide quality feedback for your learners?

Links To CPD

- Respond to the above questions and record your answers.
- Read around the topics of goal setting and feedback by accessing up-to-date educational textbooks or doing a search of academic journals or internet sites.
- Make notes on the theoretical information you have collated and make connections to your own teaching and learning.
- Reflect on whether the knowledge gained from the above activities has led to a reconceptualisation of learning.
- Prepare a reflective account that addresses how you have deepened your understanding of your subject and teaching and learning.
- If you are undertaking initial teacher training, your reflective account provides evidence for LLUK standards AS2, AS4 and elements of Domains B, C and E.

Maximising learning

A professional challenge that faces all teachers is how to maximise learning and this section looks at simple ways in which busy professionals can improve learning and encourage learners. Petty investigated the best evidence available on quality learning, then summarised the relevant research and came up with seven principles common to high-quality learning and achievement. He advocates these principles as a way to bring about high attainment, although he admits they lack an emphasis on the affective side of learning.

1. Students must see the value of the learning
2. Students must believe they can do it
3. Challenging goals
4. Feedback and dialogue on progress towards a goal
5. Establish the structure of information and so its meaning
6. Time and repetition
7. Teach skills as well as content. (Petty, 2006: 164–7)

It is clear that to be a successful teacher, one of the things you need to have is a deep understanding of teaching and learning. It is common for teachers to spend time developing their specialist area knowledge when planning for learning, but less common for teachers to spend time developing their knowledge of learning and teaching.

Viewpoint

Ensuring consistency and sufficiency of professional development

From an organisational point of view, I think the impact of compulsory CPD for teaching and training staff has yet to be felt. There appears to be an amount of uncertainty and inconsistency about what exactly constitutes professional development activities. On the one hand, the Institute for Learning (IfL) talks about activities with a great deal of depth, those requiring extensive reflection and ambitious action research projects, as fitting to contribute to CPD. If you consider that staff have to have a balance of activities in their thirty hours between teaching and learning, subject specialism and context, this suggests that an activity might only be ten hours at the most – so it does beg the question of how thorough it can be. On the other hand, when talking to colleagues in other organisations they seem to see activities that I would consider a routine part of a teacher's or trainer's work, such as updating session plans, as acceptable and sufficient for recording as professional development. My view is that gradually the IfL will not just make sure staff comply, but also get round to ensuring some sort of consistency.

Developing professional knowledge

From a member of staff's point of view, I think the requirement to get involved in CPD will prove really beneficial. I think up to now lots of staff just turned up at staff development events and didn't really take away anything from them. The requirement to record CPD means that staff have to start thinking how they can use the information or new ideas in their own work, they have to reflect on what they are doing and think how they can incorporate the changes. I don't think that's what all staff have done up to now, so I think that everyone will have to start to prioritise where they will put their effort and spend their time, which will be better.

Registration with IfL

In my college we have achieved 100% registration with IfL for all those requiring it, so staff are getting involved and have access to IfL publications which contain current information and plenty of ideas. I think that this new system will provide opportunities for more vocational up-dating. There could be chances for renewing technical skills, study visits and certainly becoming better informed about current practices in their specialist areas. When I think about how to plan and manage staff development activities, I think that having more frequent staff development opportunities throughout the year would be beneficial. However, any changes which involve redistributing and allocating time and resources need the pro-active support of senior management to make them effective and, as in any organisation, there are competing demands for resources.

A way of recording CPD within the college has been set up. We have a training area on the human resources database and if staff development activities have been organised internally we have the details at hand to input them into the staff records. If staff have attended external events then the relevant managers notify the details for input. Some staff have managed to get to grips with using the IfL's REFLECT and it is possible to download a summary of their record – though not of course their personal reflections. However, we have an excellent eILP system within the college already so it could really be a very effective medium for recording activities and then posting them in REFLECT.

Developing reflective practice

My view is that at the moment the professional formation process appears a rather demanding process and I think I would encourage staff to do PTLLS, etc. I also think that college-wide staff development is very important to address cross-college issues, e.g. functional skills, but that the personalised approach that IfL promotes does allow staff to take responsibility for their own professional development. What would really help to get the process moving would be practical sessions on how to maintain your CPD record and staff development sessions on how to reflect.

(College Staff Development Manager)

To maintain your professional autonomy, it is important to update your knowledge of learning and teaching by prioritising the following professional development activities:

- reading educational columns and articles in national newspapers to keep abreast of changes and developments in the sector;
- keeping up to date with the latest news and information from the Institute for Learning's website, e-bulletin and newsletter;
- checking in your library or learning resources centre for new stock of the latest textbooks on learning and teaching and making notes from them;
- accessing academic journals and research through the internet.

However, in this chapter it is only possible to provide an overview of learning and teaching knowledge and ideas. I have chosen to focus on a selection of acronyms that provide practical prompts for you when planning for learning and assessment. They are simply presented but highly effective models, which are sufficiently flexible so that they are applicable to many settings. The simplicity of the acronyms is not meant to limit your own inventiveness by suggesting that you conform to a prescribed format. Rather, the merit of the acronyms is that they are easy to remember and if you remember them you are likely to apply them. The value of the acronyms is in the *knowledge you gain from applying them*. The purpose in applying them to your own situation is to deepen your understanding of teaching and learning. The best outcome would be that this:

- encourages you to think about how you approach teaching and learning;
- increases your knowledge;
- persuades you to approach teaching and learning differently in future;
- enables you to achieve one of the three criteria that Hattie asserts set expert teachers apart from other teachers, i.e. a reconceptualisation of learning.

Set these outcomes as your goals and, as you read through the eight acronyms set out below, consider how you could apply them to your own setting.

1. The CLASS test

The idea behind the CLASS test is to apply it to your planning documents before you deliver your sessions to identify any missing element(s). In her book on professional development in the Lifelong Learning Sector, Hitchings suggests that if all the ingredients seem to be present in your session 'yet the chemistry fails to work', then if you apply the CLASS test your learners will tend to have a better learning experience, there will be a more positive outcome and you should feel more professional as a result.

Sounds good – why not have a go yourself and apply the CLASS test to your learning plans!

Challenging to learners.	Not beyond their abilities but stretching their knowledge and skills enough to be invigorating.
Linked to what they already know or have experience of.	Build on their existing knowledge and understanding when introducing new concepts. Compare or contrast the new concepts with recent or previous learning and show how the ideas are related.

Action or activity-based.	Build a number of different activities into every session so that every learner can participate by doing, as well as looking and listening.
Structured clearly.	All tasks should be structured clearly, so each learner is clear about their role, how much time they have, what they need to do and why. The way you introduce concepts also needs to have a logical structure. What skills or knowledge do they need to already possess before they tackle this next stage?
Supported by resources that meet different learning needs.	Who is likely to need more explanation or examples and how can you provide them? Who will need extra support with basic skills and how can you secure it? Have you resources that will stretch the faster learner and keep them motivated? Are the resources that you intend using sufficiently diverse to satisfy a range of learning style preferences?

Source: Hitching (2008: 96)

2. The SPERT checklist

If you accept the premise of constructivism, then you have to work really hard at planning *before* your sessions and get learners to work really hard *during* the session. This poses several questions, which Minton raises:

> What are your students going to do in order to learn?
> What are you going to do to help them to learn?
> Who is doing most of the work in the class? (Minton, 2005: 45)

You have to be aware of the balance of activity between you and the learners. If you think of SPERT as the word that it sounds like, i.e. spurt, you may begin to think of some of the answers. One of the meanings of 'spurt' is to *make a sudden effort* – and that's just what you want your learners to do – make an effort. Your role is to get the right balance between intrinsic motivation (which comes from the learners) and extrinsic motivation (which comes from you). The energy that you expend in a session needs to be focused on energising your learners:

> Teacher motivation can energise a class and pull it out of the spiral of negative feelings and lack of success. I've seen very challenging classes turn around within a term when teachers have:
>
> - planned together and worked as a team
> - moved away from easy blame and labelling

- involved students in the re-establishment process [a collaborative process to refocus the group through discussion]
- provided challenging material that seeks to 'connect' with students' understanding and (where possible) their needs
- acknowledged and affirmed the effort of individuals and the group
- not given up. (Rogers, 2006: 49)

Rogers reinforces some of the principles common to high-quality learning and achievement. Let's see if the SPERT checklist, adapted from a Teachers' Toolkit (QID, 2007), provides the answers to motivating your learners when it is applied *before* your session to make sure your planning is effective.

- *Success* – at the beginning of the session share the learning objectives formally or informally with the learners and at the end of the session check achievement. Have stretching and extending activities for the most able learners.

- *Purpose* – outline the purpose of the session and ensure that the language you use conveys this to the learners. Make sure the session has a clear structure.

- *Enjoyment* – decide whether to start with a bang or a quiet settling activity. Use a variety of teaching methods which encourage activity and avoid passivity. Select content which is suitable to the characteristics of the learners and will promote their interest and get them motivated.

- *Reinforcement* – recap the previous session to check progress of learners. Monitor by checking and correcting learning. Set homework or research.

- *Target setting* – check whether there is an explicit link between the short-term goals agreed with learners and the long-term goals the learners want to achieve by the completion of the programme.

3. The ABC approach

The ABC approach is helpful in deepening your understanding of learners' behaviour, particularly inappropriate behaviour, during a session. It reminds you that learning usually takes place in the social setting of a group and so you need to take into account all of the social interactions within the group and develop your knowledge about managing the learning environment.

- *Antecedent* – Look at what leads up to the inappropriate behaviour and try to identify what was the trigger and context for it. Remember, it is possible that the antecedent may have been outside of your session and before it began, so it's not always immediately observable. On the other hand, your teaching approach may be the trigger, e.g. keeping talking once the learners have lost concentration or not being confident when organising and timing activities: changing the antecedent is a way of controlling inappropriate behaviour.

- *Behaviour* – Examine the inappropriate behaviour or incident that caused the disruption.

- **C**onsequences – Look at the outcome of the inappropriate behaviour and the end result it had on your session. Consider what 'reward' the learner(s) gained from the behaviour, e.g. attention, delaying everyone from getting down to work, sidetracking you from teaching.

You obviously need to develop your knowledge about managing inappropriate behaviour, but if a session went particularly well you could also use the ABC approach to evaluate the triggers for success.

4. The BRR approach

This is an approach to behaviour management that is discussed by Gray (2007: 26) and which complements the ABC approach. The approach recommends that you work with the learner(s) to establish positive relationships, and the BBR approach would, therefore, be a good way to follow up inappropriate behaviour in a one-to-one situation, say after the session or outside of the session in a tutorial.

- **B**ehavioural – focus on actual behaviour;
- **R**eflective – reflect on the learner's thoughts, feeling and motives;
- **R**elationship – negotiate with the learner what behaviour would contribute to a more productive working relationship.

You have to accept that a learner's motives and feelings are important and see things from their point of view, but at the same time you have to ensure that the inappropriate behaviour is stopped if you are to create a positive learning environment in your sessions. The BRR approach should prove helpful. It should help you move away from the cold and frosty atmosphere that is generated when there is inappropriate behaviour which causes disruption to your sessions (and you may go 'brrr … brrr…' because the atmosphere in the group is so chilly) to establishing warmer relationships which are conducive to a positive learning environment!

5. The PAR model

The components commonly found in an effective session have been identified by Petty (2006) and are presented as a structure for teaching a topic which is said to work in almost any learning situation. The three components are: present, apply and review.

Present	*Apply*	*Review*
Orientation: preparation and challenging goals given or negotiated New material is taught and practical and intellectual skills are demonstrated	After the orientation stage students work towards goals that apply the new learning Tasks involve practical tasks to carry out a skill and reasoning tasks for cognitive skills	Learning is summarised and clarified Check whether goals are met and key points and structure emphasised
Typical learning strategies include: listen to teacher, watch video or demonstration, study exemplars, asking not telling, using Information and Learning Technology (ILT) or other resources	Typical learning strategies include: listen to teacher, watch video or demonstration, study exemplars, asking not telling, using ILT or other resources	Typical learning strategies include: note making, creating mind map, poster, summary of key points, discussion, revising advance organisers, reviews, peer explanations, quiz, test
Feedback for learner and teacher: learning in progress is checked and corrected	Feedback for learner and teacher: inform learners of what is good and what is not	Feedback for learner and teacher: learning is checked and corrected

Adapted from Petty (2006: 169)

In this model, good teaching has been characterised as being like a three-legged stool: if one leg is missing the stool falls over! It is important, therefore, to include all three components in one session but the sequence is not fixed and you may revisit each component more than once. Can you see how flexible the PAR model is and how you could apply it to your context?

6. SOLO taxonomy

This classification of things to look for when assessing learner's work was promoted for use in university, but over the years has been successfully adopted by teachers who assess in colleges. It is another useful tool for anyone in the Learning and Skills Sector who is also an assessor. Again, it can be used across a range of specialist areas and levels. SOLO stands for **S**tructure of **O**bserved **L**earning **O**utcomes and each category is a 'representation' of learning. A hierarchy of verbs that may be used to form curriculum objectives, e.g. identify, enumerate, compare/contrast and theorise, has been added more recently (Biggs, 2003: 48).

Categories in the taxonomy	Examples of objectives	Suggested examples of work
• Pre-structural–there is no appropriate structure. The learner misses the point.		A portfolio is presented as a jumble of evidence – not sorted, filed, cross-referenced – the learner just wants to get the task over as quickly as possible.
• Unistructural – only one general element is represented.	Identify, do simple procedure.	A project only addresses one point of view, e.g. hairdresser's not those of client and salon owner.
• Multistructural – more than one general element is present but the elements are poorly integrated in a serial or unrelated manner.	Enumerate, describe, list, combine, do algorithms.	Written work jumps from one topic to another and although there may be more than one point of view addressed they are not evaluated, e.g. is cost of sports equipment more important than its effectiveness or flexibility?
• Relational – there are relevant elements present and they are integrated in a coherent and interdependent manner; development of any appropriate new structure is competent but not generalised to new situations.	Examples of objectives: compare/contrast, explain causes, analyse, relate, apply.	Relationship between factors is recognised, e.g. a project on inclusive practice in an Early Years setting deals with how factors, such as level of learning difficulty, extent of behavioural problems, gender, age, carer attitude, etc., contribute to a child's progress.
• Extended abstract – the coherent structure is developed into an effective and coherent new structure in a competent manner, from which generalisations to new situations are made.	Theorise, generalise, hypothesise, reflect.	The learner goes beyond what has been covered in the sessions or is included in the criteria and provides an holistic overview or innovative perspective, e.g. provides ideas about how a new business initiative can be developed in a certain location.

The SOLO taxonomy has three phases:

- The first phase contains the category 'Pre-structural' and is the informal phase as work does not warrant formal marking or grading, just formative feedback.
- The second phase contains the categories of 'Unistructural' and 'Multistructural' and is the quantitative phase, i.e. a number of marks are pre-allocated for each bit of information and the assessor tends to measure for quantity of information provided and gives marks for relevant points made – 15/20 or 75%.

- The third phase contains the categories of 'Relational' and 'Extended abstract' and is the qualitative phase, i.e. the assessor measures overall quality – Pass, Merit, Distinction.

The representation of learning illustrated in the SOLO taxonomy is linked to the idea that an individual's approach to learning can be a limiting factor or a positive factor. This theory was initially introduced by Marton et al. (1984) and developed by Entwistle (1997).

- **Surface approach** – Learners cope with learning programme requirements by working without reflecting on the purpose, treating content as unrelated bits of knowledge and memorising facts or procedures. Learners take a passive approach and are concerned about covering the content and finding the correct answers. Learners tend to feel undue pressure and worry about work.
- **Deep approach** – Learners relate ideas to previous knowledge and experience and look for patterns and underlying principles. Learners become actively interested in the content and are questioning, critical and want to understand the whole picture.

A surface approach to learning relates to the Pre-structural end of the taxonomy and a deep approach to learning relates to the Extended abstract end of the taxonomy, i.e. learning and teaching needs to go from concrete to abstract.

7. The GROW model of coaching

This model of coaching is used in training and development as a means of developing coaching skills and is based on a cycle of four elements:

- Setting **G**oals.	The **G**oal: what do you want to do or achieve? - What is your goal? - How will you know when you have achieved it? - What is the aim of today's discussion?
- Assessing current **R**eality	Current **R**eality: what is happening now? - What are you doing at present? - What difficulties are you encountering? - What's holding you back? - What have you achieved so far? - What have you done so far? - What results have your actions produced?
- Generating **O**ptions	**O**ptions: what could you do? - What options or courses of action do you have? - What else could you do? What alternatives are there? - What if ...? - What would be the benefits/advantages of these options?

Setting a **W**ay forward	**W**ay forward: what will you do?
	• What options or strategies have you chosen?
	• Will they meet your objectives?
	• What do you need to make this happen? What steps will you take?
	• Can you foresee any difficulties?
	• What resources do you need?
	• Do you need to develop new skills/knowledge to achieve this?
	• Do you need any support?

Adapted from Scales (2008: 144–5)

Scales suggests that the GROW model of coaching can be used as a form of self-coaching by more experienced learners. It would be a useful tool for teachers in the Lifelong Learning Sector to use themselves to ask questions and explore options for CPD.

8. Just ASKe

This last one's a bit of a cheat because the acronym stands for **A**ssessment **S**tandards **K**nowledge **e**xchange which is a Centre for Excellence in Teaching and Learning based in the Business School at Oxford Brookes University rather than a practical prompt – but it is an excellent source of practical advice. The work of ASKe has been organised into three strands of activity: replicating proven practice; pioneering evidence-based practice and cultivating a community of practice. As well as online information, ASKe publishes a range of pamphlets about assessment processes. One example is given below.

'Using generic feedback effectively'

Would you like to help your students gauge how well they are doing?
Would you like to encourage them to become independent learners?
Have you ever considered how generic feedback might improve individual performance?
If so, why don't you try this three-step exercise?
It's easy to do, and it works …

… here's how you do it

1	• When assessment of the cohort is complete, describe the overall strengths and weaknesses of your students' work, highlighting what was done well and what needs to be improved. Provide this feedback to your students both orally and in writing and allow them to ask questions.
2	• Ask your students to evaluate their own work in the light of the generic feedback, and so write a self-assessment with action points for future work.
3	• Provide individual feedback to your students which builds on the earlier generic feedback.

Source: www.business.brookes.ac.uk/aske.html (accessed 15 January 2009)

Remembering and applying the acronyms provides opportunities for informal learning through your everyday workload and, in a relatively pain-free way, helps you make informed choices about designing a responsive curriculum from a learner's point of view.

How smart are you?

Did you recognise any of the eight acronyms listed? Did you miss the SMART acronym in the last section? If you did, it just shows you how effective acronyms are. There can't be many teachers in the sector who aren't aware of the need for objectives to be SMART, i.e. Specific, Measurable, Achievable, Realistic and Time-bound. I hope the other eight will be just as useful!

Successful Strategies
- Specialist area knowledge and teaching and learning knowledge need to be developed alongside each other.
- Constructivism has a social element which requires activities involving interaction between teacher and learner, and between learners, but it also has a cognitive element so activities must be designed to provide opportunities for thinking about the experience and developing meaning.
- To assess the quality of teaching and learning, you need to distinguish between the effectiveness of your practice and the ability of the learners in contributing to their achievement. Don't just take the credit when things go right and don't necessarily blame the learners when things go wrong.
- Doubts about your knowledge of teaching and learning tend to creep in when you meet new learners, or when you have to deliver a programme at a different level, with different learners or on an unfamiliar topic. Therefore, thorough planning is particularly important for induction sessions.

- Asking learners to second-guess what's in your mind, or what you know already, wastes time. Instead get learners to express what's in their heads and by questioning and encouragement help them to consolidate their learning.
- Sometimes it's the simple ideas that really work. Acronyms are easy to remember and if you remember them there is more likelihood that you will apply them, which means that you can develop your knowledge of teaching and learning through your everyday workload.

In Chapter 8 the importance of developing positive professional relationships with learners, colleagues and other stakeholders is introduced.

8 Constructing Professional Relationships

In this chapter you will find sections on:
- purposeful development of professional relationships;
- building professional relationships with learners;
- developing collaborative professional relationships with colleagues;
- widening professional relationships.

The chapter addresses issues relating to Domain A: AS3 Equality, diversity and inclusion in relation to learners, the workforce, and the community.

For those undertaking initial teacher training, the chapter provides opportunities to generate evidence for LLUK standards AS3, AP3.1 and AS5.

Purposeful development of professional relationships

We are reminded by Fawbert that professional relationships are an extremely important aspect of practice and require *purposeful* development:

> Despite their apparent isolation in the classroom, teachers and teaching teams frequently work in partnership with external groups such as employers, parents, other members of the educational community and related agencies. They are automatically involved in different levels of practical and theoretical collaboration in order to ensure the relevance and responsiveness of their learning programmes. The purposeful development of collegial relationships is therefore an extremely important aspect of practice. (Fawbert, 2008: 10)

Teaching is a job where you are involved in developing professional relationships every time you meet your learners: you earn your living through developing successful professional relationships, primarily in the classroom. A key element in your success, however, depends not just on your relationship with your learners but, as Fawbert says, on developing relationships with others, which enables you to work collaboratively – rather than in isolation – to support your learners' achievements and ensure the relevance and responsiveness of your learning programmes. It is pretty obvious that when you teach you mainly work in isolation from your colleagues in your organisation and others outside it, but in point of fact when you are in the classroom the quality of your teaching is dependent not just on the working relationships you form with your learners but also on the collaborative relationships you form, say, when you are planning your learning programmes with colleagues or liaising about work experience with employers.

Luckily, you don't seem to have to work at some professional relationships. Just as with some learners, communication with colleagues and others is easy as you seem to understand each other and are mutually sensitive to each other's position. But life is not always like that and, sometimes, the more you try the worse it gets:

> However capable or talented individual lecturers may be, if they are unable to communicate with each other, say because of personality clashes and conflicts, then it is difficult to achieve what they set out to do. (Steward, 2006: 56)

Working well with colleagues is not always easy. However hardworking or keen you are, if your team or department doesn't function as a whole, your efforts will be wasted. No doubt you have experienced 'off-days' when problems appear insurmountable and communication with learners, colleagues or others is exhausting rather than exhilarating. If you become stressed about this situation, then poor professional relationships become a source of aggravation, which can lead to tension between you and others. If this goes on, it can badly affect your motivation at work and even your health. You need to stand back sometimes and avoid becoming too emotional when things don't go as planned. You have to resolve to build positive professional relationships in the workplace to support your learners – not just to enjoy chatting and being with them (although chatting over a cup of coffee and sharing your concerns with an empathetic colleague is an excellent way of getting things into perspective), but to develop a supportive and collaborative culture in your organisation.

There is no doubt that you have to work at developing positive relationships. In this chapter, you will get the opportunity to find out how to make choices which enable you to work effectively with others and to learn how individuals in the Lifelong Learning Sector have set about purposefully developing professional relationships.

Building professional relationships with learners

The reason why developing professional relationships with your learners is so important is that learning occurs when individuals are *engaged in social activities*. As I discussed in Chapter 7, a social constructivist approach to learning and teaching emphasises the importance of the relationship between learners and teachers. Both are involved in the learning process and learning from each other. Learning is not achieved just by the learner sitting passively and trying to absorb information, nor does it just go on in the learner's mind. Learning occurs when there is a convergence of shared and practical activities:

- learning needs to be intrapersonal, i.e. within the learner;
- learning needs to be interpersonal, i.e. between the learner and others.

This requires a positive learner-teacher relationship in which awareness of each other's viewpoints is critical, which means that good communication is essential. You have to remember that when you are trying to create conditions where individuals are engaged in social activities, you are trying to create a *learning environment* – not a club, a bar or even a coffee shop. You have to remember what you're all there for and it's not just to meet friends, because as a student whom Hayes quotes reminds us: 'College is where you go if you want to learn stuff'.

Hayes counsels teachers that college should provide different experiences from those that young people encounter outside of college 'on the street':

> in trying to get 'kids' off the streets to widen participation in FE, colleges seem to be attempting to recreate the street in the very place that should be giving students the opportunities to achieve far greater things in life. (Hayes, P., 2007: 70)

Although relationships between learners and teachers are among the most difficult aspects of teaching to get right, they are among the most important aspects of teaching if you want to provide opportunities for learners to achieve greater things. Sometimes, it has to be said, just getting individuals off the street and into learning is a great achievement. But an even greater achievement is getting them to stay and learn. Also, unless there's at least some mutual trust and respect it is difficult for learning to take place. As a teacher there are always demands on your time but building relationships should be at the top of your list for professional development.

Success Story

How I got into teaching

I got into teaching by accident really!

I hated school and left with two GCSEs. I lost confidence at school, I didn't know why I had failed or passed anything. I didn't get any feedback on anything when I was there. I thought I would be an unqualified worker all my life, but like an 'accidental tourist' I arrived where I am inadvertently without really having planned it.

I worked as an unqualified nurse at a hospital and another nurse suffered from depression and wasn't able to work. As her friend and to support her, I went along with her to an Access Course and I realised my assignments were OK and began to think that I could go to university myself. Getting into university meant I had an academic mentor and, although I didn't really know what to do in that relationship at first, after the first year I was making progress. I only realised then how outrageous it was that no-one had given me any help at school.

I had a car crash and couldn't go into the career I'd planned. I saw an advert for Community Adult Education and asked if I could shadow a teacher, which I did every Thursday for quite a time. The teacher was very encouraging and said at one point 'Do you want to take the class today?'

Starting out in teaching

Shadowing and filling in for Community Adult Education was really the best introduction to teaching: practical, developmental, hands-on. I was in the classroom straight away and the teacher proved to be a brilliant mentor. So I took my C & G teaching qualification and I loved it, it was fantastic. I had trouble getting a job but did part-time work on Access Courses and got temporary contracts and eventually got a full-time job in an FE College in my home town. I had to do a one-year PGCE and I soon realised that teaching had moved on and I was not as up to date as I thought and was having to figure it all out again.

When I first joined the college, I found the students' behaviour in class was atrocious as I was teaching on BTEC Level 1 and 2, BFD and E2E and it was such a contrast to teaching Access Level 3 students. I gradually learned that the students were rebelling against the system; they had been told 'No, you mustn't do that!' for years. Once I grasped that, I became more tolerant of their behaviour and explained *why* I want something done and put it in positive not negative terms. I would advocate a facilitative approach as a teacher and I now say to students 'I'm here to help you'. I accept that I can't teach them to be brilliant in a vocational area in twelve hours a week, but I can teach them the social skills they need so that they can gain qualifications later. I can help them to understand what appropriate behaviour is and how to act in certain situations. Towards the end of their college course, we do a joint ILP and talk about progression, and some go on the Level 2, others go into the workplace and some progress to Level 3.

Developing awareness of learners' viewpoints

I feel I have a responsibility to be aware of the *students'* surroundings and ask them about their background and what's going on for them. I live in the same area as them and I am a volunteer in the area so I know where they come from. I get them to tell me what their day consists of and get a picture of what they've experienced in school and what they've observed in their neighbourhood. When you understand that most of what they do is learned behaviour you see them differently. I suppose I do all this because I am so interested in sociology and what goes right and why, and what goes wrong and why. I think it stems from when I was an auxiliary nurse and you had twenty minutes to take a case history from nervous patients and there I developed emotional intelligence and became very aware of body language and sensitive to the feelings in the room. So now I don't blame my students, I try to understand them.

Developing professional relationships with learners

I tell the Level 1 students that I didn't do well at school as I think it breaks down barriers and definitely makes a difference to how they see me. I think you have to give quite a bit of yourself with Level 1 students and you can't keep a strict divide between you as the teacher and them as the student – it just doesn't work. You can't say I know everything and you're here to learn it all from me, or say 'I'm the great I am' in front of the students and tell them how lucky they are to be here and how hard you've worked to get where you are and how you work hard to get money for a car and go on holiday. The teacher behind the desk who thinks they are No.1 in the room has always been a problem for Level 1 students and they've seen it as a barrier and rebelled. But it's hard for them to dislike you if you tell them something about yourself that they can *relate* to. Despite all this, one lesson I learned early on was to set ground rules, talk about what is expected of them, as you can't harden up if things get out of hand. It doesn't work like that. Don't be too pally at first but be professional, and get to know each other, develop a positive relationship.

If you asked me ...

My advice to other teachers who want to be successful would be:

- be yourself;
- don't get over-friendly;
- don't blame, try to understand.

(Programme Leader – Levels 1 and 2, BFD and E2E – FE College)

The case study above illustrates how important it is for learners and teachers to be aware of each other's viewpoint in order to establish good learner-teacher relationships. Developing an insight into the learners' backgrounds and community and being realistic appear to be successful strategies for this teacher. Interestingly, although this teacher clearly works at breaking down barriers, they don't advise being over-friendly or pally with learners but advocate developing positive relationships in which expectations are clear and ground rules are set, i.e. relationships are professional. When it is clear that the relationships have developed in a positive way you can plan less structured and more flexible sessions. This is because as you get to know your learners better you can afford to relax more. This teacher also acknowledges that you cannot teach Level 1 learners in a conventional manner as they usually bring with them poor experiences of education from their schooldays and they want to be treated as adults, even if they don't necessarily respond as adults all the time. Creating a learning environment for Level 1 students may be a very different task to creating a learning environment for Level 3 or Level 5/6 learners. But, as Hayes says, you have to take all learners seriously:

> What does it mean to treat students like adults? Fundamentally, it is to take them seriously, what they have to say should be critically engaged with and clear reasons should be given for any praise or criticism given to them. (Hayes, P., 2007: 77)

To do this you have to have an understanding of how they see themselves as individuals, as members of a community or workforce and, particularly, how they see themselves as learners. Their attitude to learning is often evident through such comments as:

- 'I'm rubbish at this. I hate this lesson.'
- 'What are we doing this for? What's the point? I'll never pass the exam.'
- 'This is a useless college. Why do we have to keep coming?'

You may be familiar with some of these comments – or have heard much worse! It's not just young learners, those still at school or coming straight from school, who have a negative self-image of themselves as learners. At any age or level, learners may express how inadequate they feel about achieving, display anxiety and, indeed, may never have experienced any enjoyment from learning or any feeling of success. What you have to remember is that their behaviour is learned, perhaps from modelling others, e.g. association with peers, home environment and local community, and from reinforcement over time. That means behaviour can be unlearned or re-learned, but the learner has to be open to change, i.e. motivated to change, and any change will take time and effort. The time and effort will seem worthwhile if you think of learners' current attitudes towards learning as telling you something about them as an individual and as an indicator of how being in a college or training workshop makes them feel. As a teacher, you haven't really got much control over who enrols in your class, but you do have control about how you develop relationships with them. Learners don't necessarily have the characteristics we would dearly like them to have, so:

> Rather than be normative, ascribing to all adult students characteristics we would like them to have rather than as they really are, I would prefer to start where my students are, with what they wish to do, with the ways in which they have constructed themselves as adults and students. ... I too have my own constructs of adult and of student which suggest to me that I might try to encourage them to become more self-directing and autonomous. I do not wish to have their constructs

imposed on me, but even more importantly I do not wish to impose my constructs on them. (Rogers, 2003: 67–8)

To *start* where your learners are, as Rogers suggests, is pretty good advice; but it's not good to *finish* the programme and find that learners are still in the same place because they can't be bothered and neither can you. You can skirt around issues and keep learners occupied as best you can and not impose any of your ideas about learning on them. But I would disagree with Rogers and say that as a teacher you should try to encourage them to become more self-directing and autonomous. It may not be easy – and you may not always achieve it – but you have to be clear about your expectations and not always just go along with what learners wish to do. That's not what 'personalising' learning or listening to the 'learner voice' are all about. It doesn't mean *ignoring* their way of thinking either – but *listening* to them and trying to get them to work on tasks that are both relevant to them and to their learning programme.

It takes time and effort to foster good relationships with learners, especially if they are disruptive and aggressive at the outset. You have to understand who you're working with, why they're shouting and bawling, why they're not cooperating and why they're up in arms about the smallest thing. You've probably experienced what a relief it is when you realise that your most disruptive learner hasn't turned up for your session! If you think about it, your relief is because you can get on with the business of teaching and learning without constant interruptions or friction in the class. Implementing inclusion policies is often professionally demanding.

Check It Out   8.1

Dealing with disruptive learners

The question on everyone's lips is: How do you get disruptive learners to behave? The answer is: 'With difficulty!'

Teachers agree that dealing with disruptive learners is not easy and sometimes one strategy works and sometimes it doesn't. Here is a list of things that different teachers have recommended:

- Go in really hard;
- Use rewards and punishments;
- Send disruptive learners out of the class;
- Move them from their friends;
- Make them work in silence;
- Don't start shouting but be firm;
- Think whether there are any sanctions before you start disciplining;
- Keep a professional distance and don't be afraid to be strict;
- Tell them what's acceptable behaviour rather than what isn't;
- Get to know them and let them get to know what you expect;

- Tell them forget how you were before, say I don't anticipate bad behaviour, it's a new start for everyone here.

I'm not saying that there aren't barriers to be overcome, but if you want to get on well with learners and treat them equally you have to use your professional judgement when selecting successful strategies.

Links To CPD
- Identify a colleague who manages behaviour successfully and values equality and diversity, and discuss their ideas with them.
- Arrange to observe your colleague during a teaching session and note how they put their ideas into practice.
- Reflect on the ideas and observations and draw up your own 'Behaviour Code' that's relevant for your specialist subject and your learners.
- Discuss your new code and any ideas they put forward with your learners and negotiate a workable 'Behaviour Code' that's inclusive and acceptable to everyone.
- Reflect on and record the process of developing your new code in your Professional Development Journal and log the activity on your CPD.
- If you are undertaking initial teacher training, your responses to the above activities provide evidence for LLUK standards AS1 and AS3.

Violent incidents are reported to be increasing, but for most teachers they are not an everyday occurrence. If a learner's behaviour is a threat to the safety of others, then tell the rest of the group to take a break and leave the room:

> The safety of everyone is paramount, so get students away from the violent incident as quickly as possible, and then get help. If you experience violent behaviour in your class, or are aware of serious incidents involving students outside class, then you have a responsibility to report these to the college management. (Steward, 2006: 10)

Isolate the learner and get help from colleagues because you cannot deal single-handedly with sudden outbursts of rage or violence on your own.

However, it's not always the serious breaches of an acceptable behaviour code that you have to contend with. Not everyone encounters the 'class from hell' or the 'nightmare learner'. Sometimes it's the petty infringements and lack of self-control by learners that you have to spend time dealing with and which prevent you from concentrating on creating a positive learning environment:

- regularly turning up late for sessions;
- forgetting to bring essential equipment or uniform;
- eating or drinking at the wrong times;
- not getting down to work or showing any interest in completing tasks;

- distracting everyone and being unable to concentrate themselves;
- talking over you, contradicting everything you say or arguing about requests.

At the start of a learning programme, you need to be explicit about your expectations and develop a rapport with learners in order to identify their expectations. Learning agreements are usually completed during an induction session but they do not usually deal with the expectations of everyday classroom behaviour and routines. If you negotiate a clear Code of Behaviour which can become a framework for working in your sessions, then you can start a discussion about what it means for learners to be part of a particular learning or vocational community. Here are some ideas for such a code that I prepared earlier!

Guidelines for our group
- Turn up to sessions on time.
- Bring the necessary equipment/materials to each session.
- Complete assigned tasks by the agreed deadline.
- Complete work between sessions as required.
- Be prepared to participate in activities.
- Take responsibility for your own progress.
- Respect each other.
- Safety rules are to be followed at all times.
- Finish work and clear away on time, not well before time. (Steward, 2006: 93)

Setting a strong model of acceptable behaviour in teaching and learning sessions that values equality, diversity and inclusion and not being afraid to challenge unacceptable behaviour, whilst demanding in the short term, is rewarding in the long term.

Check It Out   8.2

Assessing your relationship with learners

One thing you have to address is whether your approach to teaching and learning creates friction and contributes to the conflicts and disagreements in your sessions and poor relationships with learners. Are you aware whether your reaction to an unpleasant incident makes it worse and prolongs the confrontation, rather than curtails it? Your responses to the questions below may reveal your approach to teacher-learner relationships and uncover some areas for professional development.

- Do you see all learners as potential troublemakers?
- Do you pick on learners when they're least expecting it?
- Do you embarrass learners or laugh at them – not with them?
- Do you demonstrate that you have favourites and treat learners unfairly?
- Do you forget names and say 'you' or make a fuss about how to pronounce unfamiliar names?

- Do you show learners up in front of other group members?
- Do you display your prejudices about learners from different ethnic groups?
- Do you ridicule a learner's attempts when they don't reach your high standards?

Links To CPD
- Reflect on your response to the above questions.
- Ask a colleague to do the same and set up a time for a professional discussion about the issues raised.
- Identify actions points and use as preparation for an appraisal.
- Record the process in your CPD log.
- If you are undertaking initial teacher training, your responses to the above activities provide evidence for LLUK standards AS1 and AS3.

Your professional relationship with your learners is a major influence on learning. A positive personal approach is conducive to learning. As a teacher you must be aware of the way you come across. There are a number of strategies you could use in your teaching and learning to improve relationships with learners. General strategies are to make certain in your planning that you make links with prior learning and get the sequence of activities right so that learners are able to progress through the tasks. You can teach a whole class, but remember you cannot 'learn' a whole class – learners have to do the work themselves. Try the following strategies that emphasise learners working together.

Peer collaboration

Getting learners to work in small groups allows learners with different levels of experience, knowledge and ability to interact and, therefore, learning is not just encouraged by your guidance as a teacher, but also by the peers' own initiative in observing others in the group, imitating them and making suggestions about how to proceed. As a teacher you still have to provide achievable goals for the group and ensure the task is manageable so as to avoid frustration and degeneration into disruptive behaviour. If you have a group who can easily 'get out of hand', make sure that you observe what's going on and are there to offer support if necessary. Effective learning involves the *progressive transfer of responsibility* from teacher to learners as the learners develop their competence and confidence – don't just throw them in at the deep end by putting them in groups, giving them instructions and leaving them to it. You need to provide support as necessary through 'contingent instructions'. Giving contingent instructions involves three steps:

- give learners clear instructions and explanations about tasks;
- when learners get into difficulty offer help straight away by giving further instructions and explanations;

- when learners manage to finish a task with some help, offer less help and fewer instructions in any subsequent task and allow the group to help each other.

As learners achieve, gradually withdraw your help and explicit instructions and allow them to take responsibility for the tasks. Peer collaboration offers opportunities for learners to develop their social skills in a positive manner through working with peers in small groups. Learners are often anxious about 'showing themselves up' in front of their peers during activities involving the whole group and tend to feel less wary about making contributions in a small group. Peer collaboration in mixed groupings is a suitable teaching method for a wide range of specialist areas and levels. Collaboration between peers of differing intellectual abilities may be used in activities to foster development of theoretical concepts as well as vocational skills.

Reciprocal teaching

You start off teaching, but as the session progresses a learner takes on the role of teacher. The purpose is to make sense of some activity or task and to ensure that it is clearly understood before moving on. An example might be that you prepare a set of questions on a particular topic before the session and print them up on cards. You introduce the topic briefly and then give the learners a summary of what you've said, which could be in the form of a chart or diagram, a sheet of illustrated notes or a section from a newspaper, magazine, textbook or journal. Then you get the learners to organise themselves into small groups and appoint a group leader. Give the group leader the cards with the questions on and invite them to take on the role of teacher in getting the group to work out the answers, organise note-making and then share the recorded answers with the rest of the class. Reciprocal teaching needs to be handled sensitively so that those in the role of teacher don't get into difficulty and this requires some guidance from you about handling groups – but to my mind taking on the role of teacher provides an excellent extension activity for learners by stretching them.

Quizzes and games

If you can incorporate activities that encourage guesswork or intuition then it is easy for everyone to get involved and have a go. Simple true/false, yes/no quizzes are a good place to start. Tasks can be light-hearted but still focus on your subject and can be good for checking learning in a fun way. Getting small groups to set their own quiz at the end of a topic and appoint a quizmaster to pose the questions to the rest of the group makes the activities more interactive. You can offer silly answers yourself to break down barriers and get everyone laughing. Don't jump in with the answers when the learners can't think of them straight away as then they will have to reason them out. You might be called on to be a referee, either as an adjudicator, if there's a difference of opinion about answers, or as an umpire, if arguments arise. I've observed some successful quizzes and games and most are linked to TV shows and so aren't viewed as too juvenile or patronising by learners. You can keep on task if you sum up at the end and explain where answers went wrong – if they did.

Developing collaborative professional relationships with colleagues

As a teacher in an organisation in the Lifelong Learning Sector, you play different roles which are determined by:

- the requirements of the situation you're in, e.g. assessor or internal verifier;
- the management style of the organisation, e.g. programme manager or staff development officer;
- the communication system of the organisation, e.g. coordinator for functional skills, 14–16 liaison officer.

Check It Out   8.3

Set of professional roles
Teachers in the Lifelong Learning Sector have a job title, but everyone also has other roles that they perform as part of their regular duties.

Identify the many different roles you play. It might surprise you just how many different 'hats' you have to wear in the course of your role as a teacher!

Links To CPD
- Once you have identified all the different roles you play, you could focus on one particular role and develop your expertise in this. For example, you could focus on assessment and become the expert in assessment in your team.
- Consider how you could develop your role, either by attending specialist training events or taking on responsibilities in the workplace.
- During the year log your progress towards developing expertise in one element of your role as teacher and reflect on how successful you were.
- If you are undertaking initial teacher training, your responses to the above activities provide evidence for LLUK standard AP3.1.

In addition to the set of roles that you play in your organisation, you are in a set of role relationships with other colleagues in your organisation. These are the colleagues that you have a professional relationship with in the performance of your day-to-day workplace duties. Some colleagues you might meet up with every day, whilst your association with others may be only a few times a year when a special duty has to be carried out. These role-related relationships are known as your 'role set'.

Check It Out 8.4

Exploring your role set
- Identify the different colleagues you work alongside in your organisation.
- Identify the different contacts you have outside your organisation.

Links To CPD
- Use the lists you collated above to answer the following questions: Are different patterns of behaviour expected? Is the behaviour of members of your role set consistent with expected pattern of behaviour?
- Networking is an excellent way of keeping up to date in your specialist area. Make an appointment to meet up with members of your role set outside your organisation.
- See how many visits to other organisations you can arrange during the year and record your reflections on the importance of networking and collaboration and the benefits to you, your learners and your organisation.
- If you are undertaking initial teacher training, your responses to the above activities provide evidence for LLUK standards AS3 and AS5.

Developing collaborative practices and dissemination of good practice bring benefits to your everyday practice because:

> Teaching can ... be a 'lonely' profession. Yet we teach 'next door' to the very people who experience, know and understand our common concerns and struggles. Research has shown that the *degree of consciousness* – regarding colleague support – can significantly affect the wellbeing of an individual or a group of individuals. Moral support; professional support; structures; processes and supportive plans ... can all affect how an individual copes in a naturally stressful profession like teaching. (Rogers, 2006: 166)

Discussions with colleagues, or observing them, provide opportunities for acquiring new ideas about teaching and updating your subject specialist knowledge. Moran suggests that you put your collaboration onto a more formal footing and develop a partnership for professional development. See what you think!

A collaborative professional development programme		
Step 1	Use a teaching portfolio to identify professional development goals	Present materials that illustrate: your strengths and weaknesses, what is unique about your practice and the skills you hope to acquire and use.
Step 2	Write a learning plan to attain selected goals	Select a small number of goals, identify the highest priority and plan the learning activities that will enable you to achieve your objectives. Specify resources, strategies and what constitutes evidence of accomplishment.
Step 3	Establish a collaborative arrangement with a peer	To establish if you are ready, ask yourself: 'Am I willing to have a peer watch me teach? Am I willing to have someone discuss my teaching with me? Am I willing to experiment with changes in the way I teach? Am I willing to serve as a coach?' Ask for peer feedback on the portfolio and learning plan you have developed. If the peer is willing to serve as a resource to support your learning plan and write their own comparable plan, then you have the basis of a collaborative professional development programme.
Step 4	Refine the learning plans	Collaborate in refining your learning plans. Reconsider, and perhaps reorder, your priorities. If you haven't collaborated before begin with non-threatening activities, e.g. comparing schemes of learning or programme documentation. Agree a timescale for collaboration and concentrate on objectives that can be achieved in that time.
Step 5	Consult administration	Most collaborative professional development programmes are private arrangements between teachers, but it is wise to try to anticipate the concerns administrators (Team Leaders and Programme Managers) might have and explain to them what learning goals have been identified and the benefits that might accrue – perhaps in your appraisal.
Step 6	Carry out the learning plans	Depending on the plans, one partner acts as coach and collects information, e.g. by observing the other one teaching. This would be analysed through discussion and evaluation made of its significance for practice. It is important to keep records of these meetings to highlight the changes made. They can contribute to your professional development journal.
Step 7	Serve as coach and/or co-researcher	As a coach you provide feedback to your partner. You must remain supportive in difficult times. Set aside time to meet to analyse coaching you receive from, and give to, one another. Both of you develop skills in fostering critical thinking and providing support, which are needed to conduct effective tutorials with your own learners.

Step 8	Revise the teaching portfolio to reflect accomplishments	When the learning plans have been completed you should do a self-assessment to evaluate what has been achieved individually. Self-assessment ensures both of you are always supporting and never judging each other. Revise your portfolio and develop your professional journal.
Step 9	Repeat the above steps as desired	After revising your portfolios, you can decide whether to enter into another professional development cycle with your partner, take a break, begin collaborating with a different partner – or take another professional development route entirely.
Step 10	Close the collaboration	Take care in reaching closure on the learning plans and ensure you thank each other and then work out how each of you might help one another after the formal relationship is over.

Adapted from Moran (2001: 21–37)

Collaborative relationships are an optional but excellent way of developing self-awareness. You learn a lot about yourself but partners have to strive to be critical and caring – not always an easy balance to achieve!

Success Story

Developing interpersonal skills
I had a variety of jobs before I did a PGCE and trained to be a specialist in Art and Design. I taught in a school initially and was quite successful, but I found that the job wasn't really for me. Eventually I found work in a Day Service setting for students with learning difficulties and I began to realise how many opportunities for learning were being missed. The students had skills – but they were not being developed. What I learned about working in the Day Service setting was that you have to have an interest in people and I certainly developed my own skills when working there.

Creating a cooperative learning environment
My current job is as a Manager of a Regional Centre for Learners with Asperger's Syndrome (AS). The centre is a specially designed learning environment situated in a college. I think that the environment is very important and working on the design was a shared experience with input from students and staff. What we have achieved is a brilliant, contemporary space with high-quality fittings and equipment which is multi-functional and enables us to work in a cooperative and very flexible way. When we started out there were 18 students who had disclosed about AS and now we have 125 students who have 'come out' about AS. The facility has become known and people now know that support is available. I'm sure that if students couldn't come here in their breaks or out of class time, they probably wouldn't come to college at all or they'd soon drop out.

Relating to students
AS students are all different, but to be honest if I was teaching GCSE Art it would be

the same. You have to think how you can engage students who are almost failing and build their self-esteem, discover their ability and how to overcome their lack of confidence. The secret is to listen to students and hear what they say. When you listen, you are listening to individuals, not disabilities. But you can't enter their world – you are on the periphery as it were – so it does take an effort to get the relationship right.

Collaborative working and professional learning

All the best staff have a genuine interest in people and treat people as individuals with potential and see their job as trying to develop their skills. When we appoint staff they all go through a baseline assessment and an interview, but it is not always the best qualified or most experienced staff we're keen to have but the most empathetic. In this sort of work it's having the right sort of personality that counts and good staff have empathy. We work very much as a team and have appointed staff with diverse skills and from across the age range. We encourage discussion about students all the time and have weekly meetings where ideas and experiences are shared and teaching and support staff can air their views. We set ground rules for the centre and agree approaches which break down staff-student barriers and encourage cooperative working. These meetings are a real professional development opportunity, especially for younger staff, and they become immersed in the culture and absorb our working values through listening to others and joining in the discussion.

Changing student-staff relationships

My own professional development this year has involved work with 'Training in Systematic Instruction' (TSI). TSI originated in the USA and has been developed there for students with severe learning difficulties, but it is becoming more widely used in the UK now. What the original research revealed was that people were failing in the workplace not because they couldn't do the job, but because they weren't given the right training. In this country, where there is more and more a focus on progression into work, it seems right to move away from a neuro-typical way of thinking about AS, to one which recognises individuals with particular talents. One of the significant elements of TSI is that you don't over-praise. Historically, in this sector praise has been given for the smallest thing. In TSI you don't praise unless the individual is doing something exceptional. Over-praising limits the students' aspirations in a way and in the centre we're careful about praising now. It's not that you don't encourage or support students, but when you're preparing individuals for the outside world TSI encourages staff to be realistic and not give students inflated ideas about their abilities. For example, a student who had attended another organisation for Motor Vehicle training applied to the college and didn't get a place and was quite distraught and bewildered because 'They said I was really good'. He felt let down rather than supported: the student-staff relationship had failed him in that respect.

As a manager, you have to have the confidence and expertise to know what's up to the minute and right for your students as, quite recently, one of our staff was criticised by the Ofsted inspector for not praising when they were being observed! Doing a project like this for professional development makes you look at things differently – it's a changing world and a lot of training with AS is based in another era.

> **If you asked me ...**
> For a member of staff who was new to working with students with learning difficulties, I would suggest:
> - you need basic information about AS (or SLDD);
> - you need to be able to put yourself in the learner's position;
> - you need to look for reasons behind a learner's behaviour, not the behaviour itself;
> - you need to think about your job as an enabler into the community or society for your learners.
>
> As a mentor of a trainee-teacher, I would suggest that you try to:
> - be flexible;
> - not criticise what you observe until you see it's not working;
> - remember your way of doing things is not necessarily the right way;
> - keep in mind newcomers bring new ideas which you can learn from;
> - be a positive, not a limiting factor, in others' development.
>
> (Manager of a Regional Centre for Learners with Asperger's Syndrome Disorder)

The case study provides an excellent example of professional vision and values put into action. Opening the Regional Centre in college is symbolic of equality, diversity and inclusion embedded in practice. This manager ensures collaborative relationships are developed not just between colleagues but with learners, the workforce and the community.

> **Check It Out 8.5**
>
> **Collaborating with others**
> Collaboration and cooperation with others about your learners is an excellent way to develop your relationships with colleagues and, at the same time, your knowledge of teaching and learning.
>
> **Links To CPD**
> - Why not try out Moran's idea of collaborative professional development.
> - The collaborative partnership could contribute to your annual hours for CPD.
> - Identify a target for your Action Plan to share good practice with others by, e.g. contributing a specialist item to a course team meeting or organising an informal meeting with colleagues.
> - If you are undertaking initial teacher training, your responses to the above activities provide evidence for LLUK standards AS3 and AS5.

Widening professional relationships

In vocational education and training, it is important to build professional relationships outside of a formal training course in order to ensure the learners have an opportunity to develop the skills and workplace practices they will require in the future. Employability and employer engagement have become prominent features, particularly in FE Colleges, and many teachers spend a lot of their time trying to organise work placements, making visits to various workplaces and building up contacts.

Viewpoint

Employability and employer engagement

Employer engagement is vital. However, the way it is done is also important as this has an impact on its value for learning and teaching and also for the employer. For learners, e.g. on Public Service courses who have had no experience of part-time or full-time employment, the benefit of a work placement is that working alongside those already in the job they aspire to opens their eyes to the pressures and experiences of the workplace and the glamour of the role is replaced by the reality. For those who are changing careers, they get a real chance to assess what is involved on a day-to-day basis on which they can base decisions about their future.

When I first came into teaching I built up good relationships with employers by organising visits to various workplaces and inviting guest speakers into the college. This took up a lot of time and the relationships obviously depended on my own personal contacts and networking and the goodwill of the employers. Gradually I realised that as the policy of employer engagement became more prevalent, these relationships needed to be on a more professional footing. My aim now is to build relationships at a strategic level, rather than on a personal level, so that links with employers are on a sound footing for the future.

Developing strategic partnerships

In my area of Public Services, the college has developed long-term strategic relations with, for example:

- Police Force – for managing training from pre-entry level to progression to Foundation Degree;
- Fire Handling – for Level 2 qualifications;
- Community Safety – for accreditation at Level 2 for security firms, housing wardens, event staff;
- Ambulance Service – for driving and maintenance

It is easy to focus on one course or employer but more difficult to cater for all Public Service students. The benefits of developing strategic partnerships between organisations at senior management level are that learners can relate their college work to the world of work and visits, etc. take on a whole new perspective, e.g. skills of analysis, evaluation and synthesising are becoming evident in their written work and presentations as they use their first-hand experience and primary evidence. Also, staff in the workplace are challenged by being involved in the placement and training of college learners and it has been reported back to me that they are more enthused and motivated by sharing their expertise with college learners. Another benefit is that we have recruited some part-time teachers from Public Services professionals who bring to their teaching excellent, up-to-date experience.

My view is that strategic partnerships involve commitment from senior management

> from both organisations over time and are more stable and transparent than staff trying to make links individually. I would recommend this as a way ahead to develop employer engagement.
>
> (Programme Manager for Public Service Courses in an FE College)

The Viewpoint reveals that as employability and employer engagement become requirements rather than desirable 'add-ons' to programmes, an excellent tactic is to take a whole college approach to developing strategic partnerships with local employers. The real benefits to both sides of the partnership are evident. Successful teachers do not work in isolation but adopt practices that help them stay positive about their professional relationships.

Successful Strategies
- Ways in which you can adopt a collaborative working approach are to join in team projects, attend team meetings and contribute ideas to team meetings.
- Developing positive relationships with others is more successful if you value others' contributions to collaborative projects and recognise other people's strengths.
- Work out ways of encouraging learners to become aware of their behaviour and develop codes of behaviour for your groups.

In Chapter 9 there is a discussion about the idea that if you want to develop professional autonomy you need a repertoire of intellectual skills to help you.

9 Constructing a Repertoire of Intellectual Skills

In this chapter you will find sections on:
- professional development, control knowledge and intellectual skills;
- developing critical thinking;
- evaluation of professional practice;
- embedding reflective practice;
- using research to develop practice.

The chapter addresses issues relating to Domain A; AS4 Reflection and evaluation of their own practice and their CPD as teachers.

For those undertaking initial teacher training, the chapter provides opportunities to generate evidence for LLUK standards AS4, AS7 and elements of Domains B and C.

Professional development, control knowledge and intellectual skills

The quote from Eraut below, which defines what he terms *'control knowledge'*, depicts the complexity of the process of developing professional knowledge and competence, and through it Eraut encapsulates the notion that one's own learning is not a single – or even simple – act:

> self-awareness and sensitivity; self-knowledge about one's strengths and weaknesses, the gap between what one says and what one does, and who one knows and does not know; self-management in such matters as the use of time, prioritisation and delegation; self-development in its broadest sense, including how to learn and control one's own learning; the ability to reflect and self-evaluate, that is

to provide oneself with feedback; and generalised intellectual skills like strategic thinking and policy analysis, which involve the organisation of one's own knowledge and thinking. (Eraut, 1994: 92)

There is a lot packed into this definition of control knowledge, which incorporates the *means by which you use all the other forms of knowledge*. As there's such a lot to take in, you might have to read the definition several times to get your head round the many ideas it contains. Eraut's definition exemplifies metacognition, which is a term used to describe knowledge of your own thoughts and the factors that influence your thinking. It involves the evaluation of what one is doing and thinking, i.e. what is often called 'thinking about thinking'. But thinking alone is not enough for professional development according to Eraut, he says that what you need are actions which encourage you to evaluate yourself and organise your own knowledge and thinking. Control knowledge is a wide-ranging concept, which is as relevant today as when the passage was written because it puts in a nutshell the many and varied aspects surrounding CPD that have now taken on a new importance with the introduction of the LLUK standards for teaching and learning in the Lifelong Learning Sector.

The LLUK standards – e.g. Domain A: Standards relating to professional values and practice – emphasise the need for teachers to contribute to the continuous improvement of quality by evaluating their contribution to their organisation's quality cycle and engaging in CPD through reflection, evaluation and the appropriate use of research; all of which require the generalised intellectual skills that Eraut describes, such as strategic thinking and policy analysis.

Knowledge: Teachers in the Lifelong Learning Sector know and understand:
AK4.3 ways to reflect, evaluate and use research to develop own practice, and to share good practice with others. (LLUK, 2007b)

You may well question how you recognise the outcomes of activities to develop your own practice in teaching and learning. Who notices or benefits? How do you know if your practice is good enough to share with others? As you embark on CPD activities you need some reassurance that engaging in them will make a difference. You have to know what makes teaching and learning more skilful and accomplished. For example, what are the attributes that makes someone an expert in your specialist area of teaching and learning, so much so that others want to share their good practice?

Check It Out   9.1

Subject specialist expertise

Explore the opportunities for developing your subject-specific expertise by doing one of the following:

- searching for an appropriate subject-specific conference and seeking sponsorship to attend with the purpose of identifying latest developments in your area and ascertaining what it is about the speakers that makes them experts in their subject;
- booking an appointment to speak to your external examiner or external verifier when they next visit your organisation to discuss with them what the latest developments are in assessing your subject area and asking them what attributes are required to be considered for appointment as an external examiner or verifier, and what they would advise you to do to develop your own expertise.

Links To CPD

After attending a conference, or after a meeting with your external examiner or verifier, record what you learned and evaluate what particular attributes you might focus on for professional development. Enter your reflections in your Professional Development Journal and develop an Action Plan with your aims.

If you are undertaking initial teacher training, your responses to the above activity provides evidence for LLUK standard AS4 and elements of Domain C.

There appear to be attributes of expertise that everyone would recognise, which are useful to know about if you wish to develop your expertise, and there are some models to help you here. A classic example is the typology developed by Dreyfus and Dreyfus (1986) which depicts five stages of developing expertise:

- novice;
- advanced beginner;
- competent;
- proficient;
- expert.

In this typology, which has been applied to developing expertise in teaching by Berliner (2001), it is claimed that experts grasp situations and don't need to rely on rules to perform; they only need to analyse what is going on when *new situations occur or problems arise*. That probably hasn't made things much clearer, I suspect, as it's probably difficult to judge what 'type' you fit into or what stage you are at in developing expertise. For example, if you are a newcomer to the Lifelong Learning Sector you may consider yourself an expert in your specialist area but a novice in teaching and learning.

Rather than concentrating on the stages of expertise, Atherton (2003) explores the *components* of expertise, which he identifies as competence, contextualisation, contingency and creativity. His model identifies the 'parts' or 'resources' that contribute to expertise, which are also the means to achieve it. In this simpler model the lower level of competence in performing is taken for granted and the expert doesn't have to think about it, which means experts can spend time thinking about the higher levels in the model. See if you have any of the components of expertise outlined below; an example of how a teacher might exhibit them is provided.

- **Competence:** the simple ability to perform the requisite range of skills for practice. The 'competence teacher' has a range of skills.
- **Contextualisation:** knowing *when* to do *what*. The 'contextualising teacher' knows which skills to draw on in a given situation.
- **Contingency:** the greater flexibility to be able to cope when things go wrong. The 'contingency teacher' has sufficient depth of understanding of the situation to be able to develop a strategy for action and does not have to rely on a fixed set of rules about what to do.
- **Creativity:** the capacity to use competence, contextualisation and contingency in new ways to solve new problems. The 'creativity teacher' not only responds to change with imagination and resourcefulness but also anticipates it. (Adapted from Atherton, 2003: 5–6)

It is reassuring to know that if you have a range of skills and are a competent teacher then you have the initial component and are on the start of your journey to expertise! The significant aspect of this model for teachers considering CPD, however, is that to move from competence to creativity requires what Atherton calls a 'game plan' or a strategy, i.e. the development of plans to deal with possibilities, which he jokes is identifying *what you do when you don't know what to do*!

It seems that if you want to progress to expertise, having a strategy is one key. In a sector as diverse as the Lifelong Learning Sector, there is no one best way of improving practice and, therefore, CPD needs to be carefully tailored to address local issues and the needs of different teachers in different types of organisation. Throughout this book you have been encouraged to develop an Action Plan and various activities have been suggested, and I have to reinforce here that it is best for you to develop your own strategy to fit your own personal and professional circumstances and your own organisational context.

The next step is to consider what you include in your strategy. Eraut makes it clear that you need to think of developing professional knowledge in its broadest sense. To recap, he identifies control knowledge as the means by which you use all other knowledge and defines this as incorporating:

- self-awareness;
- self-knowledge;

- self-management;

- self-development;

- self-evaluation;

- generalised intellectual skills.

This list could be said to include the 'components' of control knowledge as they are the means by which other forms of knowledge are used. Developing professional knowledge means developing these components (which you can think of as parts of yourself, resources to draw on or personal attributes) and it is suggested that they make an excellent starting point for formulating your own strategy and developing your Action Plan. The question is, can you identify how you will develop these attributes and are they possible to learn? Can you attend staff development events and be taught expertise? Atherton suspects not, but I would say that, in part, you can. For example, you can attend a staff development workshop and learn about self-management techniques, such as use of time, prioritisation and delegation. However, I would add that you need the intellectual skill of *strategic thinking* to apply the techniques efficiently. You have to know not just that it is important to prioritise tasks, but also *what* is important to prioritise and *why*. To develop the attribute of self-management effectively, you also need to be capable of the intellectual skill of *policy analysis* to decide what is important to attend to, i.e. you need to have experience of contextual issues such as what's new in your vocational area and deploy intellectual skills to interpret what the latest government policy means for teaching and learning in your organisation.

It is clear that contextual issues, e.g. your workplace practices and policy frameworks, are another key to achieving expertise through CPD. Other theories are useful to apply here, too: Lave and Wenger's (1991) well-known model of 'situated learning' and Wenger's (1999) 'communities of practice'. Their contention is that learning involves participation with others, e.g. colleagues, team members, mentors and managers in your professional community. As a newcomer to the teaching profession you are on the edge (or periphery) of the community but, through working alongside other teachers (practitioners), and through observing how they perform and modelling their behaviour, you gradually become part of the professional community of teachers (a participant) in your organisation. Such experiences must be had: they cannot be taught. Your professional learning involves participation in a community of practice: you learn from the *experiences* you engage in with more experienced or knowledgeable members of the community ('old-timers' as Lave and Wenger called them!). If you are undertaking your initial teacher training, can you now see why it is important to shadow your mentor and observe colleagues and discuss these encounters with your mentor so that you can evaluate which aspects of their practice to model?

Lave and Wenger's position is that knowledge is 'distributed' amongst the community of practice, and participation in the community of practice, through interaction and dialogue with colleagues, exposes you to that knowledge. But just as you require your learners to 'think for themselves', you don't just want to accept unquestioningly other people's thinking or rely on the way they do things. Whether you are in a community where practice is poor or out of date, or whether you are in a community sharing good practice, if you want to improve your expertise you need to be creative and use that knowledge in new ways to solve new problems. That is why the generalised intellectual skills of strategic thinking and policy analysis are so important: developing professional knowledge requires that you work out what is relevant to your situation.

Success Story

Professional and academic progression

I have undertaken several different roles during my career, become a teacher on higher education courses, lead postgraduate courses and moved into management. I think that enjoying the process of professional development and enjoying the journey you take through your career is most important.

What I would say to anyone starting out on their career or thinking about their professional progression is to continue to be curious about things: new knowledge, new opportunities, the way people operate together and new initiatives. Being curious about things and open to new opportunities is crucial.

Reflection, analysis and strategic thinking

Another important thing that I would have to say is that you need to have the capacity to 'helicopter'. By that I mean that you have to have sight of what is potentially new and significant. If you're immersed in day-to-day things and bogged down with the routine, what you do is limit your horizons. You have to have some kind of ability to stand apart from the everyday things and think about where the future of teaching and learning is going and your role in it. I think it's about curiosity but also the ability to be anticipatory. You have to reflect and be prepared to analyse your strengths and weaknesses and figure out what needs to be worked on. You need to reflect on what needs improving. I suppose it's the idea of looking back so that you can look forward.

I think there is an element of serendipity in all of this, however, as often the most interesting opportunities emerge at a tangent to what one's involved in or anticipates. You can't necessarily forecast everything. You can't be too linear in your approach as you close yourself off to new learning experiences. It's means going with the flow and being alert to things that come up. True learning experiences are engaging and take you in a new direction and open up different opportunities.

Evaluation and decision making

For those of us who've been in the sector for some time, you are aware of the tension between your professional background and the impact of 'new managerialism'. You may hold your professional values very dear and to get on this may be difficult to manage. Do you say 'no'? Do you compromise dearly held views? It may be more of a dilemma for those of us who have seen considerable changes in the sector and whose careers have straddled the professional-managerial divide. Perhaps for younger teachers, or those new to teaching, they may not be so aware of the issues as they have grown up in a managerialist environment.

I think if you are in a position where you feel advancing your career would compromise your professional values you would be advised to talk things through with a 'critical friend'. The decision would still be yours but talking through things would help you weigh up the pros and cons and in the end make a decision about whether compromise threatens your fundamental beliefs or not.

If you asked me ...

As a manager, my advice for those wanting to move into management in the Lifelong Learning Sector is:

- try and focus on both the task in hand and the relationships amongst staff. What tends to happen is that the task predominates – probably because of pressure from within the organisation.
- management is not about just successfully meeting targets but also it's extremely important to make sure that to a large extent staff are empowered to do things for themselves.
- you have to recognise staff commitment and contribution to achieving targets and not abandon them, e.g. acknowledge the part they play and their involvement in meeting targets. If staff have no sense of whether any of the work they do is worthwhile this depresses their inclination to set and achieve higher targets and have an input into the organisation's success.
- I think you have to recognise that staff invest time in their work and take on a role of nurturing, developing and facilitating their professional development.

(Manager and Course Leader in a college)

The case study depicts the importance of strategic thinking in practice very well indeed. What this manager is telling us is that you have to develop a strategy and be able to stand back from the hustle and bustle of the workplace and think ahead. This manager concedes that some things happen by chance and you can't plan everything, you have to go with the interesting opportunities that arise, which demonstrates perfectly the 'creativity' in Atherton's model, i.e. they not only anticipate change but respond to possibilities with imagination and resourcefulness. As a manager they recognise that professional knowledge is 'distributed' amongst the staff and see their role as facilitating professional development for staff, and also keep their own enjoyment in learning and curiosity about new developments in teaching and learning alive. If you see your future as a manager in your organisation, then you will not find better guidance than that given here.

It has been argued that professional learning is part of your everyday workplace practice through observation of colleagues and critical dialogue, and that CPD lies as much within the organisation as in your individual practice. A role for teacher-trainers during initial teacher training is to prepare teachers for *future learning* and provide the environment for teachers to collectively recognise their workloads as a vehicle for CPD. The central tasks for this are grounded in the practice of so-called 'expert' teachers and offered as guidelines for constructing a repertoire of intellectual skills:

- Provide opportunities for analysis, reflection, evaluation, defining, justifying, examining and exploring own practice and others' practice.
- Provide opportunities to test hypotheses about current practice through learning conversations with others about concrete primary experiences.
- Provide opportunities for teachers to challenge current assumptions about practice, to take risks and feel comfortable with change through the use of primary experiences, e.g. case studies, student profiles, evaluations, assessments and authentic resources. (Steward, 2004: 298)

If you are undertaking initial teacher training, or have recently achieved your teaching qualification, you have no doubt developed intellectual skills through the opportunities provided by the programme, such as those outlined above. However, as CPD is now seen as a continuation of professional learning it is essential that you create opportunities during your career to further develop intellectual skills through engaging in similar activities. It may be that 'developing thinking skills' is one of the criteria for your learners to achieve and you are aware of what's required, but sometimes it is different applying skills to your own context. However, it's good to know that thinking skills 'can and should be taught; the main question is how?' (Scales, 2008: 262).

In the rest of this chapter I consider the overarching concept of critical thinking and how thinking skills can be learnt and developed, and also the associated skills of evaluation, reflection and research that have been identified in the LLUK standards, which I consider are part of your repertoire of intellectual skills for 'constructive practice' that I introduced in Chapter 5.

Developing critical thinking

You are almost certainly thinking about something all the time you are at work, so what is it that makes *critical thinking* different? You have probably applied critical thinking to solving problems in your day-to-day life such as:

- going on the internet and checking out which of two differently priced insurance policies will suit your needs better;
- reading the labels on the packets of breakfast cereals and working out which one is both better value for money and for your health;
- listening to the weather forecast and considering how likely it is to rain in your neck of the woods.

When you are engaged in such activities you are probably not aware of the strategies you use to make the decisions because the situations are so *familiar* to you. You don't realise at the time that you are comparing and contrasting information, attending to similarities and differences in text or making judgements about whether to trust information or be sceptical about it. You'll be pleased to know that your capacity for critical thinking can be improved with practice, even though it can be hard work at times:

> Critical thinking is a process that relies upon, and develops, a wide range of skills and personal qualities. Like other forms of activity, it improves with practice and with a proper sense of what is required. ... Developing good critical thinking skills can take patience and application. On the other hand, the rewards lie in improved abilities in making judgements, seeing more easily through flawed reasoning, making choices from a more informed position and improving your ability to influence others. (Cottrell, 2005: 16)

When you're really busy at work, you don't always want your manager to ask your opinion on how a new policy or a new initiative should be implemented; you sometimes just want to be told how they see things happening and what they want doing so that you can get on with it. It's because you're on *unfamiliar* ground that you become aware that you don't really know what it entails to implement a new initiative and you realise you need to really think things through and weigh up the pros and cons before making a decision. Put simply, that's what critical thinking involves. The best thing to do in such a situation, especially if you are too worn out to grasp the meaning of what is going on, or of judging whether your manager's point of view is reasonable, is to bide your time because critical thinking is not about thoughtless agreement, or disagreeing with someone and getting into an argument about what action to take. When referring to critical thinking, an argument is setting out *reasons* to support your ideas or to persuade someone else to come round to your point of view. It's about being logical and rational and not being personal and too emotional.

On the other hand, critical thinking is 'perhaps the most significant marker of an educated person' according to Morgan et al. and they consider that in the working world 'the most consistently valued asset of an organisation is the capacity of individuals to use their critical and creative thinking abilities to improve collective performance' (Morgan et al., 2004: 156–7). Therefore, if you want to become an expert in your field, you have to get out of your comfort zone and put new ideas and initiatives to the test, and challenge them if necessary. Contributing to the continuous improvement of quality in your organisation requires you to use your critical thinking skills.

If you want your decisions to be made in a more informed way, then Cottrell's framework of critical thinking as a process is an excellent place to start as it makes it very clear what's entailed; if you have a 'proper sense of what is required' you can practise and get better.

> Critical thinking is a complex process of deliberation which involves a wide range of skills and attitudes. It includes:
>
> - *identifying other people's positions,* arguments and conclusions;
> - *evaluating the evidence* for alternative points of view;
> - *weighing up opposing arguments* and evidence fairly;
> - *being able to read between the lines,* seeing behind the surface, and identifying false or unfair assumptions;
> - *recognising techniques* used to make certain positions more appealing than others, such as false logic and persuasive devices;
> - *reflecting on issues* in a structured way, bringing logic and insight to bear;
> - *drawing conclusions* about whether arguments are valid and justifiable, based on good evidence and sensible assumptions;
> - *presenting a point of view* in a structured, clear, well-reasoned way that convinces others. (Cottrell, 2005: 2)

Thinking about critical thinking as a process helps you gain a sense of what is required to demonstrate critical thinking and provides a checklist that can be used to help you develop a course of action in dealing with new problems or when working in different situations. However, you will only develop your critical thinking skills if you put them into action as, surprisingly, you can't develop them just by going through a checklist! You need some content or subject matter on which to try them out. You can compare this with the teaching of thinking skills to your learners – you are likely to be more successful if the skills are embedded into activities within your specialist area than if you try to teach them as a discrete unit.

For example, before a team meeting about introducing changes to a learning programme, you could address the first item in the process – *identifying other people's positions* – by sounding out your colleagues and managers and getting their views on the changes. This can be done informally over coffee or at lunchtime. If you have this information before the meeting you can work out your 'game plan' or strategy of how to deal with different points or questions that might possibly come up at the meeting. Planning for a meeting has the same purpose as planning for a teaching session: you have worked out your objectives and you know what is required to achieve them. When colleagues put their view at the meeting, you are in a much better position to respond in a professional manner and present your point of view in a clear and well-reasoned way. If this happens, your contribution to the meeting will be recognised and your views are more likely to be considered seriously, but they won't be if you don't develop strategic thinking and end up getting in a muddle and all hot under the collar about what's being decided. Remember, developing a strategy is a mark of expertise!

Check It Out 9.2

Developing critical thinking
Considering the development of thinking skills as a process which requires a range of skills and it would be useful to try to recognise the steps identified by Cottrell (see above) when you are attending team meetings. You can learn a lot from observing what goes on! The next step is to try out something new.

Links To CPD
- Develop reasons for adopting a new assessment strategy in your specialist subject area to improve learner achievement.
- Practise putting across your case for change to a colleague and take note of their response.
- When appropriate, put your case to a team meeting and take particular note of how you handle both positive and negative reactions.
- Did you notice if any of the stages in the process identified by Cottrell were evident in the meetings?
- If you are undertaking initial teacher training, your responses to the above activities provide evidence for LLUK standard AS4.

The Lifelong Learning Sector is always subject to change and a case has been made by Coffield for a new set of priorities, and one of them is:

> [t]o inspire and enable individuals to develop their capacities to the highest potential levels throughout life, so that they grow intellectually, are well equipped for work, can contribute effectively to society, and achieve personal fulfilment. (Coffield, 2008: 59)

This is the first priority Coffield identifies, which concerns teachers in the sector and reinforces the importance of developing intellectual skills for both personal and professional development.

Evaluation of professional practice

Teacher training textbooks provide different concepts of evaluation. Evaluation is identified as a skill for effective teaching (Rogers, 2002; Minton, 2005). According to Rogers, evaluation can focus on the learning programme and encompass skills such as:

- identifying goals;
- monitoring progress;
- judging the usefulness of the learning process.

Or, alternatively, Rogers suggests that it can be considered as self-evaluation skills:

- the need to take stock of what has happened;
- exploring where we are now;
- deciding where to go from here.

Armitage et al. (2007) provide a more sophisticated approach to evaluation in their model:

- **scientific evaluation** – scientific evaluation comprises two elements: first classical evaluation which is solely interested in measuring and testing, and second evaluation via behavioural objectives.
- **qualitative evaluation** – The aim of qualitative evaluation is to present a holistic picture through methods such as observation, interviews, questionnaires, assessments and other data and is language-based rather than statistical. The essential element of qualitative evaluation is of evaluating learning as a social activity. It takes into account the course intentions and organisation and a range of outcomes through evaluating the perceptions and experiences of the learner(s) and others involved.

In qualitative evaluation it is the quality of the experience that is central to capture, including unintended outcomes:

> the aim is to present an holistic picture of the new course in operation which is designed to illuminate the reality of the course for all those involved. (Armitage et al., 2007: 227)

Nowadays, as well as addressing scientific and qualitative evaluation, the distinction between formative and summative assessment is emphasised in teacher training texts. This distinction is used more and more in relation to evaluation, e.g. there is a growing trend to undertake evaluation of learning programmes mid-way through them as well as at the end. Formative evaluation is intended to help in development of learning and learning programmes, whereas summative evaluation concentrates on assessing the effects and effectiveness of learning and learning programmes. But, Robson (2002: 208) suggests the distinction is primarily one of purpose and is not absolute. In Robson's view summative evaluation could well have a formative effect on future developments and, even if evaluation is neither totally negative nor positive, he asserts that evaluation highlights issues to do with change and carries within it strong implications for change. One purpose of summative evaluation is that it contributes to development, but unlike the purpose of formative evaluation, it will be implemented in the *future*, so it will not benefit learners whose experiences contributed to the evaluation.

Nevertheless, making sense of your practice through both formative and summative evaluations and preparing responses to them becomes a learning process, and helps you to become more aware of the experience of teaching and learning and what you can take from the experience to move your thinking and practice forward.

Check It Out 9.3

Evaluation to improve practice

Before carrying out a formative evaluation, you have to be realistic about what can be achieved within organisational constraints:

- be transparent with learners about what is possible to change and what is not, e.g. staffing;
- explain where it might be possible to negotiate change, e.g. room or venue;
- focus on what is possible to change, i.e. your teaching and their learning!
- If you are new to teaching, it would be wise to stick to your sessions initially, rather than evaluating the whole learning programme.

Links To CPD

- Design a formative evaluation form that takes the above factors into consideration.
- To instigate a formative evaluation of your sessions, discuss with colleagues involved when the best time would be, e.g. after the first four weeks of a twelve-week programme, or after one term of a three-term programme.
- After the evaluation, discuss the outcomes with the course leader or your manager and negotiate any improvements.
- If you are undertaking initial teacher training, your responses to the above activities provide evidence for the LLUK standards AS4, AS7 and Domains B and C.

Additionally, to learn from experience, and to promote personal and professional development, requires teachers to make time for deliberations about teaching and learn through self-evaluation. However, self-evaluation, self-awareness, self-knowledge and self-management on their own will not bring change; there also needs to be an *intention* for self-development and the *ability to behave in a different manner*

(Moon, 1999: 82). Doing the evaluation will improve nothing on its own; you have to intend to do something about the responses and make changes.

Embedding reflective practice

Reflection, as a concept, helps those in teaching and learning and other professional situations to make sense of an area of human functioning through critical thinking and it is applied to gain a better understanding of complex ideas through reprocessing knowledge, ideas and, possibly, emotions that you already have (Moon, 1999, 2005, 2008). Moon contends that whilst reflection seems to be understood in common sense terms, in academic terms there are problems of definition as models of reflection, such as those of Schon (1983) and Kolb (1984), are founded largely on non-empirical work. Problems of definition appear to be because the concept is invariably related to a task, e.g. professional development or learning from experience, and what can *be done* with reflection rather than on the concept itself.

Using reflection in an educational context is not a new idea, but in recent years reflection has been a key factor in the training of teachers and is now embedded in the LLUK standards. Dewey's (1933) view is that reflection occurs when a problem needs solving, i.e. when a person experiences cognitive discomfort. However, this seems rather a narrow view if we consider creative solutions to a problem that may emerge unexpectedly. Habermas (1972) also linked reflection with cognitive function whilst others additionally linked affective function (Boud et al., 1985; Mezirow, 1990).

More recently, reflective practice has been considered as a way of finding a link between professional knowledge and self-knowledge; between thinking and taking personal action to improve (Osterman and Kottkamp, 1993; Ghaye and Ghaye, 1998, Moon 1999, 2005). These authors base their argument on the assumption that reflective practice is an open-ended approach to personal and organisational change and improvement that encourages adults to continue to learn and grow. In this way it stands in sharp contrast to many of the assumptions shaping the traditional models of professional development, e.g. compulsory attendance at one-off training events. Their writings suggest that as a strategy for achieving behavioural change, reflective practice enables teachers to develop a new awareness of their own performance and to improve the quality of their practice. This is not to say that change is easy, but reflective practice promotes the notion that organisational change connects with personal change and is about making sense of professional life: its context, values, practice and ways of improving (Ghaye and Ghaye, 1998; Fullan, 1999). Reflection is regarded as a valuable capability for individuals in organisations as it enables us to see ourselves from outside as objects of our own experience (Buchanan and Huczynski, 2004).

However, not everyone agrees that reflective practice enables practitioners to improve practice:

> I don't accept that 'reflective practice' is a good thing. It is a meaningless term that promotes a dangerous anxiety-making, navel gazing that undermines a lecturer's ability to be a good teacher. (Hayes, D., 2007: 169)

Hayes argues that reflective practice promotes anxiety and considers that reflecting all the time on personal experiences is the opposite of theorising and takes away a teacher's knowledge, authority and ability. Reflection is also considered too vague, too privatised, too individualised, and there is confusion about the meaning of the concept (Cornford, 2002; Elliott, 2002; Armitage et al., 2007). These authors believe that the explicit teaching of thinking and analytical skills, rather than reflective practice, may assist teachers to become more critical and thoughtful practitioners. The assumption that adult learners are in possession of effective cognitive skills that develop naturally and without the need for specific teaching is challenged by them. Nevertheless, the notion of reflective practice is embedded in the LLUK standards and Cornford's critique of reflection raises the question of whether it is an approach to professional development that satisfies immediate policy imperatives, whilst denying the long-term development and possession of truly critical skills of analysis for teachers in the sector.

Martinez (1999: 13) suggests that reflective practice may be a useful model for CPD where teachers continue to operate within an unchanging set of assumptions and basic beliefs about their practice, but it is neither helpful nor accurate where teaching and learning strategies and core beliefs are subject to substantial change. A dilemma for the teacher that he identifies is that pressures of time and change create barriers to reflection in a thoughtful, measured and unhurried way in the workplace but, at the same time, those self-same things stimulate the need for reflection and CPD.

The paradox is that, on the one hand, reflective practice is seen as a way of:

- problem-solving;
- gaining understanding of complex ideas;
- providing the link between thinking and action, which results in self-knowledge and professional knowledge.

However, on the other hand, it is seen as:

- taking away teachers' knowledge, authority and ability;

- assuming that teachers have the skills to reflect;

- not helpful where teaching and learning strategies are subject to change;

- requiring time – but pressures of time are seen to inhibit measured and unhurried reflection.

As reflection underpins the LLUK standards and IfL's notion of CPD, it is important to address these criticisms. If the last point is considered first, Hobley (2008) admits that the role of the teacher involves constantly coping with a range of competing demands and, therefore, it might be tempting to think of reflective practices as 'the sort of luxury you can enjoy when you have time available, much as you would quiet contemplation'. However, she asserts that finding the time to stand back and reflect is not an indulgence but a *prerequisite* for effective teaching: it is a necessity and not an option:

> As you become conscious of this developing ability, you become more confident, relaxed, flexible and responsive and as your students learn to trust you, they will often respond with an openness that makes the whole process easier to manage and more rewarding. Refining this highly valuable 'responsive expertise' is the purpose of reflective practice. It is the ability to identify *and prioritize* all subtle indicators within your learning environment. (Hobley, 2008: 17)

Hobley's response to the pressure of time in today's hectic environment is to maintain that *over time* teachers become 'experts' in their specialist area and are better informed and more aware; it is only when teachers become *conscious* of their developing ability that they become more responsive.

It would seem that, through immersing yourself in your organisational culture and participating in a community of practice over time, you become more alert to the finer points about teaching and learning that perhaps an outsider would not pick up. Developing 'responsive expertise' over time allows you to take a holistic view of teaching and learning and evaluate what you have learned and encourages continuous personal and professional growth. For Hobley, cultivating this awareness of professional knowledge is the purpose of reflective practice.

Sotto also suggests that you need to immerse yourself in a new situation and just look at what is going on around you, and pay attention to what is happening and what people are saying, rather than trying to understand everything straight away. If you are inexperienced or facing unfamiliar circumstances, then give yourself time and try not to jump to conclusions and a clearer picture of what is happening may gradually unfold:

> But when we immerse ourselves in a new situation, when we can allow it to come to us freshly, not through the screen of our past experiences, expectations or

desires; and when we are able to allow it to unfold itself before us, so that all its facets become clear, we might be able to understand it. (Sotto, 2007: 53)

It seems that a good way to develop professional knowledge and expertise is to gradually absorb it by observing and participating.

Nevertheless, it has to be admitted that reflection could result in navel gazing if thinking and analytical skills are not employed. Moore (2000) admits that there is a danger that teachers and tutors or mentors may practise 'amateur psychoanalysis' which improves nothing, or may even make things worse. However, if intellectual skills are embedded in initial teaching training, or are incorporated into sessions for CPD, then teachers can raise their awareness of the necessity for developing intellectual skills – such as critical thinking and evaluation – just as your learners develop them through the cognitive elements integrated into activities in your own specialist area.

In an attempt to counter the argument that reflection is too personal and can lead to teachers over-blaming themselves, what needs to go hand in hand with initiatives to embed critical thinking skills into initial teacher training and CPD, is consideration of the wider educational context, e.g. address how social and political influences and ethical issues influence your organisation and have an impact on your teaching and learning:

> critical thinkers make explicit the connections between the personal and political in their lives. They are aware that individual crises often reflect wider social changes. (Brookfield, 1991: 57)

If teachers, particularly those undertaking initial teaching training, understand that political initiatives with laudable motives to bring about social cohesion and economic prosperity may have unintentional consequences which result in what Brookfield terms 'individual crises', then they are less likely to blame their own performance and dwell on their personal failings.

A simple framework for reflecting on professional practice is suggested by Brookfield (1995). He asserts that teachers should develop an approach which demands the 'hunt for assumptions', which is a bit like detective work as you seek out clues to your current behaviour. But, so you don't dwell only on yourself he suggests that you look at a situation from what he calls 'four critical lenses':

- your own viewpoint;
- your colleagues' viewpoint;
- your learners' viewpoint;
- through theoretical literature.

Using research to develop practice

Research provides an opportunity for teachers to use and develop the intellectual skills of critical thinking and analysis, evaluation and reflection. Action research as an approach is a popular choice amongst teachers researching into their own practice as it lends itself to small-scale research focusing on improving aspects of the researcher's own practice. Action research offers a systematic approach to the definition, resolution and evaluation of everyday problems in your organisation: practical issues involving teaching and learning that have been identified by you and which are somehow both problematic and yet capable of being changed (Elliott, 1991). It is an attempt to bring about change in practice and to monitor the results. The process of enquiry is generally carried out as a cycle of:

- planning;
- acting;
- observing;
- reflecting.

There is a view that action research should be a collaborative, professional activity and involve cooperation with one or more colleagues and that the outcomes should be disseminated to all your colleagues through writing up the research in simple terms and making it accessible to all in your specialist area, e.g. by posting it on your organisation's intranet, publishing it in a newsletter or presenting it at a team meeting or staff development session.

To give you some idea about how to get started, here are seven principles in the REFLECT method of action research for change in FE for you to follow and help you on your way.

- **R = Reflect, read up on change and its impact:** Reflexive informed selective contemplation on issues identified.
- **E = Establish purpose and audience:** Establishing collaborative purpose and audience for research.
- **F = Focus questions, plan, monitor intervention:** Focused planning and monitoring of intervention for empowerment.
- **L = Lead on getting method and timing right:** Leading the shared ownership of a precisely worked out research method and timescale.
- **E = Ensure ethical and political sensitivity:** Ethical and political sensitivity in implementing data collection.
- **C = Critique report and dissemination:** Critical practitioner writing and dissemination of findings.
- **T = Targeted evaluation:** Targeted evaluation of the impact of the research on change management practice and refinement of action.

(Adapted from Jameson and Hiller (2003: 446–7)

The principles above are based on the acronym REFLECT, which is most appropriate for those wishing to undertake action research for their CPD.

Success Story

Developing as a teacher requires more than teaching skills

I didn't really plan to be where I am today, but I feel that I have made a successful career as a teacher in Further Education in the specialist area of Hospitality. In fact, although I had professional experience in my field, when I started I didn't have any teaching qualifications. I started out as a part-timer, which I enjoyed, and then went to full-time. I did an MSc in Microbiology before I did my teacher-training. I learned how to teach on-the-job. I was really lucky that I was working with two very focused people. I can remember on the first day just being told 'Go and teach'. Now I realise I was doing all the wrong things, such as writing on the board with my back to the class!

I have to admit that I didn't find my teacher training course very relevant. It was the first year of the NVQ-style assessment by portfolio and you got your work back with it stamped FAIL if you had only put in one lesson plan instead of two. Very disheartening! You couldn't take away much about practical classroom teaching from the course. I think I missed out because I had not done the initial City and Guild Further and Adult Education course and so didn't learn about basics such as lesson planning and teaching techniques. What I've found most useful in my teaching have been tutoring and counselling skills.

Developing research skills

I've always planned some professional development and always done qualifications or other activities. I did a Diploma through on-line training about ten years ago. It was very odd studying at a distance – one tutor was in Australia – and I found it a weird experience. I did start an EdD but I found the 'education speak' and the language of schools and universities did not fit with my experience as an FE teacher. I did, however, get interested in social science and, although I didn't continue with the doctorate, I learned valuable skills and got into research projects. For example, I did some small action research projects for the Learning and Skills Development Agency and also for Centre for Excellence in Leadership [now merged as The Learning and Skills Improvement Service]. I got involved in a project involving ten partner institutions about employer engagement and have had links with the Higher Education Academy as a specialist subject HE in FE Liaison Officer for Hospitality, Leisure, Sport and Tourism. This provided opportunities for collating good practice and insight into subject networking.

I have been 'bought out' for the hours and do research one day a week. Personally, the action research projects have filled in the bit missing from the doctorate. They bring an understanding to the FE working environment and applicable research methods. These professional development opportunities have helped me fill my gap in knowledge and I have got involved in wider educational issues through action research.

Developing reflection through mentoring

What I am particularly involved in at the moment is mentoring. I volunteered to mentor one part-timer and was picked to mentor another. Both mentees are competent and have been working in the department a long time. You have to make time for mentoring and what we do is discuss and reflect on what they are doing. In turn, this makes me reflect on what I'm doing and keeps me up to date. I have learned more about successful teaching and learning from the process of mentoring than from anything else I've done and my teaching has changed course because of it.

I do have a dilemma about what makes a successful teacher. There is an issue about the fitness of the observation process: Ofsted observations are procedural – you follow a tick box regime. Basically, I find that for internal observations, colleagues re-jig everything they normally do to jump through the hoops. In HE in FE the value in teaching and learning is within the debate you have, which is a different construction, i.e. the teacher and teaching is not the 'whole package'. My belief is that this could be a useful way of looking at teaching and learning in FE and I also think peer assessment would be more appropriate for FE colleagues. I believe that learning goes on all over the place and the teacher's role is facilitation, planning and being organised – in fact is very much like a mentoring role in HE in FE.

The case study provides a vivid illustration of the value of having a repertoire of both practical and intellectual skills as a teacher. Rather than non-completion of a higher degree being a setback for this teacher, the unintended outcomes were the acquisition of valuable skills. This teacher has achieved professional development through taking on new challenges, such as research and mentoring, and has risen to them. It is interesting how taking on different roles, both inside and outside their college, makes teachers reflect about their own practice, evaluate their skills and develop their own teaching and learning. Being open to new experiences and moving into unfamiliar areas has enabled this teacher to develop a rewarding professional role.

If you undertake research yourself, you may be using a variety of methods of enquiry in your own action research, such as informal interviews, group interviews and documentary analysis, and seeking the views of learners and other staff. None-theless, your focus will be to understand issues you are personally involved in and then to explain the issues being investigated. The new ideas that are generated by those involved in the action research from critical thinking, analysis and evaluation of the data collected are a form of theorising about your professional practice. The outcome of your findings results in developing new strategies to improve practice; action research is essentially applied research designed to bring about change:

> it is only through personal commitment to change that teaching can be improved. Imposing one methodological approach, or insisting on undifferentiated training workshops, is not the way to encourage any of us to change what might often be unconscious but deeply held beliefs about the nature of teaching and learning. Instead, we need to come to change through our own observations and research.
> (Campbell and Norton, 2007: 88)

The approach advocated in action research is a reflexive one and as such involves a mixture of reflecting on your own teaching and learning as a form of self-evaluation and dialogue with colleagues about professional values. The most significant benefit of action research is that it integrates activities which are often regarded as separate:

- teaching and learning, programme development, programme evaluation, subject specific updating;
- intellectual skills of critical thinking, reflection and evaluation;
- data analysis, creative problem-solving and writing skills.

Successful Strategies
- Use the LLUK standards to assist your professional development and provide criteria for you to evaluate your own performance.
- Constructing a repertoire of intellectual skills can be developed through a better understanding of what is entailed and by practice.
- Making wise choices about which aspects of teaching and learning to improve, which policies to focus on or what qualifications to study for requires professional judgement – not just off-the-cuff choices.
- CPD is most effective when it involves activities that develop a teacher's ability to take control of what they do, e.g. increase their capacity for self-management, provide feedback about one's own performance through self-evaluation and develop self-knowledge and self-awareness.
- Action research is often challenging, but the rewards in improved practice, developing positive relationships with colleagues and increased professional knowledge are well worth the risk-taking.

The Conclusion brings together the ideas presented throughout this book about a positive approach to CPD through 'constructive practice'.

Part IV Future Practice

Conclusion – Continuing your Professional Development

In this chapter you will find sections on:
- inquiring into professional practice as a lifelong learner;
- practical guidance and advice from teachers in the sector;
- envisioning alternative futures;
- considering the way forward;
- putting your plans into action;
- the future is yours – it's up to you.

Inquiring into professional practice as a lifelong learner

It seems that it is the questions you ask about teaching and learning and how probing and searching your questions are about your professional practice that influence the kind of teacher you are:

> construct theory sees man not as an infantile savage nor as a just-cleverer-than-the-average-rat nor as the victim of his biography but as an inveterate inquirer, self-invented and shaped, sometimes wonderfully and sometimes disastrously, by the direction of his inquiries. (Bannister and Fransella, 1971: 10)

It was hearing Fransella talk about the importance of the continuing exploration of your professional role when I was studying for my Diploma in Education many years ago that my interest in professional development started. Her contention was that if you wanted to consider yourself a professional – and not an 'infantile savage' or a 'just-cleverer-than-the-average-rat' – you had to become an 'inveterate inquirer', which seemed to me much more preferable than the alternative!

My experience over the years is that if you think of yourself as an 'inveterate inquirer' or lifelong learner, your questions can enhance your performance in your organisation, whereas if you focus on your performance all the time you might end up blaming yourself for letting your learners down. For instance, many teachers take all the blame when learners don't achieve and all the credit when they do. If you stand back and question what you might learn from this, then you realise that learners are all different and some achieve and some don't. You can't 'learn' learners, they have to do this for themselves, but you can identify the positive aspects of your teaching that *support* learning and which you could develop and incorporate into your future teaching. You can also identify aspects of your teaching that need improving – or ditching! You can come to an understanding that success is not all about your brilliant performance but your contribution to learners' learning. When you question your professional practice and think for yourself and don't just carry out others' bidding, or do what you've always done, then there is more than a chance that your teaching may turn out 'sometimes wonderfully', rather than disastrously, as Fransella predicts – and this is what CPD is all about in my experience.

According to Cranton different forces bear down on your professional practice and any improvement in practice is influenced by your individual circumstances: your own attributes, the subject you teach, the resources available to you, the type of organisation you work in and the wider social context. Although in the Lifelong Learning Sector teachers work in different organisations and hold different views about teaching and learning, Cranton asserts that the core of professional development for everyone is critical self-reflection and self-directed learning:

> professional development [is] a process of critical self-reflection and self-directed learning, potentially leading to a revision of one's assumptions about teaching or one's larger perspectives on education. (Cranton, 1996:180)

Although your individual circumstances make a difference, it is the self-directed learning, e.g. through the questions you ask about teaching and learning and critical self-reflection on them, that can lead to new ways of thinking and working which help you achieve your goal of improved practice. As a lifelong learner you are not alone and have to remember that colleagues across the sector may be in a similar position, or have been there before you.

Practical guidance and advice from teachers in the sector

Throughout this book there have been activities to help you plan for your professional learning and the development of your own practice. It has been advocated that more informal approaches to CPD recognise an individual's professional needs and engage them in activities that are important and relevant to them. It has been argued that much professional learning takes place through your informal workplace experiences and through collaborating with others in your team, section or department. Although organisational structures may be there for CPD, Bloxham and Boyd (2007) maintain that it is not possible to control the practice that emerges in response to them. They suggest, like James and Biesta (2007) and Coffield (2008), that everyday interaction in the workplace is essential for professional learning for teachers and:

> although institutional contexts may be significant, it is the professional cultures and leadership at departmental or teaching team level that are crucial. (Bloxham and Boyd, 2007: 222)

That is why this book includes Success Stories and Viewpoints through which experienced, expert and successful teachers and managers have offered their guidance about improving practice and developing as a professional. You don't have to accept their advice, you can question it, but it is worth considering because it comes from colleagues who are currently engaged in teaching and learning, leading specialist area teams or managing programmes or departments in a variety of organisations across the Lifelong Learning Sector. They are experiencing the same changing conditions as you, and you might need help in coping and surviving in this uncertain world, so a first step might be to think about the practical wisdom, insights and good sense offered by colleagues. Their words of advice are tabulated under the framework of 'constructive practice' and are presented here as a handy guide.

Constructive practice
Constructive practice is identified in successful teachers who approach CPD in a positive way, which is beneficial to themselves and their organisation. Constructive practice requires teachers to have an intention to continue to learn and an ability to control their workload so that learning can be applied to achieve personal and professional development.

Constructing a professional role
Successful teachers create their own role, identify their vision and purpose and develop their personal skills and attributes. Their words of advice include:
- be realistic about what you can achieve and maintain a work-life balance;
- be open-minded – don't get stuck in a rut;

- know all about your role and start to think where you want to go;
- accept that you can achieve some of your targets and ambitions and not others;
- acknowledge your weaknesses;
- identify what you want and if you're determined you can get there;
- trust your instincts, trust other people and trust your knowledge;
- develop self-belief, resilience, self-reliance, self-assurance and stamina;
- consider mentoring and coaching as areas for CPD.

Constructing professional knowledge

Successful teachers intuitively adopt a constructivist approach to teaching and learning, develop their understanding of their specialist area knowledge and keep it up to date. Their words of advice include:

- never stop learning – don't think that because you've got the qualification that's it;
- develop knowledge of your industry;
- develop knowledge of current training practices;
- be able to manage a class of learners and address individual needs;
- be flexible, innovative and try out new things and don't rely on whole class teaching and telling;
- be organised with preparation, paperwork and planning;
- be proactive and find out what's new, what's changing and look ahead;
- start small and make little changes and build up a repertoire of resources and skills;
- think about your job as an enabler into the community or society for your learners;
- keep up to date and renew your enthusiasm through professional development.

Constructing professional relationships

Successful teachers concentrate on building relationships with learners, maintaining positive relationships with colleagues and establishing good working relationships with other stakeholders. Their words of advice include:

- be yourself;
- be aware of how you are with people and stay open-minded;
- be aware of the boundaries and establish what is acceptable/not acceptable between teacher and learner in the classroom;
- empathise with learners and try to understand the mindset of 16 year-olds;
- don't get over friendly with learners;
- you need to look for reasons behind a learner's behaviour, not the behaviour itself;
- take an interest in the development of other people;
- care for people and help them to progress;
- ask for help from colleagues and share your concerns with other teachers;
- develop a professional relationship with someone you can talk to about issues at work;
- you win more battles by being nice – remember why you are a teacher.

Constructing a repertoire of intellectual skills

Successful teaches engage in reflection, develop critical thinking skills and value research and evaluation. They also:

- learn when things go wrong and reflect on unintended outcomes.

A glance at the table above provides a lot of practical advice from colleagues about ways to develop your professional practice – but rather less about developing intellectual skills. This obviously reflects the learning culture across many organisations. But my additional advice is that professional development is not just a fast, quick fix and achieved only through hints and tips provided by others. To develop a sense of what it means to be a professional in the Lifelong Learning Sector today, your questioning must move on to broader, wider issues, and engage critical thinking about your role. This reinforces the idea that you need to be an 'inveterate inquirer' into wider educational issues and consider how your role in the classroom influences, or is influenced by, changes in society. For example, teachers talk about the empowerment of learners, but what does this really mean for them and their future? As a teacher you do have to be:

- pragmatic and address practical issues;
- strategic and think about your future role;
- critically reflective about wide educational issues confronting society.

The practical guidance and advice that I would add to that provided by colleagues across the sector is that you need to develop a repertoire of intellectual skills to be an effective professional in the sector in the future.

The use of constructive practice that has been promoted in this book means that you can look at quality in teaching and learning differently. It implies that CPD is not simply a process of recording information until it adds up to 30 hours' worth. Neither is a focus on quality a matter of management control over you or getting you to conform to the sector's and your organisation's requirements. My argument is that CPD should increase professional autonomy over time. Two key factors to bear in mind, which have been identified as contributing to a successful approach to professional development, are:

1. level of control over your workload;
2. an intention to continue to learn.

You can't control what happens in your organisation but, as Stenhouse (1975) wisely said many years ago, what you can control is the direction of your learning. But how do you know which is the best direction to take? If you can't predict the future, what direction do you take?

Envisioning alternative futures

Brookfield (1995: 119) considers education to be an ongoing activity and urges you to 'envision alternative futures' and image how the dream of a lifelong learning society could be created. What he exhorts you to do is to picture in your mind's eye an image of your 'desired future'. By that he means that you imagine yourself, say, five years or so from now. Imagine what you will be doing differently and what will be happening that is not happening now. You can dream about how you would like your situation to be and consider what teaching and learning might be like, what your classroom will look like and how your role might be different.

But it's not just a daydream. You have to really think about what brought you to the future, the progress you made and what pleased you along the way. From the vantage point you've reached in the future you have to look back over the years until you come back to the present so that you can see how you reached that desired state of affairs. If you imagine that your goals have been achieved, you have to identify the specific things that helped you achieve them. For example, was it gaining a higher qualification, taking on different responsibilities, joining a new team, developing a new programme or getting promotion? Envisioning alternative futures is a technique Brookfield advocates for developing critical thinking and considers that the capacity to speculate on alternative futures is particularly important for teachers because education is always *futuristic*. If you think about it, you are always preparing your learners for the future: skills for life, vocational and academic qualifications for progression to the workplace and higher education.

There is a view that using creative imagination as part of critical thinking is rather illogical (Jarvis, 2002), but if you're a bit fed up in your present job, or feel stuck in a bit of a rut, do you want to believe that you could still be in the same unrewarding place five years from now? Questioning where you might be in the future is not meant to be something you invent now, struggle with or get depressed about. The general idea of creating your own future scenario is that it helps you plan ahead and identify potential opportunities and make a long-term action plan. Can you project your own situation into the future? Unless you envision an alternative future, you can't achieve it.

Considering the way forward

Let's be more realistic now and look back at what has actually happened in the sector in the last few years before imagining what's ahead for everyone. Four major policy themes in the Learning and Skills Sector between 2005 and 2007 have been identified:

1. 'Prioritisation'.
2. A 'demand-led system', including 'market making' and 'contestability'.
3. The drive for quality and excellence, including 'specialisation', 'personalisation', 'clarity of mission', 'the trust agenda' and 'self-regulation'.
4. 'Simplification'. (Coffield et al., 2009: 77)

From the vantage point of today, Coffield et al. have looked back and identified four major policy themes. You are probably familiar with these and aware of how they have had an impact on your organisation and your teaching and learning. The question for everyone now is 'What will the major policy themes be for the next few years?' Here are four themes that teachers have speculated about!

1. '**Learners**' – Across the sector the term 'students' will have bitten the dust! In 2013 learners who otherwise would not be in education will be attending colleges and other organisations, which will inevitably result in a growth in 16–18 learner numbers. This will create pressures on resources in organisations. The concern for some is that these young people will not see this as an opportunity and, as a consequence, will present behavioural challenges. Williams (2007: 37) predicts that you might be 'pushed into the role of disciplinarian'. The LLUK standards based teacher qualifications framework includes a module on Behaviour Management, but for teachers who have been in the sector for some time this topic might need to be the focus for future professional learning. The personalisation strategy will develop through a requirement for a learner involvement strategy in colleges. Establishing a National Learner Panel will ensure that the 'learner voice' is heard more widely in future.

2. **Vocational training** – The current economic climate means that whole sectors of employment are declining, e.g. retail and construction, and this will impact on the opportunities for future jobs and apprenticeships. There is a view that, if unemployment figures rise, the sector will have to radically change its vocational training offer. The difficult thing to predict is whether this will result in the expansion or decrease of vocational training. Will vocational training expand because of increased numbers of 16–18 year-olds and unemployed adults, or will there be a decline because of the lack of paid employment opportunities?

3. **HE in FE** – Some teachers predict that colleges in the sector seem to be firmly committed to 16–19 education training and will become vocational sixth-form centres. Standards of HE in FE have been under scrutiny and it may well be that in future these courses will diminish and HE targets will be cut. The result in the future may be a return to a divide between HE and FE.

4. **CPD** – The introduction of a requirement for CPD has not yet been fully assessed and there is a view that it needs to be regulated more rigorously, planned more carefully and that organisations need to monitor its impact on teaching and learning. In reporting research for LLUK into CPD opportunities Fiddy (2008: 5) points out that the 'measurement of impact is currently neglected, with few appropriate instruments of measurement identified in any sector. A variety of indicators were cited, but they were imprecise and not carried out systematically'. Teachers in the sector have always engaged in professional development and staff training, the difference now is that in the future there will be an opportunity to monitor its value.

When you read this you will be able to assess how correct these predictions from teachers in the Lifelong Learning Sector were!

Putting your plans into action

You don't have to wait for things to happen in the future, you can start on your own professional development right now by reviewing the CPD opportunities presented throughout the book. They are brought together below so that you can make a quick review and cross check the standards – anything to make Action Planning easier!

Suggested CPD activities	Check It Out	Suggested topics	Links to LLUK standards
Developing an Action Plan	0.1	Initial thoughts and identifying issues	
	1.1	Analysing workforce practices	
	1.2	Prioritising CPD activities	AS4, AP4.2, elements of Domains B, C, D, E
Investigating your teaching role and the teaching and learning environment	3.1	Addressing changes and/or improvement to practice	AS7, AK7.2, AP7.3, elements of Domains B and C
	3.2	Formulating personal goals to align with organisational goals	AS6, AK6.1, AP6.1, elements of Domain E
	3.3	Reflecting on personal goals	AS4, AP4.2, AP5.2, elements of Domains B, C
	3.4	Identify teaching and non-teaching tasks	Link to 3.5
	3.5	Reviewing record keeping	AP7, AK7.1, AP7.1, elements of Domain C
	3.6	Reviewing formal evaluations	AS4, AK4.2, AP4.2, elements of Domain B
	3.7	Identifying priorities for CPD	AS4, AK4.1, AP4.1, elements of Domains B and C
	3.8	Identifying a curriculum development project	AS4, AK4.1, AP4.1, elements of Domain D
	3.9	Contributing to quality cycle	AS7, AK7.2, AP7.2, elements of Domain B
Exploring approaches to CPD	4.1	Identifying conditions for CPD	AS5, AK5.1, AP5.1
	4.2	Reflecting on areas of professional control	AS4
	4.3	Justifying what constitutes CPD	AS4
	4.4	Reflecting on route for CPD	AS7, AK7.2, AP7.2
	4.5	Investigating organisational opportunities	AS7, AP7.3

Suggested CPD activities	Check It Out	Suggested topics	Links to LLUK standards
	4.6 – 4.10	Identifying your approach to CPD	
Thinking of CPD as constructive practice	5.1	Recognising successful practice	AS4, AK4.3
	5.2	Defining personal success	AS4, AS7
	5.3	Targeting technical skills development	AS7 and elements of Domains B, C and D
	5.4	Working more constructively	AS2, AK2.1, AP2.1 and elements of Domain F
Aspects of role development	6.1	Identifying personal qualities	AK4.2
	6.2	Updating knowledge of professional standards	AS1, AS 4 and overview of Domains A – E
	6.3	Teaching as a strategic activity	AS1, AK1.1, AP1.1, AS7, AP7.1 and elements of Domains B, C and, D
	6.4	Individual biography and career planning	AS1, AS4
	6.5	Evaluating professional values	AS3, AK3.1, AP3.1 and elements of Domain F
	6.6	Incorporating values in practice	AS7, AK7.3, AP7.3 and elements of Domain D
	6.7	SWOT analysis	AS7, AK7.2, AP7.2
	6.8	Personal skills and attributes	AS1, AS7
Developing professional knowledge	7.1	Developing knowledge through practice	Overview of Domains A – F
	7.2	Adopting a constructivist approach to CPD	AS2, AS4, AK4.3, AP4.1 and elements of Domain B
	7.3	Updating specialist area knowledge	AS2, AP4.3, AS5 and elements of Domains B, C and F
	7.4	Inducting learners into your specialist area	AS2, AS4 and elements of Domains B, C, D and E
	7.5	Identifying strategies for specialist area	AS1, AK1.1, AP1.1, AS2 and elements of Domain C
	7.6	Deepening understanding of teaching and learning	AS2 AS4 and elements of Domains B, C and E

Suggested CPD activities	Check It Out	Suggested topics	Links to LLUK standards
Building professional relationships	8.1	Dealing with disruptive learners	AS1, AS3 and elements of Domain B
	8.2	Assessing your relationships with learners	AS1, AS3 and elements of Domain B
	8.3	Exploring set of professional roles	AP3.1
	8.4	Exploring your role set	AS3, AS5
	8.5	Collaborating with others	AS3, AS5
Developing a repertoire of intellectual skills	9.1	Developing specialist subject expertise	AS4
	9.2	Developing critical thinking	AS4
	9.3	Evaluating ways to improve practice	AS4, AS7
	9.4	Reflecting on practice from different perspectives	AS1, AS2, AS4, AK4.1 and elements of Domains B and C

The future is yours – it's up to you

Let's hope that the book has given you ideas, tips, guidance and positive advice for your professional development. I have offered you a framework of constructive practice that successful teachers demonstrate, and recommend you assess your future CPD activities using the cluster of factors that underpin successful practice:

- constructing a professional role;
- constructing professional knowledge;
- constructing professional relationships;
- constructing a repertoire of intellectual skills.

Successful practice is subjective and you have to identify what success means for you. Even if you're not very ambitious, or not thinking about changing your job at the moment, I am sure you would rather be successful than unsuccessful. However experienced or content you are at the moment, your job changes around you all the time, so you cannot ignore professional development altogether. All I can say now is that teachers who are successful and have developed expertise in their specialist area said that they found continuing to learn and working towards their goal of successful practice is very rewarding. They seem to have developed a CPD mindset. Ecclestone captures this notion well:

> Learning alongside your learners promises to be a valuable experience you will surely enjoy. (Ecclestone: 2008: viii)

However, I can only pass on my ideas about how they manage this:

> The important thing to realize, I think, is that books are not static, once-and-for-all-time universal statements of an author's ideas. Books are just as contextually and historically specific as other external forms of thought, such as speeches or even conversations. Books are also, ultimately, personal statements. How we write, what we choose to write about, what examples we select to prove our case or disprove that of our opponents, what we emphasize, what we ignore, what we deride, and what we approve are all reflections of our own personalities. Books should be regarded as elements in an ongoing dialogue – invitations to further reaction and discussion and not the last word on the matters discussed. (Brookfield, 1991: 248)

As Brookfield says, books are a personal statement. What I have chosen to write about is what I have found works for me. The personalisation agenda that this book argues for recognises that your CPD arises from your individual needs. Aligning these individual needs so that your professional development benefits your learners, meets your organisational priorities and the aspirations of employers and the wider community is the secret of success. This book is my invitation to you to start an ongoing dialogue about your own future success.

References

Anderson, A. (2002) *Working Together to Develop a Professional Learning Community*. Wanganui, NZ: HERDSA

Armitage, A., Bryant, R., Dunnill, R., Flanagan, K., Hayes, D., Hudson, A., Kent, J., Lawes, S. and Renwick, M. (2007) *Teaching and Training in Post-Compulsory Education* (3rd edn). Maidenhead: Open University Press McGraw-Hill Education

ASKe www.business.brookes.ac.uk/aske.html, accessed 15 January 2009

Atherton, J. (2003) *Doceo: Competence, Proficiency and Beyond* [On-line] www.doceo.co.uk/background/expertise.htm, accessed January 2009

Avis, J. (1999) Shifting identity: new conditions and the transformation of practice – teaching within post-compulsory education. *Journal of Vocational Education and Training*, 51(2): 245–64

Bannister, D. and Fransella, F. (1971) *Inquiring Man: The Theory of Personal Constructs*. Harmondsworth: Penguin Education

Barrett, R. (2006) *Building a Values-driven Organization: A Whole System Approach to Cultural Transformation*. Oxford: Butterworth-Heinemann

Barth, B.-M. (2000) The teachers' construction of knowledge, in B. Moon, J. Butcher and E. Bird (eds), *Leading Professional Development in Education*. London: RoutledgeFalmer

Bennett, G. (2009) Young(ish), gifted, and black. *UC Magazine*, January 2009: 20–1, London: UCU

Berliner, D. (2001) Teacher expertise, in F. Banks and A. Shelton Mayes (eds), *Early Professional Development for Teachers*. London: David Fulton

Biggs, J. (2003) *Teaching for Quality Learning at University*. Buckingham: Open University Press McGraw-Hill

Billett, S. (2001) *Learning in the Workplace: Strategies for Effective Practice*. Sydney: Allen and Unwin

Bloomer, M. and James, D. (2003) Education research in educational practice. *Journal of Further and Higher Education*, 27(3): 247–56

Bloxham, S. and Boyd, P. (2007) *Developing Effective Assessment in Higher Education: A Practical Guide*. Maidenhead: Open University Press McGraw-Hill Education

Boud, D. (ed.) (1988) *Developing Student Autonomy in Learning* (2nd edn). London: Kogan Page

Boud, D., Keough, R. and Walker, D. (eds) (1985) *Reflection: Turning Experience into Learning*. London: Kogan Page

Bowden, D. (2007) Your place in your school, in A. Thody, B. Gray and D. Bowden, *Teacher's Survival Guide* (2nd edn). London: Continuum

Brain, G. (1994) *Managing and Developing People*. Blagdon: Staff College in association with Association of Colleges

Brookes, D. and Hughes, M. (2001) *Developing Leading-edge Staff in Vocational Education and Training*. London: LSDA

Brookfield, S. (1991) *Developing Critical Thinkers: Challenging Adults to Explore Alternative Ways of Thinking and Acting*. San Francisco: Jossey-Bass

Brookfield, S. (1995) *Becoming a Critically Reflective Teacher*. San Francisco: Jossey-Bass

Bruner, J. (1971) *Toward a Theory of Instruction*. Harvard: Harvard Paperbacks

Buchanan, D. and Huczynski, A. (2004) *Organizational Behaviour: An Introductory Text* (5th edn). Harlow: Pearson Education

Butcher, L. (2008) Continuous improvement, in F. Fawbert (ed.), *Teaching in Post-compulsory Education: Skills, Standards and Lifelong Learning*. London: Continuum

Campbell, A. and Norton, L. (eds) (2007) *Learning, Teaching and Assessing in Higher Education: Developing Reflective Practice*. Exeter: Learning Matters

Carr, W. (1993) What is an educational practice?, in M. Hammersley (ed.), *Educational Research: Current Issues*. London: Paul Chapman

Coffield, F. (2008) *Just Suppose Teaching and Learning Became the First Priority … .* London: Learning and Skills Network

Coffield, F. Edward, S., Finlay, I., Hodgson, A., Spours, K and Steer, R. (2008) *Improving Learning, Skills and Inclusion: The Impact of Policy on Post-compulsory Education*. London: Routledge

Coles, A. (2004) (ed.) *Teaching in Post-compulsory Education: Policy, Practice and Values. London: David Fulton*

Colley, H., Hodkinson, P. and Malcolm, J. (2002) *Non-formal Learning: Mapping the Conceptual Terrain*. Leeds: University of Leeds Lifelong Learning Institute

Cooper, P. and McIntyre, D. (1996) *Effective Teaching and Learning*. Buckingham: Open University Press

Cornford, I. (2002) Reflective teaching: empirical research findings and some implications for teacher education. *Journal of Vocational Education and Training*, 54(2): 219–35

Cottrell, S. (2005) *Critical Thinking Skills: Developing Effective Analysis and Argument*. Basingstoke: Palgrave Macmillan

Cranton, P. (1996) *Professional Development as Transformative Learning: New Perspectives for Teachers of Adults.* San Francisco: Jossey-Bass

Dadds, M. (2002) Taking curiosity seriously. *Educational Action Research*, 10(1): 9–28

Davies, L. (2008) Foreword, in J. Hitching, *Maintaining Your Licence to Practise: Professional Development in the Lifelong Learning Sector*. Exeter: Learning Matters

Day, C. and Sachs, J. (eds) (2004) *International Handbook on the Continuing Professional Development of Teachers*. Maidenhead: Open University Press McGraw-Hill

Denby, N., Butroyd, R., Swift, H., Price, J. and Glazzard, J. (2008) *Masters Level Study in Education: Guide to Success for PGCE Students*. Maidenhead: Open University Press McGraw-Hill

Department for Children, Schools and Families (DCSF)(2007) *CBI Conference Press Notice 2007/0195*. www.dcsf.gov.uk, accessed 28 March 2009

Department for Education and Employment (DfEE) (1998) *The Learning Age: A Renaissance for a New Britain*. London: HMSO

Department for Education and Employment (DfEE) (1999) *Learning to Succeed: A New Framework for Post-16 Learning*. London: HMSO

Department for Education and Skills (DfES)(2002) *Success for All: Reforming Further Education and Training – Our Vision for the Future*. London: HMSO

Department for Education and Skills (DfES)(2004a) *Equipping Our Teachers for the Future: Reforming Initial Teacher Training for the Learning and Skills Sector*. London: HMSO

Department for Education and Skills (DfES)(2004b) *14–19 Curriculum and Qualifications Reform* (Tomlinson Report). London: DfES

Department for Education and Skills (DfES)(2005) *14–19 Education and Skills*. London: HMSO

Department for Education and Skills (DfES)(2006) *Further Education: Raising Skills, Improving Life Chances*. London: HMSO

Department for Education and Skills (DfES)(2007) *Further Education Training Act*. www.dius.gov.uk, accessed 7 January 2009

Department for Innovation, Universities and Skills (DIUS)(2007) *Implementing the Leitch Review: World Class Skills*. London: DIUS

Department for Innovation, Universities and Skills (DIUS)(2008) *FE Colleges: Models for Success*. London: DIUS

Department for Innovation, Universities and Skills and Department for Children, Schools and Families (DIUS and DCSF)(2008a) *The Children, Skills and Learning Bill*. London: HMSO

Department for Innovation, Universities and Skills and Department for Children, Schools and Families (DIUS and DCSF)(2008b) *Raising Expectations: Enabling the System to Deliver*. London: HMSO

Dewey, J. (1933) *How We Think: A Restatement of the Relation of Reflective Thinking to the Educational Process* (2nd edn). Boston: Heath

Dreyfus, H. and Dreyfus, S. (1986) *Mind over Machine: The Power of Human Intuition and Expertise in the Era of the Computer*. Oxford: Blackwell

Dutton, S. (2000) Invest in skills. *FEnow*, Winter 2000. Association of Colleges

Ecclestone, K. (2008) Foreword, in F. Fawbert (ed.), *Teaching in Post-compulsory Education: Skills Standards and Lifelong Learning*. London: Continuum

Elliott, G. and Crossley, M. (1997) Contested values in further education: findings from a case study of the management of change. *Educational Management and Administration*, 25: 79–92

Elliott, J. (1991) *Action Research for Educational Change*. Buckingham: Open University Press

Elliott, J. (2002) Action research in education, paper presented at seminar at City College, Norwich, December 2002

Engestrom, G. (2001) Expansive learning at work: towards an activity-theoretical reconceptualisation. *Journal of Education and Work*, 14(1): 133–56

Entwistle, N. (1997) Contrasting perspectives on learning, in F. Marton, D. Hounsell and N. Entwistle (eds), *The Experience of Learning: Implications for Teaching and Studying in Higher Education*. Edinburgh: Scottish Academic Press

Eraut, M. (1994) *Developing Professional Knowledge and Competence*. London: Falmer Press

Eraut, M. (1998) The characterisation and development of professional expertise in education management and in teaching, in M. Strain (ed.), *Leaderships and Professional Knowledge in Education*. London: Paul Chapman

Eraut, M. (2000) Non-formal learning, implicit learning and tacit knowledge, in F. Coffield (ed.), *The Necessity of Informal Learning*. Bristol: Policy Press

Evans, K., Hodkinson, P. and Unwin, L. (2002) *Working to Learn: Transforming Learning in the Workplace*. London: Kogan Page

Fawbert, F. (ed.)(2008) *Teaching in Post-compulsory Education: Skills, Standards and Lifelong Learning*. London: Continuum

Feiman-Nemser, S. (2001) From preparation to practice: designing a continuum to strengthen and sustain teaching. *Teachers College Record*, 103 (6): 1003–55

Fiddy, R. (2008) Introduction, in *Access to Effective and Equitable Continuing Professional Development Opportunities for Teachers, Tutors and Trainers in the Lifelong Learning Sector*. London: Lifelong Learning UK

Foster, A. (2005) *Realising the Potential: A Review of the Future Role of Further Education Colleges*. www.dfes.gov.uk/further education/fereview, accessed 8 January 2009

Fullan, M. (1991) *The New Meaning of Educational Change* (2nd edn). London: Cassell

Fullan, M. (1999) *Change Forces: The Sequel*. London: Falmer Press

Further Education National Training Organisation (FENTO)(1999) *Standards for Teaching and Supporting Learning in Further Education in England and Wales*. London: FENTO

Gewirtz, S. (1996) Post-welfarism and the reconstruction of teacher's work. Paper presented at the British Educational Research Association (BERA) Conference, Lancaster, September 1996

Ghaye, T. and Ghaye, K. (1998) *Teaching and Learning through Critical Reflective Practice*. London: David Fulton Publishers

Gray B. (2007) Creating a positive learning environment, in A. Thody, B. Gray and D. Bowden, *Teacher's Survival Guide* (2nd edn). London: Continuum

Gulati, S. (2004) Constructivism and emerging online pedagogy. Paper presented at the Annual Conference of the University Association for Continuing Education, Centre for Lifelong Learning, University of Glamorgan, 5–7 April 2004

Habermas, J. (1972) *Knowledge and Human Interests*. Oxford: Heinemann

Handy, C. (1993) *Understanding Organizations* (4th edn). London: Penguin

Hannagan, T. (2008) *Management Concepts and Practices* (5th edn). Harlow: Pearson Education

Hanson, A. (1996) The search for a separate theory of adult learning: does anyone really need andragogy?, in R. Edwards, A. Hanson and P. Raggatt (eds), *Boundaries of Adult Learning*. London: Routledge/Open University Press

Harrison, R. (2002) *Learning and Development* (3rd edn). London: Chartered Institute of Personnel and Development

Hayes, D. (2007) Teacher training for all?, in D. Hayes, T, Marshall and A. Turner (eds), *A Lecturer's Guide to Further Education*. Maidenhead: Open University Press, see p.151

Hayes, P. (2007) What's motivating students?, in D. Hayes, T. Marshall and A. Turner (eds), *A Lecturer's Guide to Further Education*. Maidenhead: Open University Press

Hicks, L. (2002) The nature of learning, in L. Mullins, *Management and Organisational Behaviour* (6th edn). London: Financial Times/Prentice Hall

Hillier, Y. (2005) *Reflective Teaching in Further and Adult Education* (2nd edn). London: Continuum

Hitching, J. (2008) *Maintaining Your Licence to Practise: Professional Development in the Lifelong Learning Sector*. Exeter: Learning Matters

Hoban, G. (2002) *Teacher Learning for Educational Change*. Buckingham: Open University Press

Hobley, J. (2008) Responsive reflection, in F. Fawbert (ed.), *Teaching in Post-compulsory Education: Skills, Standards and Lifelong Learning*. London: Continuum

Hodkinson, P. and Hodkinson, H. (2001) Individuals, cultures and types of learning: a study of teachers' learning in their workplaces. Paper presented to the Learning and Skills Development Agency Conference, Cambridge, December 2001

Hoyle, E. (1969) *The Role of the Teacher*. London: Routledge and Kegan-Paul

Huddleston, P. and Unwin, L. (2007) *Teaching and Learning in Further Education: Diversity and Change* (3rd edn). London: RoutledgeFalmer

Hunter, D. (2008) *Letter from Chief Executive to Colleagues in Lifelong Learning Sector.* London: Lifelong Learning UK

Institute for Learning (IfL)(2008) *Member Handbook*. Version 2.0 July 2008. London: IfL

James, D. and Biesta, G. (2007) *Improving Teaching and Learning in Schools: A Commentary by the Teaching and Learning Research Programme.* London: London University, Institute of Education, TLRP

Jameson, J. and Hillier, Y. (2003) *Researching Post-compulsory Education.* London: Continuum

Jarvis, P. (1995) *Adult and Continuing Education: Theory and Practice* (2nd edn). London: Routledge

Jarvis, P. (1997) *Ethics and Education for Adults in a Late Modern Society.* Leicester: National Institute for Adult and Community Education

Jarvis, P. (2002) *The Theory and Practice of Teaching* (2nd edn). London: Routledge

Kelly, G. (1955) *The Psychology of Personal Constructs.* London: Norton

Kelly, J. (2008) Planning your CPD, *InTuition*, Winter 2008. London: Institute for Learning

Kolb, D. (1984) *Experiential Learning: Experience as a Source of Learning and Development.* New York: Prentice Hall

Lave, J. and Wenger, F. (1991) *Situated Learning: Legitimate Peripheral Participation.* Cambridge: University of Cambridge Press

Leitch Review of Skills (2006) *Prosperity for All in the Global Economy – World Class Skills.* London: HM Treasury

Lifelong Learning UK (LLUK)(2007a) *Further Education Workforce Reforms.* www.lluk.org/feworkforcereforms, accessed 30 January 2009

Lifelong Learning UK (LLUK)(2007b) *New Overarching Professional Standards for Teachers, Tutors and Trainers in the Lifelong Learning Sector.* London: Lifelong Learning UK

Lincoln, Y. and Denzin, N. (1998) The fifth moment, in N. Denzin and Y. Lincoln (eds), *The Landscape of Qualitative Research: Theories and Issues.* Thousand Oaks, CA: Sage

Marsick, V. and Watkins, K. (2001) *Informal and Incidental Learning in the Workplace.* London: Routledge

Martinez, P. (1999) *Learning from Continuing Professional Development.* London: FEDA

Marton, F., Hounsell, D. and Entwistle, N. (1984) *The Experience of Learning.* Edinburgh: Scottish Academic Press

Mezirow, J. (1990) *Fostering Critical Reflection in Adulthood: A Guide to Transformative and Emancipatory Learning.* San Francisco: Jossey-Bass

Miner, J. (1971) *Management Theory.* London: Kogan Page

Minton, D. (2005) *Teaching Skills in Further and Adult Education* (3rd edn). London: Thomson Learning

Moon, J. (1999) *Reflection in Learning and Professional Development: Theory and Practice.* London: Routledge

Moon, J. (2005) *Guide for Busy Academics No 4: Learning through Reflection.* York: Higher Education Academy

Moon, J. (2008) *Critical Thinking: An Exploration of Theory and Practice.* London: Routledge

Moore, A. (2000) *Teaching and Learning: Pedagogy, Curriculum and Culture.* London: RoutledgeFalmer

Moran, J. (2001) *Collaborative Professional Development for Teachers of Adults.* San Francisco: Kreiger Publishing

Morgan, C., Dunn, L., Parry, S. and O'Reilly, M. (2004). *The Student Assessment Handbook.* London: RoutledgeFalmer

Mullins, L. (2007) *Management and Organisational Behaviour* (8th edn). Harlow: Pearson Education

National Institute for Adult and Continuing Education (NIACE)(1999) *Lifelong Qualifications: Developing Qualifications to Support Lifelong Learning.* Leicester: NIACE

Office for Standards in Education (Ofsted)(2003) *The Initial Training of Further Education Teachers: A Survey.* London: HMSO

Oldroyd, D. and Hall, V. (1991) *Managing Staff Development.* London: Paul Chapman

Osterman, K. and Kottkamp, R. (1993) *Reflective Practice for Educations: Improving Schooling through Professional Development.* Newbury Park, CA: Corwin Press Inc.

Peeke, G. (2008) *Professionalisng the Workforce: Report of the Case Studies Project.* St Ives: East of England Centre for Excellence in Teacher Training (EECETT)

Petty, G. (2004) *Teaching Today: A Practical Guide* (3rd edn). Cheltenham: Nelson Thornes

Petty, G. (2006) *Evidence-based Teaching: A Practical Approach.* Cheltenham: Nelson Thornes

Pollard, A. (2008) *Reflective Teaching: Evidence-informed Professional Practice* (3rd edn). London: Continuum

Pollard, A. and James, M. (eds) (2004) *Personalised Learning: A Commentary by the Teaching and Learning Research Programme.* London: Economic and Social Research Council

Quality Improvement Department (QID)(2007) *Teachers' Toolkit: Professional Development Portfolio.* Norwich: City College Norwich

Rammell, B. (2006) Ministerial Foreword, in *New Overarching Professional Standards for Teachers, Tutors and Trainers in the Lifelong Learning Sector*. London: Lifelong Learning UK

Ramsden, P. (2000) *Using Research on Student Learning to Enhance Educational Quality*. http://www.lgu.ac.uk/deliberations/ocsd-pubs/ramsden.html, accessed 3 February 2009

Reece, I. and Walker, S. (2007) *Teaching, Training and Learning: A Practical Guide* (6th edn). Sunderland: Business Educational Publishing

Robson, C. (2002) *Real World Research: A Resource for Social Scientists and Practitioner-Researchers* (2nd edn). Oxford: Blackwell Publishing

Rogers, A. (2002) *Teaching Adults* (3rd edn). Buckingham: Open University Press

Rogers, A. (2003) *What is the Difference? New Critique of Adult Learning and Teaching*. Leicester: National Institute of Adult Continuing Education

Rogers, B. (2006) *Cracking the Hard Class: Strategies for Managing the Harder than Average Class* (2nd edn). London: Paul Chapman

Scales, P. (2008) *Teaching in the Lifelong Learning Sector*. Maidenhead: Open University Press/McGraw-Hill

Schon, D. (1983) *The Reflective Practitioner: How Professional Think in Action*. New York: Basic Books

Senge, P. (1990) *The Fifth Discipline: The Art and Practice of the Learning Organisation*. London: Random House

Sotto, E. (2007) *When Teaching Becomes Learning* (2nd edn). London: Continuum

Squires, G. (2003) *Trouble-shooting Your Teaching: A Step-by-step Guide to Analysing and Improving Your Practice*. London: RoutledgeFalmer

Stenhouse, L. (1975) *An Introduction to Curriculum Research and Development*. London: Heinemann

Steward, A. (2004) Constructive practice: workloads, roles and continuing professional development for college lecturers, Anglia Ruskin University, unpublished EdD thesis

Steward, A. (2006) *FE Lecturer's Survival Guide*. London: Continuum

Townley, B. (1994) *Reframing Human Resource Management: Power, Ethics and the Subject at Work*. London: Sage

Tummons, J. (2008) *Becoming a Professional Tutor in the Lifelong Learning Sector*. Exeter: Learning Matters

Vygotsky, L. (1962) *Thought and Language*. Cambridge, MA: MIT Press

Wallace, S. (2007) *Teaching, Tutoring and Training in the Lifelong Learning Sector*. Exeter: Learning Matters

Wenger, E. (1999) *Communities of Practice: Learning, Meaning and Identity*. Cambridge: Cambridge University Press

Williams, J. (2007) A beginner's guide to lecturing, in D. Hayes, T. Marshall and A.

Turner (eds), *A Lecturer's Guide to Further Education*. Maidenhead: Open University Press/McGraw-Hill

Index

ABC approach 182–3
action research 91, 161, 178, 226–7, 229–30
alternative futures 237–238
apprenticeships 22–3, 239
assessment
  competence-based 136
  LLUK standards 52–3
  reforms 21, 28
attributes 120, 153, 155–6, 211, 213, 229
autonomy
  learner 48, 94–5
  professional 90, 179, 237

behaviour
  guidelines 198
  and IFL code 40–1
  learner 47, 110, 182–3, 193–7, 239
  values-driven 152
behaviourism 94
biography 144–5, 233

coaching 48, 150, 186–7, 203, *see also* Learning Coaches
Code of Professional Practice 39–41
collaboration
  peer 199–200
  professional 26, 46, 49, 89, 95, 127, 174–5, 202–4
community of practice 187, 213–4, 224
constructive practice 114, 118–19, 128, 129–31, 235, 237, 242
constructivism 119, 163–7, 175–6, 181
control
  knowledge 209–10, 212–13
  of workload 113
contingent instructions 199
critical thinking 19, 125, 203, 216–18, 219, 222, 225, 230, 236, 238

curriculum 17, 21, 27, 57, 73–4, 107, 167, 187–8
Diplomas for 14–19s 21, 27–8
diversity
  of learners 25, 40, 45, 49, 51, 67, 70, 128, 148, 164, 197–8, 206
  and teacher's role 1–2, 62, 64, 89, 115, 164, 177
dual professionalism 157–9, 161, 168

employability 15, 21, 207–8
employer engagement 207–8, 228
epistemology 168, 175
equality 25, 128, 148, 156, 198, 206
ethical
  issues 225, 227
  practices 76, 151
evaluation
  of practice 46, 51, 67, 78, 88, 92, 105, 108, 120, 123, 128, 137–9, 173, 210, 221, 227, 229–30
  qualitative 220–1
  scientific 220
  self- 95, 111, 164, 213, 220, 221, 227, 229–30
experiential learning 94–5
expertise 201, 205, 207, 211–4, 219, 242, *see also* responsive expertise

Foster review 21
Further Education National Training Organisation (FENTO) 14, 15, 17, 18, 20, 37

games 168, 172, 200–1
game plan 212, 219
GROW model of coaching 186–7
goals
  challenging 176–8
  of CPD 90, 92, 95, 203

goals—*cont.*
of improved practice 22–3, 93, 94, 112–13, 234
learning 45, 48, 51, 111, 123, 129–30, 154, 164, 171, 182, 184, 199
organisational 59–60, 98, 161
personal 59–60, 62, 92, 98, 112–13, 119, 161, 186, 238

Humanist school of learning 94

inside-out learning 7
Institute for Learning (IFL) 24, 39–40, 43, 158, 159, 161, 178–9, 224
intellectual skills 118, 128, 184, 209–10, 213–16, 219, 225–6, 229–30, 236–7, 242
interdependent learner 96

knowledge
professional 2, 37, 74, 118, 123, 159–61, 175, 178, 209, 212–5, 222–3, 224–5, 236, 242
subject specialist 69, 116, 158–9, 202, 211

learning
active 19, 42, 45, 110, 176
coaches 41–3
culture 3, 236
Learning and Skills
Act 15
sector 15, 17–18, 20
Leitch review 21–2, 24
licence to practice 70

maximising learning 177–8
mentor
attributes 206, 229
role 37, 41, 43, 48, 88, 94, 95, 135, 138, 143, 175, 193, 213, 225, 228, 236

needs
individual 51, 236, 243
learner 67
novice 211

Office for Standards in Education (Ofsted) 18, 37–8, 129, 149, 205
occupational standards 13–15
outside-in learning 7

PAR model 183–4
personal construct theory 102, 164, 165, 234
personalisation
agenda 15, 238, 239, 243
of CPD 1–3, 112, 113
professional learning system 86–7, 116
professional standards for teachers
components 36
development 20, 23
Domain A 45
Domain B 47
Domain C 49
Domain D 51
Domain E 52
Domain F 53
public service agreements 22

qualifications and credit framework 29
Qualified Teacher Learning and Skills (QTLS) 37, 39
quality improvement 29, 80–1, 142–4
quizzes 200–1

REFLECT online tool 41, 43
reflexive teacher 137–9
responsive expertise 224–5
role
congruity 119, 140
overload 101–3, 119–20
set 126, 202
teacher's 14, 38, 56–58, 62–6, 69, 72–3, 76, 94, 133, 141, 228

school-leaving age 16, 26
self-
awareness 36, 120, 153–4, 209, 212, 221, 230
formation 153–4

Skills Funding Agency 26–7, 58
SOLO taxonomy 184–6
specialist learning and teaching
    area knowledge 123, 157–8, 167–78, 188,
    224–5, 236, 242
    standards 49–50
strategic
    partnerships 207–8
    thinking 210, 213–5, 219
stress 68, 72, 95, 99, 101–3, 105, 119, 191,
    202
SWOT analysis 154

teacher
    associate 36, 37
    as strategist 139–40, 144
teaching standards see professional standards
    for teachers
Train to Gain (T2G) 22
transformative learning 131
Tomlinson report 21, 23

values
    -driven organisation 152
    personal 91, 149, 151, 152
    professional 4, 36, 38, 40, 45–7, 92, 137,
    148, 152, 210, 214–5, 229
vision
    -guided 149, 152
    professional 110, 111, 117, 119–20, 123,
    141, 145, 147, 148, 151, 155, 206, 235

widening participation 16, 38
workforce
    reforms 5–31, 35, 38, 45
    strategy 24–5, 58
workplace
    culture 11–13
    learning 41, 44, 96, 98
    practices 30, 98, 159, 169, 206, 213, 215

Young People's Learning Agency (YPLA) 26,
    58